Praise for *Stop the Retirement Rip-off*

"401(k) plans are costly, inefficient clunkers. Fortunately, there is a way out, and Loeper's book provides us a great map."
—Evan Cooper, Senior Managing Editor
of *Investment News*

"If you want to know what's lurking inside of your 401(k), read this book."

—John F. Wasik, author of
The Merchant of Power and
Bloomberg News columnist

"Loeper's new book shows plan participants how to actually do something about these [401(k)] costs."
—W. Scott Simon, J.D., CFP®, AIFA®,
author of *The Prudent Investor Act:*
A Guide to Understanding

"This book should spur an entire new industry of 401(k) police . . . This is just too important an issue to be ignored."
—Len Reinhart, Former President of Lockwood Advisors
(an affiliate of Pershing) and Past President of
Smith Barney Consulting Group

Stop the Retirement Rip-off

Second Edition

HOW TO AVOID HIDDEN FEES AND KEEP MORE OF YOUR MONEY

David B. Loeper, CIMA®, CIMC®

WILEY

John Wiley & Sons, Inc.

The first edition of this book titled, *Stop the Retirement Rip-off: How to Avoid Hia* *and Keep More of Your Money*, was published in 2009 by John Wiley & Sons, Inc., N New Jersey.

Published by John Wiley & Sons, Inc., Hoboken, New Jersey.
Published simultaneously in Canada.

For general information on our other products and services or for technical support, please contact our Customer Care Department within the United States at (800) 762-2974, outside the United States at (317) 572-3993, or fax (317) 572-4002.

Wiley also publishes its books in a variety of electronic formats. Some content that appears in print may not be available in electronic books. For more information about Wiley products, visit our web site at www.wiley.com.

Library of Congress Cataloging-in-Publication Data:

Loeper, David B.
    Stop the retirement rip-off : how to avoid hidden fees and keep more of your money / David B. Loeper. – 2nd ed.
        p.   cm.
    Includes index.
    ISBN 978-1-118-13304-0 (pbk.); ISBN 978-1-118-17784-6 (ebk);
    ISBN 978-1-118-17786-0 (ebk); ISBN 978-1-118-17785-3 (ebk)
        1. Pensions—United States.   2. Banks and banking—Service charges—United States.   I. Title.
    HD7125.L59   2011
    332.6—dc23

                                                                2011038885

Printed in the United States of America

10 9 8 7 6 5 4 3 2 1

This book is dedicated to my children, Brian and Megan. I am incredibly proud of both of you for the unique personal qualities you possess. Remember, it is your life and to be happy you need to fearlessly pursue your passions. You have but one life, and it is up to you to make the most of it. Don't let anyone push you around or tell you how you should live YOUR life!

Contents

Preface   xi

Acknowledgments   xvii

Introduction   **Make the Most of Your Life!**   1

Chapter 1   **Why Fees Matter—The Coming "Retirement Plan Sticker Shock"**   11

Chapter 2   **Types of Expenses Dragging Down Your Retirement Funds**   25

Chapter 3   **The Price to Your Lifestyle of Needless Expenses**   39

Chapter 4   **Complaining Without Sounding Like a Complainer**   55

Chapter 5   **Rallying Your Troops—Just One Coworker Can Help**   63

Chapter 6   **What Happens If My Employer Ignores Us?**   69

Chapter 7   Now That My Retirement Plan Is Fixed,
             How Can I Make the Most of My Life?   79

Chapter 8   Resources, Investment Selection, Asset
             Allocation, Tools, and Advice   91

Chapter 9   How Much is That Guarantee in the Window?   121

Chapter 10 Hidden Expenses in Government Union
             and Some 403(b) Plans   131

Chapter 11 Summary   137

Appendix A Lifestyle Prices of Excessive Retirement
             Plan Expenses   139

Appendix B ABC Plan-401(k) Plan Fee Disclosure Form   205

About the Author   217

Index   219

> *"I swear by my life, and my love of it, that I will never live for the sake of another man, nor ask another to live for the sake of mine."*
> —*Ayn Rand*, Atlas Shrugged

Preface

Over the last 20 years or so, there has been a major shift in the retirement plans that companies offer their employees. Your parents were probably covered by a pension plan (specifically, a defined-benefit pension plan) where the company guaranteed a certain fixed lifetime income (the "defined benefit"). Upon retirement, this would provide an ongoing retirement paycheck throughout their lives. Such plans have become less and less popular among employers because the guaranteed benefits cost the company a lot of money.

Employers have increasingly switched to 401(k), 457, and 403(b) plans (collectively known as participant-directed retirement plans), which transfer the risk of the ultimate retirement benefit (along with most of the other expenses) to employees. Such plans have been around for quite some time but were initially not very popular. Employers loved these participant-directed plans, though, because instead of the employer guaranteeing a specific benefit (and paying for 100 percent of the cost of the benefit as in many older pension plans), the employer could move both the costs and risk to its employees. Despite this, these types of retirement plans gained in popularity among employees as well, influenced partially by the high market returns some of the mutual funds experienced. Also, many companies that previously could not have afforded the cost or risk of a traditional pension plan could afford to offer a participant-directed retirement plan, since the employees carried the burden of most expenses and all of the risk. Thus, many small companies that never would have had any retirement plan at all started these retirement plans in an attempt to compete with larger employers' benefit plans. Even though the employee was assuming 100 percent of the investment risk, 100 percent of the retirement benefit risk, and, in many cases, most of the cost in the form of annual contributions (most participant-directed retirement plans have some matching contribution by the employer), the flexibility of these plans ultimately made them attractive to some employees.

There is nothing wrong with an employer trying to reduce its share of the costs of retirement benefits by moving to these plans. After all, if your employer doesn't pay attention to its costs, it won't be in business for long! Such retirement benefit plans are offered by employers in order to be competitive in recruiting talent and having employees perceive a positive benefit to encourage them to stay with the company. Therefore, your employer's goal is to offer the greatest benefit as perceived by employees and recruits at the lowest cost to the company. This is Economics 101. A retirement plan with participant direction and funding (such as 401(k), 403(b), and 457 plans*) fits the bill perfectly today, because employees view them in a positive light while generally bearing most of the costs and risks and saving the company a mountain of expenses.

Throughout this book, whenever I use the term 401(k) plan, it is also meant to cover 457 and 403(b) plans as well, even if they are not specifically mentioned. However, if there are differences applicable between these types of plans, they will be highlighted and spelled out for you.

As mentioned, when 401(k) plans first came out, they were not viewed as positively by employees as they are today. (Although the bear market in 2008 through early 2009 has had many participants change that view.) Many large companies were slow to move to 401(k) plans because of the revolt from employees. That might be hard to imagine today when it is expected that a company will offer a 401(k) plan, and such plans are normally viewed as a positive benefit to employees. But back when most employees were covered by pension plans, the companies that attempted to switch to a 401(k) plan often froze the benefits in their existing pension plans and offered employees these new 401(k) plans instead. As you might imagine, these employers experienced a fair number of complaints from their employees. At the time, the existing employees covered by the old pension plan realized that with the new 401(k), they were taking on the investment risk, the benefit risk, and most of the cost and expenses. It seemed like a rip-off

---

*401(k) plans are sponsored by companies; 403(b) plans are generally for educators, such as teachers and administrators; and 457 plans are for government workers, such as police and fire department employees.

when compared to the old pension plan in which the employer carried all of the risks and expense.

However, over time, more and more employers were able to pull off this switch, and as new people—who never had the safety of a pension plan guarantee—entered the workforce, the 401(k) became an expected, popular benefit. Also, remember that because the cost and risk to the employer is practically nothing, or at least very small relative to older types of retirement plans, many more companies that would not have offered any retirement plan at all under previous rules now found themselves in a position to offer a retirement plan to their employees.

So that is where we are today. There is more than $3 trillion in 401(k) plans covering more than 47 million employees and well more than $1 trillion in 403(b) and 457 plans covering millions more. Odds are that you—and if married, your spouse or both of you—participate in such plans. More than 600,000 employers offer these plans, meaning that a retirement benefit program is no longer just for large public companies, as was generally the case in the past. There are fewer than 6,000 public companies in the United States, which means that more than 98 percent of these 401(k) plans are offered by smaller, privately held companies.

Over the past 20 years, employers have been able to dramatically reduce their benefit costs and risks and transfer most of these to their employees, and they have done so with their employees generally being happy about it! If you are happy, the person sitting in the cube or office next to you is happy, and your employer is happy, shouldn't we just all lock arms and sing "Kumbaya"?

The Rip-off YOU CAN FIX

Complacency and the general euphoria employers and employees alike have with their retirement plans have created a massive opportunity for product vendors to excessively profit from your retirement savings.

This is not someone crying wolf. A study by the Center for Retirement Research at Boston College noted, "The bottom line is that over the period 1988 to 2004 defined-benefit plans outperformed 401(k) plans by one percentage point. This outcome occurred despite the fact that 401(k) plans held a higher portion of their assets in equities during the bull market of the 1990s."

Since you are bearing all of the risks in your 401(k), what does this 1 percent cost YOU? All things being equal, except this extra 1 percent cost, you may be surprised to find that the price to your lifestyle is HUGE.

For example, if you are 40 years old with $75,000 in your 401(k) plan, and you are earning $50,000 a year, contributing 10 percent with a 50 percent match by your employer, and planning on retiring at age 65 with the hope of a $32,000 annual retirement income, this 1 percent excess expense can cost you any one of the following:

- ☑ A 90 percent chance that this excess cost will reduce your retirement fund at age 65 by somewhere from $100,000 to $700,000
- ☑ Working three more years to age 68
- ☑ Working an extra hour every day for 25 years until age 65
- ☑ Living on 22 percent less than you desired ($25,000 instead of $32,000)
- ☑ Accepting a 72 percent greater chance of outliving your resources (31 percent versus 18 percent)
- ☑ Increasing your annual savings by 80 percent from $5,000 (10 percent) to $9,000 (18 percent)

There is a reason why you are bearing this burden, and it DOES NOT generally have to do with your employer saving money on the costs of offering you a retirement plan. Your employer wants you to perceive a positive benefit from the 401(k) plan it offers. If you and your neighbor in the next cube both perceive the 401(k) plan as an attractive benefit, then your employer has done its job, even if you are getting "taken" to the tune of more than $100,000!

Fixing This Is Up to You!

How would you spend an extra $4,000 a year for the next 25 years? How much more secure would your retirement be with an extra $100,000 or more? How much more time could you spend at your family dinner table if you could work an hour less each day? What would you do in retirement with an extra $7,000 every year? What would you do in retirement if you could retire three years earlier? THIS is the price of complacency to many retirement plan participants.

In the old days of defined-benefit plans, your employer assumed the burden of all of the risks and all of the expenses, and those employers that still offer such plans still carry that burden. Back then, and today as well, employers who accepted the risks and carried the expense of a defined-benefit plan bore a huge incentive to reduce the costs, because THEY would get the benefit of doing so. The benefit they promised was fixed, the variable of the COST of that benefit saved the company money. THEY could avoid increasing THEIR contribution for your benefit by 80 percent if they saved 1 percent in expense. That might just be the reason, or at least part of the reason, that such plans outperform 401(k) plans by 1 percent a year.

In a 401(k) plan, because YOU bear this expense, your employer has little motivation to shop for a better deal if you and your associates are content, even though it probably should be looking for that better deal in its role of a "prudent fiduciary." This prudent fiduciary standard may be a bit different for 401(k) plans than in some 403(b) and 457 plans. Regardless, the vendors of plans in this market have no reason to compete on fees since practically no one is complaining about them.

A study by the Government Accountability Office[*] commissioned by Congressman George Miller of California reported that in 2005, despite 47 million people being covered by 401(k) plans, the Labor Department received only 10 complaints about fees. If you aren't complaining, and no one else in your company is complaining, and if your employer really doesn't care as long as you are happy with the plan, your employer isn't going to bear even the tiny cost of shopping for a better deal.

This is about to change though because new fee-disclosure rules are about to go into effect. The first version of this book took you through the steps needed to uncover the numerous deeply hidden fees. This version of *Stop the Retirement Rip-off* has been written to acknowledge the new fee disclosure rules to save you what was some fairly arduous work and focus more on higher value things that you might enjoy. The new fee disclosure rules go into effect for plan years that end beginning in 2012, meaning that if your plan's

---

[*]U.S. Government Accountability Office, "Private Pensions: Changes Needed to Provide 401(k) Plan Participants and the Department of Labor Better Information on Fees," GAO-07-2, 1 November 2006, p. 21.

fiscal year end is January 2012, you will start to see statements after the end of the plan year that explicitly show you how much your retirement plan is costing you. If your plan's fiscal year falls on a calendar year, you will have to wait until early in 2013 to discover what your retirement plan is costing you. BE PREPARED FOR RETIREMENT PLAN STICKER SHOCK! Many of you will be surprised to learn that you may be paying thousands of dollars a year in fees in your retirement plan. I suspect this will create the participant revolt that is needed to get many of these ill-designed retirement plans finally fixed.

Your retirement plan is probably one of your most important future sources of financial security. This book makes it easy for you to take the steps needed to add more than $100,000 to your retirement nest egg without taking more risk or saving more money. This can allow you to improve your lifestyle, increase your benefits, identify the hidden costs, and improve your standing within your company by proactively helping your employer to take needed action.

There is no reason, other than the price of this book and a little bit of your time, why you can't capture the opportunity to improve your lifestyle, reduce how much you need to save, retire earlier, or work less. Isn't $100,000 worth a few hours of your time?

Acknowledgments

Acknowledgments, to me, are perhaps the hardest thing to write, because we are a product of all of the people we know. How do you thank everyone who has helped make you who you are? Of course, I need to thank all the people of Wealthcare Capital Management®, who have each made a contribution to this book, either directly or indirectly. We have a great team of people who truly care about helping people make the most of their lives, and they do so with unbridled passion. They live as role models for others by consistently acting with unquestioning integrity. Jerry, Christopher, Brandy, TJ, Elliott, Eric, Will, Bill, and, of course, my executive committee partners, Bob and Karen, have all made huge direct contributions to this book. Thank you all for your patience, objectivity, and coaching and for understanding how to help us to help others.

Of course, I have to thank all of my former associates from my "Wheat First" days that are now part of Wells Fargo. These associates had the courage to challenge conventional wisdom and risk being different to better serve clients. I have to credit Dave Monday, Mark Staples, Danny Ludeman, Jim Donley, Marshall Wishnack, and, of course, the late James Wheat, a blind man who had more vision than all of us put together. Respect should be earned, not given, and every one of these people has earned mine. I consider each of them heroes in their own way.

There are a handful of people in the industry I have to thank, because they, too, have truly earned my respect by their actions and courage. People like Len Reinhart, Ron Surz, and the late Don Tabone have all contributed greatly to my knowledge, and their willingness to have rational debate on numerous topics has helped me immensely.

I want to thank Dawn and Jim Loeper, who were kind enough to give the manuscript a read and provide some valuable feedback.

Also, Donna Wells, who helped to make my normal pontification understandable, is due credit for her enormous contribution.

A big part of understanding expenses came from Parker Payson of Employee Fiduciary Corporation, whose expertise in ferreting out hidden expenses was invaluable in helping to identify the hidden costs.

I want to thank my late father, Kenneth A. Loeper, for teaching me "not to let anyone push me around." Without that skill ingrained in my brain, I would have never had the courage to face the attacks of the industry groups that hate having their apple cart upset. I also thank my mother, Anna, for teaching me that the biggest responsibility we have in raising children is teaching them to be respectable people of integrity who can take care of themselves.

Finally, I want to thank the late Ayn Rand. Whether you like her or not, you have to respect her passion for and vision of a hero or heroine, so often demonstrated in her novels. The abstracts of her concepts, living a moral life and acting with integrity, helped me to understand and express why I am what I am. Who is John Galt?

Introduction

Make the Most of Your Life!

When the first version of this book was released in 2009, much of the content was dedicated to mapping out the steps you would need to take to sort your way through the maze of hidden documents to uncover the outrageous hidden expenses that exist in a majority of participant-directed retirement plans like 401(k) plans (generally corporate retirement plans), 403(b) plans (generally education, healthcare, and other non-profit employee plans), and 457 plans (generally local government plans).

The vast majority of retirement-plan participants, as of this writing, still do not know how much of their retirement savings are being skimmed away (or perhaps "scooped" would be a more appropriate word since the word "skimming" discounts the extent of the pillaging that is going on) and how the unscrupulous product vendors have been arduously working and lobbying to keep these expenses hidden from you. Despite the vendors' efforts, **this is about to change because new fee-disclosure regulations are going into effect beginning in 2012**.

The new fee-disclosure regulations will apply to all corporate and many 403(b) plans after their 2012 fiscal year end. This means that participants in these types of plans will actually be getting relatively clear and concise disclosures about their real total costs beginning in February 2012, for plans that have fiscal year ends of January 2012. If your plan has a December end fiscal year, your first real full fee-disclosure statement will not come until January 2013.

I would like to think that my consumer advocacy books, other writings, and media appearances had some impact on getting these long-overdue disclosures in the hands of retirement-plan participants. Regardless of whether my efforts contributed to the new disclosures,

1

the new regulations have created the opportunity to rewrite this book to eliminate the soon-to-be-unnecessary content about how to ferret through your expenses and instead focus on some higher value content that you can act on to improve your lifestyle.

Even though your retirement expenses will be disclosed to you in the coming years, and many people will be shocked to discover what they are actually paying, this doesn't mean that your employer will necessarily take the steps needed to improve your retirement plan to eliminate needless and wasted expenses. So the content in Chapters 4 through 6 that guide you through motivating your employer to fix your retirement plan without sounding like a complainer is still applicable. The new disclosures just make this job a lot easier for you and your co-workers and my suggestions there have been updated to recognize this.

Additionally I've added new content for participants that will not benefit from these new disclosure regulations (some 403(b) and most 457 plans), added new up-to-date content covering new resources that are available to you, added additional educational content about how you can protect yourself from vendors and your employer, as well as some valuable educational content **about the choices you have about how you can make the most of your life**.

It is important to note that not all retirement plans have excessive fees, but if the company you work for has fewer than 1,000 employees, or if you are in a 457 or 403(b) plan, the odds are high that you are paying them. It is currently still difficult to figure out what you are really paying but soon the new disclosures (for many participants) will make it as easy as reading your statement and looking for the fee disclosures.

Chapter 1 will expose to you why fees matter. The expenses scooped out of your retirement assets matter a lot and unlike so much of the rest of retirement investing that has so much uncertainty, **fees are 100 percent certain**. For most participants (especially if you take the steps needed to get your employer to fix your plan as outlined in this book) fees are something that you can control with certainty and the price to your lifestyle of **evading this responsibility could cost you thousands or even a million dollars or more!**

Chapter 2 outlines the litany of expenses that might be dragging down your retirement assets. Most (but not all) of these expenses will be disclosed to you when the new disclosures go into effect for your plan (after fiscal plan years ending in 2012) so you will no longer need to expend the effort to hunt them down. But, you should understand what the supposed purpose of these expenses is to help you be more effective in your conversations with your employer. This is important because the employer may have been convinced by a product vendor that all participants put a value on whatever sizzle they are selling, when the reality might be that few participants put a value on it and the expense of that needless "service," "feature," or "option" drags down everyone's assets, including all of those who don't want it. Being informed to discuss with your employer that, for example, you don't appreciate being forced to buy insurance you do not need is helpful in getting your employer to take action to reduce the expenses you are being forced to pay.

In Chapter 3, you learn about the uncertainty of the markets and the impact of certain fees and how together they impact the quality of your lifestyle both now and in retirement. We will also expose how the typical advisor and retirement planning tools are designed to scare and guilt you into **needlessly sacrificing your lifestyle** (is that a service you want to pay for???). Additionally, since many plan participants are already in some pretty decent-quality retirement plans, we will expose to you when the excess costs are too insignificant to bother rocking the boat with your employer which will enable you to skip some of the chapters and move on to higher value things you can do to make the most of your life. However, our example in the preface showed how a typical 40-year-old middle-class participant (with $75,000 in his 401(k) and saving $5,000 a year) had a 90 percent chance of adding anywhere from $100,000 to more than $700,000 to his retirement fund by finishing the steps in this book. In reality, the cost savings and benefits could be far greater. So, Chapter 3 will show some examples of the price to your lifestyle at various ages and contribution levels, so you can see if it is worth going any further. You will also see what the benefits might be to improving your lifestyle if you are successful in getting your employer to improve your retirement plan.

Chapter 4 introduces you to how to approach your employer by Complaining without Sounding Like a Complainer. Let's assume you, like millions of other Americans, find out in the new disclosures you will be receiving starting sometime in 2012 or 2013 that it is worthwhile to take the next step because your retirement plan is costing you absurd amounts of excess fees. You also will have discovered that these excess fees carry a huge cost to the lifestyle you want to live. Knowing these costs exist isn't going to change things unless you take action. You might view yourself as just a cog in the company wheel, and you don't want to "make waves" with those in command. But there are ways to correct these expenses, and, instead of being viewed as a complainer, you might actually end up being viewed as a hero in the eyes of both your bosses and your coworkers. **This chapter gives you all of the secrets to fix your retirement plan in a positive and proactive manner.**

If you approach your employer about the needlessly high expenses and they ignore you, as will often be the case, the subject of Chapter 5 is the next step—rallying your troops. After discovering your expenses were way too high and were materially affecting your quality of life and proactively and positively bringing it to your employer's attention, bringing just a few of your coworkers to the cause can make the difference in getting your employer to take the steps needed to fix your broken retirement plan.

This is often needed when the distractions of day-to-day business have the "powers that be" in your company complacently ignoring your initial attempt to highlight the problem of excess expenses. Getting a copy of this book to your human resources or benefits department might be a good way to get your employer to focus on the problem. We also give you a no-cost way to help your fellow associates and coworkers join in your rally to get your employer to spend a few hours working on this problem. Your associates also will be protected from being viewed as complainers, and it generally will not take more than an e-mail and a brief discussion over the water cooler to encourage a few of your coworkers to help in the cause. Your one voice may not be enough, but if your employer receives just a couple of additional questions from other employees, it is likely your employer will wake up and take notice. If they hear one complaint, they might assume you are the only one who cares. If the employer hears three or more complaints or questions, they will assume there might be many others who have not yet complained. At this point the employer may become concerned that it is losing the positive benefit it is trying to create by sponsoring the retirement plan, and it might take action to solve the problem.

In Chapter 6, we move on to What Happens If My Employer Ignores Us? This step is the course of last resort for those of you who already as individuals and with the help of coworkers have shed light on the expenses to your employer, yet the retirement plan remains needlessly expensive. If you have figured out that your expenses are far too high, if the price to your lifestyle of these expenses is too great, if you and your associates have let your employer know about these expenses and where to go to for a solution and nothing happens, it is time to take more drastic action.

While several lawsuits have been filed against employers that ignore their fiduciary obligations and as I predicted in my book *The Four Pillars of Retirement Plans*, the number of lawsuits have been burgeoning in just the last couple of years, there is an easier and less disruptive way to solve the problem that will bring in the government on your side as an added bonus. The government exists only because you pay taxes to fund their activities, so this course of action, while drastic and unnecessary in most cases and a bit more adversarial than the teamwork methods shown in prior steps, might be the only way for you to get your employer to wake up and fix the problem.

Specifics are provided in Chapter 6 that explain some of the terminology of the Employee Retirement Income Security Act (ERISA), where to go, how to remain anonymous, and what you should say to put the fear of government intervention to work for your retirement. Finally, we will also explore how to overcome one of the most common defenses for using overpriced investments (past performance or performance track records) and what the real facts are about fund ratings and track records.

Once your retirement plan has been fixed and you are free of the excessive needless expenses that drag against your lifestyle, it is time to reap the rewards of your efforts. The next step—Making the Most of Your Life—is covered in Chapter 7. Your expenses now are reasonable, and the options this creates to improve your lifestyle are vast. Should you:

- Save less money?
- Plan on retiring earlier?
- Work fewer hours?
- Add a travel budget to your plan for retirement?
- Take less investment risk so that market gyrations still let you sleep at night?
- Take the vacation of your dreams?
- Leave a bequest to your church or school?

- Buy the new sports car you have always dreamed about?
- Pay off credit card bills?
- Send your child to a private school?
- Build an addition on your house?
- Help your elderly parents improve their lifestyle?
- Upgrade the way you pursue your hobby?
- Buy a vacation home?

While this list of options just scratches the surface of the choices you have, if your retirement plan is costing you too much, then executing the steps outlined in this book will enable some (maybe many) of your dreams for a better life to confidently become a reality. While it may seem too good to be true, any one of these goals (or any others you might have that are not on the list) might be achievable if you can move the expenses of your retirement plan to *your* pocket, instead of an investment product vendor's pocket.

This Is Why It Is So Important for You to Take the Steps Needed to Improve Your Retirement Plan!

You might be skeptical that saving 1 percent in expenses in your retirement accounts could produce options like these to improve your lifestyle. A quick calculation for our sample middle-class American with $75,000 in his 401(k) would infer that the benefit of saving 1 percent in fees is worth only $750 a year. But remember that this person is contributing 10 percent of his income ($5,000 a year), and his employer is matching an additional $2,500 so that the $75,000 balance will likely accumulate to far more money in the coming year. In fact, if he earns 7 percent on his $75,000, a year later his retirement plan would be worth $87,750. His investment may have grown by 7 percent but his excess fees grew from $750 to $877 because of the growth in assets and additional contributions. That is **a 16.9 percent increase in fees!**

Think about the way compound interest works. In 10 or 20 years, your 401(k) could easily be worth $250,000 to more than $1 million! An extra 1 percent expense at that point **could cost you $2,500 to more than $10,000 a year!** If your fees are growing by more than twice the rate you are growing your investments, this will clearly compound into some serious money.

The severe market declines we experienced in 2008, often cited as being "unprecedented," are actually a reality of the capital markets and should be planned for because no one knows when such markets might occur. All investments have risk. Just in the past few years, we've seen equities experience 40 percent losses, gold decline by 30 percent (only to rebound to new highs as of this writing), oil decline by 50 percent from record closing prices, then again rebounding and declining again in spring of 2011, and of course the five-plus-year bear market in residential real estate with losses approaching 50 percent or more in some areas. With such declines randomly occurring without warning, it might seem there is nowhere one could hide. These market gyrations should really be expected, and the uncertainty should be planned for, measured, and monitored in modeling our retirement lifestyle. It is easy for us to become complacent when long periods of time pass without such devastating markets, and this creates false confidence or over confidence that sometimes results in reckless decisions. Experiencing the pain of these losses sometimes has the opposite emotional effect of becoming excessively fearful. Just as the emotions of overconfidence result in reckless decisions to ignore risk, the emotions of loss cause us to make reckless decisions to avoid risk and those emotions are exploited by product vendors peddling guarantees. A new Chapter 9 shows us that there is no free lunch and those emotional guarantees that are sold by exploiting your emotional fears also have a price.

Understand both sides of the equation, objectively and free of product marketing spin designed to exploit emotion instead of reason. For example, the bear market of 1973 through 1974 had the stock market declining by almost 50 percent. In the crash of 1929, with the ensuing Great Depression, total stock market losses over several years were even worse. These are the realities of the markets and you can choose to ignore the risk of these environments to your lifestyle, or you can plan for them and model allocations and simulations that prepare you for these markets in advance like we do with all of our clients. Since your investments will go up and down over time but will grow in the long run, your contributions each year will become a smaller percentage of your total account balances, reducing the percentage growth in your fees while increasing the dollar expense of excessive fees. There are a lot of uncertainties in the markets, your goals, and what you personally value, and also a lot of choices of how you can "spend the dividend" you get by taking the steps needed to fix your retirement plan.

Chapter 7 walks you through the process that you and your spouse or partner can go through to figure out how and on what you can confidently use the "expense saving dividend" benefit of your repaired retirement plan. Without this step, you really won't realize the benefits of the first steps you took to get your retirement plan fixed.

Your assets (and their expenses), allocation choices, goals, dreams, priorities, and how you personally value each of these items are inextricably connected. The bottom line is that while you may have fixed the problem of paying needless expenses by taking the first few steps, you may still be saving too much, working too long, vacationing too little, or merely compromising something you value to achieve something you do not value as much. **The real payoff comes from making informed choices about what makes the most sense for what you personally value**.

How do you know if you are making an informed choice? How do you choose an asset-allocation strategy? How can you tell whether your adviser is conflicted or is helping you make the most of your life? What questions should you ask? How can you select investments that avoid needless expenses and risk? Fixing the expenses in your retirement plan is not going to improve your life if the advice you get is conflicted, you have a poor asset allocation, or you choose investments that expose you to unnecessary risks. If you want to learn more about all of the conflicts that exist throughout the financial services industry as well as the media and web sites, you may want to pick up a copy of my book, *Stop the Investing Rip-off, Second Edition* (John Wiley & Sons, Inc., 2012). It could be a handy reference guide for you. It covers, in much more detail than we can cover within the topic of this book, the details of the conflicts that are present, the parts of the sales pitches you don't hear but need to know, and the specific questions to ask any vendor of financial products or services in order to protect yourself. Some key issues are covered in this book, though.

Finally, to truly make the most of your life, this initial process of making informed choices cannot be a one-time event. To make the most of your life it needs to become a continuous process responding to the changes in your life, your values, your priorities, and the markets. We call this continuous life relative advice "Wealthcare," and our process is so unique it actually has been patented. How this process works and the benefits to improving your lifestyle are explored along with several helpful tools enabling you to implement choices in Chapter 8. Fixing your retirement plan may be a one-time event, but making the most of the only life you have should be a continuous process.

1

Why Fees Matter–The Coming "Retirement Plan Sticker Shock"

Most Americans either do not know what they are paying within their retirement plan or, even worse, make the completely erroneous assumption that they aren't paying anything at all. In the coming years, due to new required fee disclosures starting for some in 2012, this will abruptly change. Many of you will be faced with **"Retirement Plan Sticker Shock."** That retirement plan with the nice match from your employer that has previously been erroneously perceived by you to cost you "nothing" (due to the lack of ethics of the product and advice vendors hiding their fees) will suddenly show you a statement with annual costs TO YOU that may be $1,000, $3,000, or even $10,000 or more EVERY YEAR!

I am confident that these new fee disclosures are going to take many people by surprise (including many employers and trustees), so that the coming years will have many retirement plans taking action to fix all of the needless expenses that are being scooped from participants' retirement savings. I'd like to think the first version of this book and my various media appearances had something to do with getting these disclosures in the hands of participants. Keeping participants in the dark about costs was the strategy of many product vendors and advisors which left most participants not knowing what, if anything, they were paying. The first version of this book walked those motivated enough to work through the maze to uncover the craftily hidden expenses. I sent the first version of the book to every member of the Senate and Congress and then the media picked up on this message of hidden expenses. I was interviewed in numerous newspaper stories and on several radio shows. I even was interviewed on CNN and Fox Business, and 60 Minutes did a story on hidden retirement plan expenses.

Now, disclosures and more transparency are coming and the unethical vendors that have been hiding their needless fees are going to have a day of reckoning. If they had originally ethically disclosed their costs to participants and employers and charged an honest price for only necessary services instead of trying to use every trick in the book to hide their repeated skimming of retirement assets, they would have nothing to fear now because the participants and employers would have known what was going on. But now, after intentionally misleading their clients for years, they are going to face not only a revolt, but also I suspect numerous lawsuits too. It serves them right!

What's a Little Fee Between Friends?

Why should you worry about fees? Does the difference of say 0.41 percent a year really impact your life much? After all, if you have $100,000, that's "only" $410 a year. How could that make much of a difference to your life now, or in the future?

Product vendors often will discount the impact of such a "small" fee in their presentations to your employer . . . and you if you confront them. They will say it is a small price to pay for their "superior service" (which will not really be measurable) and for the "strength of their firm" which in all likelihood has no material impact that really protects you. Yet, all else being equal, this seemingly small fee differential has a real price to your lifestyle.

Take for example a 35 year old that earns $60,000 a year and has accumulated $75,000 so far in her retirement account. The difference between total expenses of 1.10 percent annually, versus 0.69 percent annually (a difference of 0.41 percent) does have some significant impact to her lifestyle. At least, I think she would think it is significant.

To make up for this seemingly "small" difference, she would have to work two extra years to age 67 instead of retiring at age 65. IS WORKING TWO EXTRA YEARS JUST TO PAY NEEDLESS FEES TO A VENDOR SOMETHING YOU WOULD CONSIDER A SMALL PRICE TO PAY?

Of course, she doesn't have to work longer to make up for the difference in the needless expenses. Alternatively, since she will have accumulated less money with the higher fee by age 65, she might just opt to spend less in retirement. That "small" fee difference would force her to reduce her retirement spending for the rest of her life by $4,200 a year. Without the excess fee she could have confidently planned on a retirement income of $36,000 a year for the rest of her life, but with just an extra 0.41 percent headwind of excess expenses, to have the same confidence she would have to reduce her retirement income by 12 percent to $31,800.

DO YOU THINK YOU COULD FIND SOMETHING TO DO IN RETIREMENT WITH AN EXTRA $4,200 A YEAR FOR LIFE? IS THAT A "SMALL" PRICE?

That extra expense of 0.41 percent right now in dollars is only $308 based on her current retirement plan balance of $75,000. Maybe she could just increase her savings to make up for this "small" difference, still retire at 65 and still plan on spending $36,000 a year. That seems less painful than working two more years, or cutting her retirement income by $4,200 a year. The only problem with this is that as her account grows with contributions (and hopefully some market growth), so will the impact of that fee differential. So, the amount she would need to increase her savings by for the next 30 years until retirement is $1,500 a year . . . 30 percent more than she would otherwise have to save ($5,000 versus $6,500) and the equivalent of about a $25,000 mortgage at 4 3/8 percent interest.

IS INCREASING YOUR SAVINGS BY 30 PERCENT A YEAR FOR 30 YEARS A "SMALL" PRICE TO PAY? WOULD AN EXTRA $1,500 A YEAR FOR 30 YEARS IMPROVE SOME ASPECTS OF YOUR LIFE? THINK ABOUT HOW THAT COULD IMPACT YOUR HOLIDAY GIFTS OR VACATIONS!

Figure 1.1 demonstrates these impacts of such a "small" difference in fees in terms that might be more meaningful to you than what the product vendor or advisor will cavalierly discount in his answer to you about fees.

I would like to think that the worst plans out there are over charging for services by "only" this "small" amount. Unfortunately, that is not what I have witnessed. For example, after releasing the first version of this book, I heard from a police officer about his union-backed 457 retirement plan for a large city's police force.

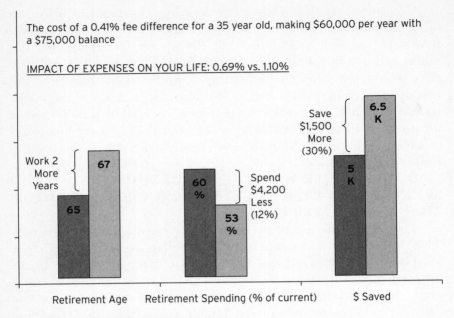

The cost of a 0.41% fee difference for a 35 year old, making $60,000 per year with a $75,000 balance

IMPACT OF EXPENSES ON YOUR LIFE: 0.69% vs. 1.10%

Figure 1.1   Cost to the Employee—Quality of Life

The officer was actually credentialed in finance and analyzed the costs that were coming from the plan. The plan was large (more than $1 billion) and should have had the negotiating power to get the lowest fees to enable the police officers to get a good deal so they could have a comfortable retirement after serving and protecting citizens over their careers. Unfortunately, it appears that the union that controlled the decision chose a vendor for some other purpose than serving their members, because the costs of this huge plan were nearly 2 percent a year.

Another example came from an objective advisor who contacted me about a State 403(b) plan where teachers and administrators didn't know their retirement assets were being skimmed to the tune of 0.50 percent by the union in the form of kickbacks, unless they read the fine print deeply buried in half-inch-thick documents. There will be more on this in Chapter 10 which is dedicated to those plans which still will not receive the fee disclosures.

Over the years since the release of the first version of my book, I have witnessed many plans with similar problems. I've seen multi-million dollar plans for several medical practices with expenses of 2 to 3 percent a year or even more. I've seen a complacent law firm that should know better with multiple tens of millions, needlessly having their lawyers' retirement assets skimmed by an extra 0.50 percent a year.

Perhaps most seriously as a violation of ERISA, I've seen multiple occasions where trustees of a corporate or non-profit retirement plan selected an expensive vendor (a bank) because they thought they could get more favorable loan and other banking terms. THIS IS A PROHIBITED TRANSACTION under the Employee Retirement Income Security Act of 1974 (ERISA) yet it happens every day, even though the trustees of the plan face *personal liability* for this action, if and when they are discovered.

You saw the impact to one's lifestyle of just a 0.41 percent additional needless expense. For some of these plans, with an excess cost of 1.5 percent to more than 2 percent, it gets even more extreme.

Do You Have an Extra $1 Million You Could Spare?

Probably not, but that could very well be the price tag you are paying over your life if your retirement plan has excess costs of 1.5 percent annually. Take an example of a diligent 25 year old that has been taught to save for retirement. Graduating from college and landing a good promotion after working for a few years, she is in a position to start saving for retirement and she starts saving $7,500 a year in her retirement plan ($625 a month) and adjusts that each year for 3 percent inflation.

Over 40 years, with an expense of only 0.50 percent, and a simple investment allocation of 80 percent domestic stocks, and 20 percent in 7- to 10-year Treasury bonds, in 83 percent of the 541 historical 40-year periods back to 1926, she would have accumulated an amazing $3,385,000. (The worst historical 40-year period for her, starting in the Great Depression and ending in the 1974 bear market, would have her accumulate "only" $2,343,000.) Unfortunately, due to the impact of inflation, the spending power of the nearly $3.4 million would be only a bit more than $1,000,000.

However, if her fees were 1.5 percent higher (2.0 percent versus 0.50 percent), and all other things being equal, instead of an 83 percent historical chance of exceeding $3.4 million, she would have only a 40 percent chance. Think about this. **The effect of the excessive 1.5 percent fee cuts her odds of accumulating $3.4 million in half!**

It gets worse as you probe into the analysis. With the drain of the excessive 1.5 percent cost, her retirement assets at age 65 at the same 83 percentile as the lower-cost plan would be more than $1 million less ($2,351,929 versus $3,385,000). Remember *the worst* outcome of 541 historical 40-year periods with a 0.50 percent expense was $2,343,000, about the same amount as the eighty-third percentile with a 2.00 percent fee.

To make up for this in additional savings, instead of saving an inflation-adjusted $7,500 a year, she would have to save an inflation-adjusted $11,000 a year. That's a 46 percent increase in the amount she'd need to save ($3,500) every year for the next 40 years, just to make up the difference in fees.

The following figures summarize these comparisons.

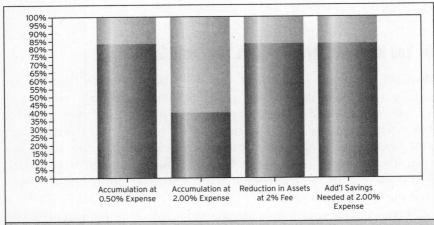

	Accumulation at 0.50...	Accumulation at 2.00...	Reduction in Assets ...	Add'l Savings Needed ...
Retirement Age				
Retirement	65	65	65	65
Target End Value				
Today's Dollars	$1,037,695	$1,037,695	$721,000	$1,037,695
Actual Dollars	$3,385,000	$3,385,000	$2,351,929	$3,385,000
Savings (Current)				
Retirement	$7,500	$7,500	$7,500	$11,000
Default Inflation Rate	3%	3%	3%	3%
Investment Adjustment	−0.500%	−2.000%	−2.000%	−2.000%
Portfolio				
All Accounts	fwc-balanced growth 80% equities	fwc-balanced growth 80% equities	fwc-balanced growth 80% equities	fwc-balanced growth 80% equities
Median Return	9.73%	8.21%	8.21%	8.21%
Risk				
Std. Deviation**	15.05%	15.05%	15.05%	15.05%
Downside (95%-tile)**	−12.34%	−13.81%	−13.81%	−13.81%

Plan Name		Over Target		< Target		Less than $0
1	**Accumulation at 0.50% Expense**	▦	83%	☐	17%	■ 0%
	We evaluated 541 40-year periods of market returns from 1926 to 2010. Your portfolio met your goals and had a targeted ending value of at least $1,037, 695 at age 65 in 450 of these periods, or 83%.					
	The first 40 year period used market returns from January 1926 to December 1965. The second period used returns from February 1926 to January 1966 and so on until the last period which used returns from January 1971 to December 2010.					
	Your plan never ran out of money.					
2	**Accumulation at 2.00% Expense**	▦	40%	☐	60%	■ 0%
	We evaluated 541 40-year periods of market returns from 1926 to 2010. Your portfolio met your goals and had a targeted ending value of at least $1,037, 695 at age 65 in 215 of these periods, or 40%.					
	The first 40 year period used market returns from January 1926 to December 1965. The second period used returns from February 1926 to January 1966 and so on until the last period which used returns from January 1971 to December 2010.					
	Your plan never ran out of money.					
3	**Reduction in Assets at 2% Fee**	▦	83%	☐	17%	■ 0%
	We evaluated 541 40-year periods of market returns from 1926 to 2010. Your portfolio met your goals and had a targeted ending value of at least $721,000 at age 65 in 449 of these periods, or 83%.					
	The first 40 year period used market returns from January 1926 to December 1965. The second period used returns from February 1926 to January 1966 and so on until the last period which used returns from January 1971 to December 2010.					
	Your plan never ran out of money.					
4	**Add'l Savings Needed at 2.00% Expense**	▦	83%	☐	17%	■ 0%
	We evaluated 541 40-year periods of market returns from 1926 to 2010. Your portfolio met your goals and had a targeted ending value of at least $1,037,695 at age 65 in 451 of these periods, or 83%.					
	The first 40 year period used market returns from January 1926 to December 1965. The second period used returns from February 1926 to January 1966 and so on until the last period which used returns from January 1971 to December 2010.					
	Your plan never ran out of money.					

Think of Your Retirement Plan Savings and Expenses Like a Mortgage

Most people, if they qualify for good terms and have sufficient equity in their homes, would refinance if it would make a significant difference in their mortgage payment.

When you shop for a mortgage, you obviously pay some attention to the interest rate and the resulting payment amount. This is completely analogous to your retirement savings. *In a mortgage, you are financing the purchase of a home. In retirement planning, you are financing the purchase of a retirement income.* In a mortgage, the interest rate you pay will impact the cost of your monthly payments and your total interest cost over the life of the loan. In a retirement plan, the expenses you pay will impact the cost of the savings needed to fund your retirement and the total amount you will be able to accumulate. It is all just simple math.

Take the example of our diligent 25 year old saving $7,500 a year ($625 a month) until retirement at age 65. That equates to the principal and interest payments for a 30 year mortgage at 4.5 percent of $121,350. To make up for the 2 percent fee instead of a 0.50 percent fee, she'd have to save $3,500 more a year. **This is the equivalent of a mortgage rate of 8.13 percent for that same $121,350!** Alternatively, at 4.5 percent interest it is the equivalent of a $180,914 mortgage, instead of $121,350. The only difference between these mortgage examples and the retirement savings examples for our diligent 25 year old is that the savings are inflation adjusted instead of being fixed, and that instead of 30 years for the mortgage the higher retirement savings lasts for 40 years.

Would you be indifferent about paying 8.13 percent interest on your mortgage if you could easily get a mortgage at 4.5 percent? Of course not. Then why would you be indifferent about the cost to finance your retirement?

It may just be time to refinance your retirement planning.

Not All Fees Are Bad

When this book was originally released, I received a lot of hate mail from financial advisors and retirement plan product vendors. There were two things they were upset about. First, most did not appreciate me exposing how they were hiding their expenses and empowering the public to discover them. The new disclosures will eventually solve this problem for most participants, so they can blame the regulators instead of me on this point. The other thing they were upset about was "denying them a living." This came mostly from financial advisors that cried they "work hard" for their "meager" earnings, and suggesting that retirement plans should have expenses that are more reasonable, in the 0.50 percent to 0.75 percent range would eliminate their income. What the advisors did not realize is that THEY are being victimized by the product vendors too!

For most corporate retirement plans that have more than just a few million dollars, many advisors are lucky to earn 0.25 percent to 0.60 percent on the plan. For this they do enrollment meetings, select and monitor the funds that are available, and replace funds that "go bad" (meaning underperform). Some advisors even do one on one personal consultations with participants to help them select an "appropriate" allocation based on the participants' "risk tolerance" and help them select the funds or portfolios. In some rare circumstances, advisors actually meet individually with participants on an ongoing basis, offering some form of continuous "advice."

The advisors that provide these services believe that they are worth the 0.25 percent to 0.60 percent they receive. Unfortunately, the way the product vendors have them fooled, there is usually an additional cost THE ADVISOR DOES NOT RECEIVE that often equals an additional 0.50 percent to 1.5 percent, depending on the products used. Advisors have been trained to think those additional product expenses are helpful and necessary to participants for the management of funds or the insurance "features" that are part of these products.

But, go back and look at our diligent 25-year-old saver and the historical analysis we did. The worst historical outcome (a 1-in-541 historical chance) with a 0.50 percent total expense had her accumulating at least $2.34 million. This would have been the result if she simply indexed domestic equities and 7- to 10-year treasuries in an 80 percent stock and 20 percent bond portfolio. There are index funds available to even smaller plans with less than $1 million that could construct this portfolio for about 0.11 percent. This would leave the advisor at least 0.39 percent for the fees for his services and keep the total expenses at 0.50 percent. For most advisors, if the plan had total expenses of 0.50 percent, they would be lucky to earn 0.10 percent to 0.20 percent, so the PRODUCT vendors (that the advisors naively believe are their "partners") are costing them somewhere between half to three quarters of their income! Instead, they blame me.

For plans with total expenses of 0.75 percent, the advisor would normally be lucky to earn 0.25 percent to 0.35 percent, because of the expense of their product vendor "partners." But, if they objectively used the lower-cost 0.11 percent expense portfolio, they could earn 0.64 percent, increasing THEIR income by 80 percent to 156 percent. Yet, they blame me . . . and here is why.

The Biggest Expenses Have the Least Value

Just as the vendors have been misleading participants and employers about how much is being scooped out of retirement plans in fees, the product vendors have misled advisors into believing their fees are worthwhile for their "professional management" or insurance "features."

Many advisors believe that the source of their value is based on their attempt to out-perform the markets and that if they play that game, then they won't be employed at all and would not be entitled to any fee. The product vendors and their firms train them in this mistaken belief.

Going back to our diligent 25-year-old saver, remember that if she simply indexed her portfolio and rebalanced annually, in the worst of 541 historical 40-year periods she would have accumulated $2.34 million. In 83 percent of the historical periods, she would have accumulated more than $3.38 million. This presumes that she indexed and **underperformed the markets every year** by the expenses of 0.50 percent AND NO MORE.

The markets cannot underperform themselves, and EVERY active (aka expensive) manager risks potentially underperform-ing. This is not knowable in advance, and past records have been academically demonstrated not to be indicative of future results despite the industry's efforts to try to mislead us about this reality.

Take Morningstar for example. They know, and have admitted in their own research papers, that the biggest predictor of relative performance is fees. Their star ratings have little if any predictive power. And it isn't hard to see this. As of this writing, Morningstar ranks the indexed exchange traded fund (ETF) iShares S&P500 Growth (symbol IVW) as being in the top 1 percent of their "Large Growth Peer Group" for the last decade. This means this index fund outperformed 99 percent of all large growth funds, according to Morningstar. This holds true for iShares Russell 3000 Value ETF as well. Morningstar ranks this fund in the top 1 percent of all large value "peers" for the last decade.

Passive pundits will argue this is why you should index. I won't, because that would be misleading. The S&P500 SPDR (symbol SPY) fell where it should over the last decade, at the 50th percen-tile based on total return. And, somewhat ironically, the iShares S&P500 Large Cap Value ETF fell at the one-hundredth percentile of its supposed "peers" over the last decade.

So which is it? Some index funds fall at the top 1 percent, some in the middle, and some at the bottom 100th percentile. What does it mean? It means only one thing. Morningstar peer rankings (and thus **star ratings**) are comparing apples to oranges and **are thus completely meaningless**. There is effectively no statistical chance that an index fund would out-perform 99 percent of all active funds over a decade. There is likewise effectively no statistical chance that every active manager would outperform the index fund over a decade. **All it shows is that star rankings and "peer groups" are**

nothing more than a misleading shell game. You, and the advisors that believe and regurgitate this sham, are the victims. The product vendors (and Morningstar, or Lipper for that matter) that convince you and the advisors otherwise are laughing all the way to the bank.

Fees are a 100 percent certainty. Future performance is uncertain. Past performance already occurred and you cannot go back in time to capture something that has already occurred. Active management has two things going against it that makes it a statistically stupid endeavor. First, there is a 100 percent certain additional cost that you could avoid. Second, along with the hope of outperformance, which does have SOME chance to occur (choose your odds . . . 50 percent? 40 percent? 25 percent?), there is also a RISK of potential material underperformance, something you can avoid with near certainty by indexing (the market cannot underperform itself).

Advisors that think they are earning their fees by being croupiers in this game have been misled by the product vendors (and their firms) that are likely getting paid more than the advisor that is actually showing up and doing work for the plan.

If you have paid attention to how this game plays out over time in your retirement plan, you may have noticed that top performers are rarely if ever swapped out. After all, why would you replace a fund that is performing excellently? Okay. So when do you replace a fund? Usually, this occurs after the performance is terrible for a few years. Advisors think this is their value. Think about the absurdity in this.

What they say:

> *"We apply diligent research and help you select some of the top-performing funds for your plan, then we closely monitor their performance and replace them with better funds if their performance deteriorates."*

Sounds pretty good doesn't it? Well, think through logically what this actually means. Would you pay for the reality of what they do? Try this on for size because this is what typically happens in reality, and even the advisors don't realize this is what they are actually doing:

"We pick funds that performed well for others, yet have no idea whether or not they will outperform in the future or not. If they do perform well for you, we will keep them in your plan. If they underperform one year, we will in all likelihood give them the benefit of the doubt and keep them in place. If they underperform a second year, we will probably put them on a "watch list." If they underperform again for a third year, we will probably replace them with a fund we didn't originally pick for you but did well for others and we will lock in the three years of poor performance for all of your participants. For this, I deserve to be paid well."

By the time you have the 100 percent certain additional cost to overcome, and, the locking in of poor performance for invariably a number of the funds over the years, it is very unlikely that the winners that are picked (either by "skill" or luck) will be able to make up the difference. And, in many cases, the investments may materially underperform, something that an index fund doesn't risk.

For any retirement plan covering a number of employees, there is no reason that the plan for Dick's Cabinet Shop needs to offer different or "custom" selected funds for their plan relative to Sarah's Catering Company. Every employee (regardless of their employer) should have access to low-cost, diversified funds across broad asset classes like domestic stocks, foreign stocks, Treasury bonds, and cash equivalents. From these simple alternatives you can design an array of efficient allocations that accommodate anyone's desire for balancing return and risk, and often pre-designed efficient portfolios can be offered as well. For example, we have six model allocations that range from 30 percent stocks up to 100 percent stocks, and the blended expense ratios for these globally diversified portfolios are around 0.11 percent to 0.13 percent. Add another 0.20 percent to 0.30 percent (depending on the size of the plan) for the responsibility of selecting the funds and keeping the portfolios in balance, and you have total expenses of 0.31 percent to 0.43 percent. A brokerage window (a discount brokerage account) offering just about any investment vehicle rounds out the investment options in case any participant has some peculiar need that the standard offerings don't accommodate for some reason, or, if a participant has a personal advisor that can help them with tax location management across all of their assets.

With this sort of structure, you get the market performance that you probably would get with any other plan at a far lower cost. You'd get participant education meetings in person, online Webinars, recorded Webinars, do-it-yourself risk-assessment kits, daily online Web access with performance reporting for each participant, and so on. Custody and administration costs (more on these in the next chapter) would be no more than 0.06 percent on assets and $35 dollars a year per participant.

The Missing Link

There is one VERY, VERY valid complaint that I have heard from financial advisors about my focus on fees. That is, most retirement-plan participants don't know whether they should increase their savings, decrease their savings, or whether they can afford to stop contributing to their retirement plan completely. They don't know whether they can comfortably plan on an early retirement at age 59 or whether they should plan to work until they are 68. They don't know whether they can afford to have a very low-risk portfolio (with, say, just 30 percent stocks), or whether the better choice for their goals might be a portfolio with 60 percent or more in stocks. They don't know whether they can comfortably plan on a $35,000 retirement income or $50,000. Lowering the fees won't tell them the answers to these questions. The advisors are right about this. You probably don't know the answers to these questions.

The problem I have with this though is that MOST advisors (not all) don't answer these questions individually for you as a participant in a retirement plan, and, even on the rare occasion when they do, they don't regularly review and change the advice as your goals, priorities, and the markets change your confidence level in exceeding your goals. So while they argue that an advisor is usually needed to help a participant figure this out for their personal situation, in most cases, advisors are not delivering that sort of advice.

Advice about these things is valuable though, because it enables you to make the most of your life based on what you personally value. You may enjoy your job and not want to retire early, so your willingness to work longer can buy you a lower annual savings amount, or less investment risk for example. Conversely, you might prioritize early retirement and be willing to compromise the retirement income from your portfolio from $45,000 to $41,000 if that enables you to retire two years earlier. These goals and priorities are clearly likely to change over time, are completely personal, and cannot be answered in "group education meetings" (that are generally sale pitches more than education) and continuous ongoing advice is the only way to make the most of the one life you have.

This type of advice is not usually offered in a retirement plan. It is personal and custom, and it isn't cheap. It might raise your total costs to 0.85 percent, or maybe even 0.90 percent. But, if it enables you to retire two years sooner, or reduce how much you are saving each year, or spend more in retirement (when you wouldn't have known you could do any of these things) it might be worth it to you to pay the extra price for the service . . . if YOU value it.

That's the problem I have with the advisor's complaints about reducing fees. I don't have a problem with someone individually choosing to pay a fee for something they value. I have a problem with the fee if it is mandated, unnecessary, based on irrational bets, and is positioned in a one-sided misleading presentation. Does the extra 0.50 percent to 1.50 percent you might pay to Putnam, American Funds, or Hartford buy you any of these goals? It might. It might not. It is unknown. If you put a value on making the gamble, you are free to do so in the brokerage window. I just don't think EVERY participant should be forced into playing the same game. Do these companies even know what your goals are and which ones you value more than others? Of course not! What are THEY doing for the fees they are taking out of your retirement plan, and maybe from the advisor's pocket too?

So, my argument with advisors that defend the products as their "source of income" as the argument they use to justify their existence is that the valued advice does not exist in their world either. Their focus is on returns, not wealth and personal goals and priorities. They confuse the two. Instead, if they really wanted to be valuable they should give the sort of continuous advice that participants want, and are willing to individually pay for instead of being a croupier hoping to outperform and locking in underperformance that could have been avoided by indexing.

2

Types of Expenses Dragging Down Your Retirement Funds

Now that new fee disclosures are coming to a retirement plan near you, it might be helpful to briefly outline the different types of expenses you might incur, the supposed service that such fees are paying for, and also some of the expenses that will remain hidden even after the new fee-disclosure rules go into effect.

Expense Ratios

Expense ratios are usually the easiest (and often the highest) expense in your retirement plan. You don't actually see these withdrawn from your account because the share price is automatically reduced by this fee in mutual funds, exchange traded funds (ETFs), variable annuity sub-accounts, and bank collective funds, for example. Variable annuities have "unit prices" instead of share prices, but the concept is the same.

I've heard some very misleading presentations addressing questions about expense ratios. Expense ratios are insidious because of their lack of visibility, but the new disclosures will correct this.

The expense ratio for any fund is reflected as an annual percentage of the amount invested, and they can vary greatly. The total expense ratio may include 12b-1 fees (which are marketing fees), administration, accounting and legal costs, and management fees. Some of these may be shared with other vendors for various services like record keeping or merely as a form of sales commission, although it technically isn't described that way.

There are funds and ETFs that have expense ratios as low as 0.07 percent annually. For $100,000, this means you would be paying $70 a year. Contrast this to some funds that charge 1.75 percent or even more, where you would be paying $1,750 a year . . . that is 25 TIMES the price. I would argue you should get something really special for that price! There are a ton of funds with such expense ratios that have dramatically underperformed the index, and some that have outperformed. But no one knows which will be a winner and which will be a loser in advance. The odds are that more will underperform than outperform with that sort of fee.

Revenue Sharing

Historically, since participants couldn't really see this fee without doing some math, retirement plans have often exploited the lack of clear visibility and loaded up on the expense ratios as a source to hide all sorts of other fees.

Excessively expensive expense ratios are used to pay advisors, administration and custody costs, and so on. When a plan does this, it is called "revenue sharing." In essence, say that the expense ratio for one of the funds is 1.25 percent. From that, 0.25 percent might go to the "advisor" for "servicing" the plan, 0.30 percent might go back to the plan to "offset" administration and custody costs, and so on, and the mutual fund might keep the remaining 0.70 percent for "management" and operating the fund.

What I find ironic, is that revenue sharing has been pitched as a "benefit" to participants because some of the expenses are being shared back to the plan. They actually spin this shell game as if it in the participant's interest. I actually heard of one vendor (who is VERY large, but shall remain nameless to protect my life and limb) that issued a mandate for nonproprietary funds to limit the maximum amount of revenue sharing a fund participating on their platform could offer. This would make their proprietary funds more attractive. I've heard they have since rescinded that policy.

The problem I see with revenue sharing is that it enables everyone who is getting a piece of that revenue to overcharge for their services, and the employer and trustees have no serious motivation (other than their obligation as fiduciaries) to competitively shop for the services for the plan.

Maybe the advisor is worth the 0.25 percent he is getting. But, by telling the employer that they will have "no administration or custody costs to pay in the operation of the plan," the 0.30 percent going to cover those costs might be TWICE the going rate. But who cares? The company isn't paying for it. The advisor isn't paying for it. And, the participant doesn't really know they are paying twice the going rate. Nice deal huh?

Revenue sharing is completely unnecessary. There are institutional classes of most mutual funds that are not laden with excessive retail add-on expenses only to be reversed out and paid to someone else. If the fund company only needs 0.70 percent for the management of its fund, why not pay them that instead of bundling it with a bunch of other expenses that are kicked back to other vendors? Pay directly (instead of hiding it in an expense ratio) for the other services at the going rate. It really is a hugely misleading shell game and creates a huge conflict of interest for all of the decision makers involved in the plan.

Custodial Costs

Custodial services amount to being a record keeper on behalf of the entire plan. Custodians keep track of how many shares of which securities are owned by the plan, process dividends and capital gains, and hold the securities on behalf of the retirement plan trust. They process distributions and contributions as well. Usually, when purchased separately, a bank provides these services. Small retirement plans may incur a cost of up to 0.06 percent a year for such services while larger plans may incur a cost of as little as 0.02 percent. This is obviously not a particularly expensive service and that is because almost everything is done electronically.

Many plans however do not incur a separate custody cost because custody is "bundled" into other fees, like wrap fees from brokerage firms, bundled into the revenue sharing from expense ratios as previously discussed or bundled into some other bank or insurance company fee. In general though, if it is bundled it is likely that the cost being paid is higher than what is necessary. Bundled fees mean that you don't really know what you are specifically paying for anything, and this creates some abuses and needless costs.

Some employers (like mine) pay the custody costs directly instead of passing it through to the participants of the plan. Others prefer to pass the cost on, but most bundle it and it ends up costing more because of it. Paying this cost on behalf of our participants only cost our company $1,200 a year for our plan, with about $2 million in assets and 40 participants.

Administration and Record-Keeping Costs

These costs cover the individual participant record-keeping costs, the plan web site and participant access, annual government filings, discrimination testing, processing loans and contributions, participant statements, and so on. Sometimes there are two different vendors providing pieces of these services and sometimes they are both offered by one entity. In this case, I don't really see much purpose in having two different vendors since the services are so interconnected and it will usually cost more by unbundling these services.

Like custody, many plans do not have a separate cost for administration and record keeping per se as many have them bundled into advisory fees, revenue sharing from expense ratios, insurance company contract fees, and the like.

The best going rate for these services is about $35 a year per participant, with some minimum amount for very small plans. For our company, with about 40 participants, we have to pay a minimum of $1,750 a year for these services. With about $2 million in assets, this would amount to about 0.09 percent of assets.

Like custody costs, companies have the choice to pay for these costs directly or they can pass the pro-rata cost on to participants directly. In my company, we pay directly for the administration, record keeping, and custody costs so our employees do not incur these expenses. Most plans however might have these bundled into expenses that could be 0.25 percent to more than 1.00 percent annually, depending on the plan. Such plans have participants probably paying nearly two to eight times the going rate if they unbundled the services. In such plans, the company doesn't have any material incentive to get better pricing for their participants, so the participants end up paying the price.

Wrap Fees, Consulting, and Advisory Fees

A wrap program account is sold by a broker or consultant and could have three or four different money managers (or more) that each manage different portfolios for participants to select for their retirement plan. Each of these portfolios might have different charges and different breakpoints that must be reached to achieve lower fee levels.

A wrap fee is charged on these accounts and is generally a combined investment advisory fee that is bundled with brokerage commissions and custody services. It may provide for discretionary portfolio management services, asset allocation advice, performance reporting (normally only to the trustees), investment-manager selection, due diligence and brokerage executions (trades), or any subset of these services. It is very common for these fees to be 2 to 2.5 percent a year or more on accounts of less than $250,000. The fees generally scale down as the account size increases, but it is not uncommon for these wrap fees to exceed 1.0 percent even for an account that is $5 million or more.

What constitutes an account? It could be that a broker/consultant sold the trustees on the wrap program where three or four different money managers are selected to manage different portfolios for participants (like you) to select for their 401(k) elections. An account under the wrap fee definition for these bundled fees represents the aggregate value of the retirement plan participants electing *a particular money manager.* This means that if you choose a manager that is not selected by many of your coworkers, your fees could be much higher than other alternatives.

There are additional twists on these wrap fees. In some cases, the broker or consultant charges a lower wrap fee but buys mutual funds with additional expense ratios instead of using independent or proprietary money managers. There are even accounts called multidiscipline accounts (MDAs) or multimanager accounts (MMAs) where multiple money managers each manage a piece of the overall account.

In many cases, wrap account fees can easily total 1.0 to 3 percent a year. **Also, it is not common that these expenses would be disclosed to you, but as I understand the new rules that will begin to go into effect in 2012, they will be disclosed**. A wrap account is often accounted for by opening up a brokerage account for each portfolio alternative, and the wrap expenses of the portfolio come right out of the account. The administrator or record keeper just tracks how much of each portfolio a participant owns and pays no attention to the fees. In essence, the fees come right out of the investment return, much like a mutual fund expense ratio.

If you have any investment selections that are not specific mutual funds with ticker symbols but are instead just an investment selection called "Conservative Growth" or "Moderate" or something similar, ask your benefits department person if that portfolio is in a wrap account, and see if you can find out who is managing it. You might also ask to obtain a copy of the investment advisory agreement that will outline the fee schedule for the advisory and brokerage services, although it will probably exclude mutual fund expense ratios if it is a mutual fund wrap program.

Mortality and Expense Charges

A large percentage of retirement plans are sold by insurance companies and thus have a nice little trick they can play with your retirement assets. In addition to the fund expense ratios and administration charges we've discussed, insurance companies tack on this additional contract charge, which is charged directly against your investment earnings. These expenses also will start to be disclosed to you when the new rules go into effect.

What does it buy you? Well, being offered by an insurance company, you might suspect that it buys you life insurance. It does a little at least. Often, the extra mortality and expense (M&E) fee you are paying on all of your retirement assets (sometimes "stable value accounts" do not have a separate M&E fee) buys you insurance so that if you die before you retire, the insurance company guarantees your beneficiaries will be paid what you put in. In essence, they guarantee your beneficiaries will get at least a 0 percent return. There are a lot of complicated and often expensive bells and whistles that insurance companies can tack on to your account for this guarantee, some of which might be valuable to you, and some that are a complete waste of money for what you are trying to achieve. The Securities and Exchange Commission (SEC) has an excellent web site that explains many of these issues at www.sec.gov/investor/pubs/varannty.htm. You probably want to know what this guarantee might cost you.

According to Don Taylor, PhD, CFA, who wrote an article about this at Bankrate.com, the average M&E charge is 1.15 percent in variable annuities.[*] Some companies have far lower M&E charges

---

[*]Don Taylor, PhD, CFA, "Are Annuities a Worthwhile Investment Option?" www.bankrate.com/brinkadv/news/DrDon/20020411a.asp.

(I haven't seen any less than 0.28 percent), and some are far higher. Keep in mind, though, that these charges are in addition to your fund expenses and perhaps in addition to administration expenses.

The best way to find out about these costs is to contact your benefits/human resources (HR) department and ask if your retirement plan is provided by an insurance company. Tell them you are doing some retirement planning and you need to understand the contract charges like M&E and surrender charges, or, you can simply wait until the new disclosure rules go into effect.

Surrender Charges

While we are on the topic of insurance company fees, I should discuss surrender fees. These fees are, in essence, penalties charged against your balances if you redeem the assets during some specified period of time—often years. They are conditional, one-time fees, so at least these expenses are not a continuous drag on your account balances. However, it is possible that if you redeem an investment, or roll over your account, you might be subject to this penalty of 1 percent, 2 percent, 3 percent, or more. Also, sometimes there are such penalties applied to transactions that are "short term." Mutual funds ran into some problems with market-timing services and they obviously do not like to have money leaving the fund. To solve this, some of the lower-cost expense-ratio funds have added on these short-term trading penalties if a fund, or portion of a fund, is sold within 90 days, for example.

Similarly, some mutual funds have a fee known as a redemption fee or a contingent deferred sales charge (CDSC), which is charged against your investment if you liquidate the investment before some longer specified time has passed, such as four years. Sometimes these fees are waived for retirement plans, but that isn't always the case.

You will probably need the help of your company's benefits/HR staff to discover these fees, because they are rarely disclosed to participants in any of the normal reporting you receive. The new disclosures that are coming though should disclose this information though, from what I understand about the new regulations.

Fund-of-Fund Fees and Life-Cycle Fund Fees

The more hands in the pie, the less you are going to keep. Fund-of-funds are often used for some of the most outrageously expensive products out there. Fees can be as high a 4 percent a year or more, and these are usually utilized for "alternative investments" like commodity funds, hedge funds, and private equity funds, which are all unfortunately gaining more and more popularity in retirement plans. There is a huge incentive for the advisor to sell these things, and their firms make a ton of money on them too. Statistically, it is doubtful that any real value will be obtained by the participant in these investments. I know a lot of advisors have been told otherwise by their firms and would like to debate me on it, so if so, feel free to reach out to me. For now, suffice it to say that I would not recommend any such investment to any client, because the certain cost is so high and the theoretical potential benefit is so low, and the uncertainty make this a poor gamble to make.

Funds of funds have several money managers, each getting their 1 to 2 percent (and sometimes a percentage of the profit too!), a sponsor that packages the managers into one product that gets their 1 percent, and then the brokerage firm and advisor that get their 1 percent. Trust me on this . . . stay away from these.

Lifecycle or Target Date Funds

Lifecycle funds (also known as target date funds) are easy and regulatory-approved automatic investment options for retirement plans. **They are also a great way of sacrificing the only life you have**. They operate under the notion that based on one's age, there should be a declining amount of equity exposure in the portfolio allocation over time. Sometimes they are standalone funds managed for this specific purpose, and sometimes the mutual fund company will assemble and select from funds they already manage to construct a target date portfolio of their own funds.

The fees in such funds can vary widely. The thing to understand about such funds is that they are nothing more than a marketing gimmick that preys on complacency of many retirement-plan participants and misleadingly makes them feel as though doing the "easy" thing is synonymous with doing the right thing.

Time is certainly ONE of the factors in what makes a potentially appropriate asset allocation decision for you. Unfortunately, for funds like this, it is the ONLY factor, thus why it is so easy! But, math doesn't work that way. You cannot solve the Pythagorean Theorem by only knowing what C squared is. You and your buddy in the office or cube next to you might be same age. Shizam! You get the same Target Date or Lifecycle fund. But, are you both saving the same amount of money? Isn't that something that should be considered? Are you both going to work to the same retirement age (ok . . . so unless auto selected you might be able to choose different target date funds in five-year increments)? Are you both planning on the same lifestyle in retirement? Are either of you potentially going to get an inheritance at some point in the future, and if so will it be the same dollar amount and will it occur at the same time? Do your spouses work in similar jobs at similar pay, happen to be the same age, save the same amount in their company's retirement plan, and plan to retire on the same dates? Do you have the same number of kids all of the same ages going to the same private schools or colleges in the future? Do you drive the same cars and have the same hobbies and spend identical amounts on them? Do you live in the same sort of house of the same age with the same property taxes and maintenance costs? Do you spend identical amounts on vacations and holiday gifts for your family? Are you both comfortable with accepting the same level of investment risk? Are your priorities amongst all of these things the same? **Are you getting the point?**

Because each of these items impacts the quality of your life and your comfort and confidence, an advisor should know your preferences for such goals. All the target date fund knows is a date or an age. Let me demonstrate how devastating such funds can be.

Let's presume there really are two employees that are truly identical in every one of the aspects listed, except for one. That would be the potential for an inheritance. One participant is not likely to receive any, and the other is likely to receive about $200,000 sometime in the next few years, since his father has passed and his mother is unfortunately in ill health. This one additional variable, with everything else being equal in age, retirement date, other goals, savings, spending, hobbies, kids, and so on, would enable him to have a portfolio with far less investment risk and maintain the same confidence level of exceeding the goals they both share. An advisor that recognizes this would not subject him to more risk, merely because of his age, or "tolerance" for the pain of risk. Risk is something that should be avoided unless it is needed, regardless of whether you are tough enough to stomach large losses.

If they were both young and in the same target date funds in 2008 (as they would be since their age and retirement dates are the same), they probably would have experienced losses of 25 to 35 percent (maybe more). Even if they were middle aged, they probably would have experienced losses of 20 to 25 percent, and even if they were near the brink of retirement, many of these funds were still down more than 15 percent.

Yet, by looking beyond the marketing gimmick of age, the participant receiving the inheritance could have confidence in funding his goals with no more than 30 percent equity exposure. A simple stock and treasury portfolio was down less than 4 percent in 2008, saving this participant 10 percent to 30 percent of his retirement assets. In essence, that one simple piece of informed advice could have potentially paid for 30 years of advisory fees.

If you value your lifestyle and comfort and confidence in exceeding the goals you personally value, do not succumb to the easy shortcut marketing gimmick that can cause you needless sacrifice in your life.

Other Hidden Mutual Fund Expenses

We have already discussed that the total expense ratio of a mutual fund will include the management, administrative, 12b-1 (distribution) fees, and the like that are charged under contract directly against the fund assets. But there are potentially significant other expenses, and you will not find these in the prospectus of most mutual funds. **Nor will these expenses be part of the upcoming fee disclosures**. These other expenses are usually available only in a document called the statement of additional information (SAI) that is not required to be given to you unless you request it.

Mutual funds buy and sell stocks and bonds just like you might do in a self-directed brokerage account, and all holders of the mutual fund own pieces, or shares, of the account. Also, just like you, the mutual fund must pay brokerage firm's commissions on the trades they make in the mutual fund's brokerage account. **These commissions are not part of the expense ratio**.

It is a painful process to find these expenses, because (1) getting your hands on the SAI isn't the easiest thing to do, since it isn't required to be given to you unless you ask for it, and (2) once you get it, you have to dig through the document and do some math to figure out the expense.

In the SAI, the commissions will not be disclosed as an annual percentage of value like expense ratios. Instead, buried in the document will be a section that states commissions paid. There may be a few sections broken into different categories (commissions paid for research, etc.), and you will have to add up all of these expenses. It will say something similar to the following:

2004 Commissions Paid:	
Directed Brokerage:	$856,757
Prime Brokers:	$120,000
Total:	$976,757

This number obviously doesn't tell you a lot. You may even need to first add them together yourself. The next step is to divide this by the total value of the fund, which is another number you have to dig up. Say the total assets of the fund were $600 million, and the commissions totaled $976,756. That would mean that in addition to this fund's expense ratio, the fund had additional undisclosed expenses of 0.162 percent ($976,756/$600 million). If the fund had $1.2 billion in assets, these additional expenses would be 0.08 percent. For many index funds and ETFs, these expenses will total less than 0.05 percent annually, some even less than 0.01 percent. However, it is quite common for an active fund to have these additional hidden expenses total 0.20 percent to more than 1.00 percent a year. According to a study done by the Zero Alpha Group, the typical **actively managed mutual fund** averaged 0.48 percent in these other hidden expenses annually.

Your benefits or HR person will not be able to help you discover these expenses, nor will many of the fund-rating web sites. In most cases, you will need to search for the SAI on the web site of the actual mutual fund you own. In some cases, it won't be available on the web site either, and you will be forced to just accept it as an unknown. You could also write or fax the mutual fund company and request a copy of the SAI for the fund you own. They do have to provide the SAI to you if you request it.

Float

The last of these hidden costs is perhaps the easiest for you to discover. Like the internal trading costs of mutual funds, this cost will not be included in the new disclosures either because it is difficult to calculate. "Float" is interest earned on someone else's money while you are processing transactions for them or waiting for transactions to clear. With interest rates so low at the time of this writing, this is not currently an issue to really worry about, but instead something to watch out for if short-term interest rates rise to higher levels.

Think about what happens when you get your paycheck from your employer's perspective. Your employer deposits your net pay into your bank account, and your bank probably credits it the same day, or maybe one day later to get one day of "float," and the money is then available to you. While that is going on with your payroll, the company also makes a deposit for your retirement plan with the vendor of your plan. They get the money the same time you do. When does it get invested in your fund selections? The next day? A few days later? A week later? Two weeks? A month?

The rules on this in the Employee Retirement Income Security Act (ERISA) are very weak, as are many other areas that are covered more in Chapter 6. There is no requirement for how quickly your money is invested other than "as soon as administratively practical," and some retirement plan product vendors are not finding it very practical to get around to it on a timely basis. During the time between your payroll and when the money is actually invested in your retirement plan selections, **the vendor gets to keep any interest earned on your money!** While most of the vendors do process your deferrals within a day or two, I have seen some that can take as long as 30 days! For a company of our size and contribution levels, the "float" with a vendor that drags their feet like this could cost us more than the administration expenses!

To find out if you are paying this expense, simply look at the time between payroll dates and the dates your contributions are actually credited to your retirement plan balance on your vendor's web site. If it is more than a few days, you have a legitimate gripe, and this delay may explain why your administration expenses might be lower than otherwise anticipated.

If you understand what your real total expenses are, and they are in the neighborhood of 0.50 to 0.75 percent annually (or hopefully even less) then your expenses are in line, congratulations! You are not being ripped off!

Regardless of whether your plan needs fixing, you still have to make the best choices about what you value and how to maximize the lifestyle benefit of having a cost-effective retirement plan. If this is the case, you can skip Chapters 4, 5, and 6. But if your expenses are excessive, it is critical to your lifestyle that you take the steps needed to fix your retirement plan.

3

The Price to Your Lifestyle
of Needless Expenses

If you are within three years of retiring or found your real total expenses were 0.75 percent annually or less, you can skip to Chapter 7, "Now That My Retirement Plan Is Fixed, How Can I Make the Most of My Life?". However, if your expenses were more than 1 percent or maybe even 2 percent, or if you are not at the brink of retirement (and even if you are near retirement), the effect of the choices you still have might make it worthwhile for you to read this chapter. If you are contributing to a retirement plan and saving for retirement in 5, 10, even 20 years, there are some key concepts we will address in this chapter that may help you understand the cost of these expenses to your life.

What are those costs? Appendix A provides a series of examples of the costs to your lifestyle of these hidden expenses in your retirement plan. Whether it means saving hundreds or even thousands of dollars more each year until you retire, spending less once you reach retirement, or even putting off retirement for one, two, or more years beyond age 65, these unnecessary expenses cost you something in your life, and this book will help you to put your finger on that cost.

You will rightly ask how we can forecast what the cost of these expenses may be, and that is the point of the discussion that follows. To understand the costs, we first need to know what you might be able to accomplish in your life, what you might value in your retirement, and what you are willing to do toward that goal. You are already contributing to a retirement plan, and you make those savings because you want to have money to spend during your retirement and a lifestyle you can enjoy.

The tables in Appendix A show what a person of various ages might already have saved and what they are contributing each year. That is only a part of the picture, though, since how the money is invested in the plan—stocks, bonds, or cash—and the level of spending once a person retires are a part of the mix as well. The examples examine how much one might spend in retirement given a particular combination of these factors and at varying levels of expense. The higher the expense charged in your retirement plan, the more something else must give, whether it is the age at which one retires, the amount one saves, or the spending level during retirement.

Why is that so? Let's begin with the markets.

Uncertainty Is CERTAIN

You may have figured out your "savings shortfall" using a retirement calculator sponsored by your friendly retirement-plan vendor who profits from you sacrificing your life by scaring you into saving too much. Perhaps you have a financial planner who examines in excruciating detail your spending budget on pet food, your cable bill, your insurance policies, and so on, and produces a 100-page document planning the rest of your life for you. Often, they will proceed by attempting to guilt or coerce you into sticking with this long-term plan despite your goals, priorities, and changes in the markets since they created the plan.

No one knows what the markets will do over any period of time and ANYONE that tells you that they do is either lying to you or lying to himself, and probably both. Some today will argue that returns will be lower in the future for one reason or another. Others will argue that they can beat the market because the gambles they made in the past worked, and it is "evidenced" in their long-term track record, as if a lucky slot machine player has figured out how to beat the odds. Study after study has shown that past performance is not an indication of future results.

We did a study comparing the very top 5 percent performing mutual funds for the three years ending March 2003. By March 2007, slightly more than 54 percent of those very top performers from 2003 performed well below their best matching index. In fact, as of March 2007, slightly more than 54 percent of all funds underperformed their best matching benchmark. It made no statistical difference whether they were a top performer in the past. This concept is why the Financial Industry Regulatory Authority (FINRA, formerly the National Association of Securities Dealers [NASD]) requires the statement, "Past performance is not necessarily an indication of future results." It is true! The reality is that there is an enormous amount of uncertainty in the two main factors that can affect you that neither you nor your adviser can control.

Remember that sample 40-year-old from the Introduction with $75,000 in his 401(k) plan, saving 10 percent of his $50,000-a-year income with an employer match of 50 percent? Assuming an allocation of 80 percent to stocks, the rest in bonds and cash, and a very reasonable 0.50 percent in expenses, historically the sample person's 25 years of accumulation produced a retirement fund at age 65 of anywhere from $1,084,000 (market returns of 1950–1974) to more than $5 million (1975–1999)! That's just based on actual historical returns for this portfolio going back to 1926 in the order they occurred. If we used the same historical returns and just randomly mixed up the order of when they occurred, the range of uncertainty of the future expands from $134,000 to more than $25 million! Of course, the markets may produce results that we have not yet seen that would just further expand this range of uncertainty.

Again, the only uncertainties represented by this are of the markets, and they are obviously highly uncertain. And they are uncertain in two ways. First, the overall long-term compound return of the markets in the future (i.e., stocks, bonds, or cash) is uncertain. Second, how that overall return happens, (i.e., when big returns or losses will happen) is unknowable but can impact your lifestyle profoundly. This "when a return occurs" part can produce surprising results.

For our sample retirement plan participant, the worst actual historical result in terms of dollars in the retirement fund at age 65 was the period of 1950 to 1974, when this person ended up with $1,084,000. The portfolio allocation, rebalanced annually, produced a compound return over this period of 8.83 percent. But, there were a lot of 25-year historical periods when the allocation produced a lower long-term compound return, yet still produced a larger retirement fund in terms of dollars. This happened because of the uncertainty of the timing of returns, or when different returns occurred. Figure 3.1 and Table 3.1 provide an example of how Great Depression-era compound returns were lower overall for the whole 25-year period, but for THIS SAMPLE CLIENT, the timing of when bear and bull markets happened and how much money he had invested during those periods produced more money in the retirement fund despite these lower Depression era returns.

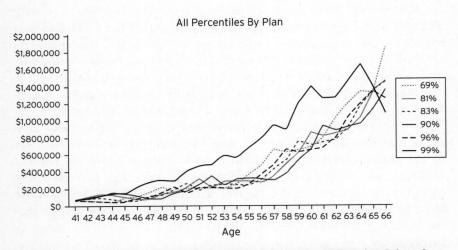

Figure 3.1   Lower Returns Can Produce Higher Dollar Values Based on WHEN Various Returns Occur

Table 3.1   Lower Returns Can Produce Higher Dollar Values

Percentile	Ending Value	Market Period	Return
69	$1,858,731	1930–1954	8.55%
81	$1,468,026	1927–1951	8.10%
83	$1,448,878	1928–1952	7.52%
90	$1,360,253	1926–1950	7.80%
96	$1,256,409	1929–1953	6.19%
99	$1,084,733	1950–1974	8.83%

For some reason, people seem to be perplexed by this reality of uncertainty, but the cause of this is really quite simple. In the crash of 1929 and the Depression era, markets in which our sample retirement plan participant would have lost half of his portfolio value over a few years, he didn't have much money invested. If the portfolio was only $50,000 to $100,000 when he experienced the 50 percent declines, the cost to his retirement fund of this decline in dollar terms was only $25,000 to $50,000. Yet the 99th percentile result during the 1950 to 1974 period experienced a decline not at the beginning when our sample participant had lower balances, but just before he was about to retire, after he accumulated nearly $1,600,000! It only takes a 3.1 percent decline to cost you $50,000 when you have a $1.6 million portfolio. The bear market of 1973 to 1974 hurt his portfolio to the tune of nearly 30 percent, which was not as bad as the Depression era, but it cost him more than $400,000 because of the timing!

So the markets are highly uncertain in two ways that no one can control. Both the overall long-term compound return AND when various high or low returns happen are certain to be uncertain, and this can dramatically affect your life.

Those little retirement savings calculators that tell you how much to save assuming some rate of return are therefore VERY misleading. You know the ones I'm talking about. You input your starting balance, how much you save each year, how long you are accumulating money toward retirement, and it uses some assumed rate of return to calculate how much money you will have at retirement. The problem is that the risk of when various returns happen is ignored in such analysis. Remember, IT IS CERTAIN that you WILL NOT receive the same return each year.

You might think the assumed rate is close enough, but it is not. Look at how misleading such an analysis can be. In the example shown in Figure 3.2 and Table 3.2, I calculated a projection of the future values for our sample middle-class retirement plan participant using the simple assumption of 10 percent a year, which is certain not to happen! Notice how smooth the line is, experiencing neither bull or bear markets.

That assumed return produced an ending value less than 77 percent of all actual historical market periods. What is more interesting, though, is the effect of this timing of when returns happen. The period of 1930 to 1954 produced a compound return

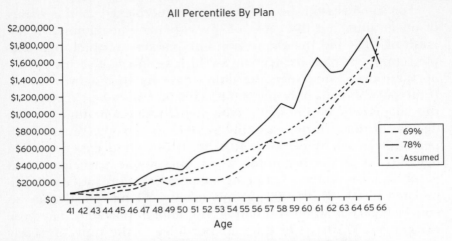

All Percentiles By Plan

Figure 3.2   Comparison of a Simple Return Assumption versus Real Market Returns

Table 3.2   Comparison of a Simple Return Assumption versus Real Market Returns

Percentile	Ending Value	Market Period	Return
69	$1,858,731	1930–1954	8.55%
77	$1,672,925	Assumed return	10.00%
78	$1,548,591	1949–1973	10.37%

that was almost 1.5 percent less per year than the return I had assumed in the calculator, but lucky timing of a bull market just as the sample participant was approaching retirement (when he had accumulated a lot of money) had him soar past the assumed return ending value by nearly $200,000! A lower return but yet a higher portfolio value: the effect of when.

Conversely, unlucky timing of a bear market as he approached retirement in the 1949 to 1973 period cost him a fortune, and he ended up short of the assumed result (at a certain 10 percent) by more than $120,000, despite compounding at a higher return. A higher return yet lower portfolio value: again the effect of when.

Do Not Trust Anyone's Projections!

The truth of the matter is that these uncertainties are real, and there is nothing you can do about them except pay attention to the changes as they happen. A recent fad in the financial services industry is to run computer simulations of this uncertainty effect, but how

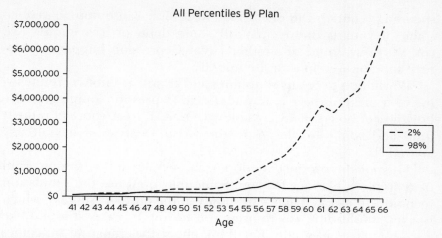

Figure 3.3   Range of Simulated Results

Table 3.3   Range of Simulated Results

Percentile	Ending Value	Market Period	Return
2	$7,055,083	Simulated	16.95%
98	$373,673	Simulated	2.74%

it is normally used doesn't give you particularly useful information. In the example shown in Figure 3.3 and Table 3.3, I simulated 25,000 years of investing for our sample retirement plan participant, just randomly ordering historical market returns for 1,000 25-year periods. All it tells us is that if nothing changes in this person's plan—income, savings, and the like—for the next 25 years, there is a 96 percent chance they will end up with a retirement plan balance of somewhere between $373,000 and $7 million. You probably don't need a calculator to tell you that. I'll bet you knew it already!

Of course, there are more uncertainties than those in the financial markets, but we will deal with those concerns later on in Chapter 7.

Soup Lines and Scare Tactics

Have you noticed another Great Depression lately? Look out your window and see if you can find any soup lines forming. If there was another Great Depression, do you think you might cut back your spending a little? Did the Great Recession cause you to reduce some of your spending, pay off some debt, or save more? Are you sincerely afraid of another Great Depression happening anytime soon or even in your lifetime?

IF you don't see any soup lines and IF you are not currently living your life as if there is another Great Depression looming on the horizon (although it IS possible), DO NOT treat your retirement fund and your lifestyle AS IF the Great Depression has already arrived.

Most of the product vendors (salespeople) will run some kind of retirement planner for you. Some may even use the simulation technique illustrated above to show you the odds of "success" which is a very misleading way to present it to you. It makes it sound like a simple pass/fail grade. But think about that range of outcomes we have discussed. It is not odds of success they are calculating but instead odds of excess. So, it isn't that you have "only" a 90 percent chance of having $1,000,000 . . . it is that you have a 90 percent chance of having MORE THAN $1,000,000. It might be that you have an 80 percent chance of having more than $2 million, or a 50 percent chance of more than $5 million. Finally, what they don't tell you is the reason they use "conservative assumptions" or attempt to get you to the "highest probability of success through simulation tools" is for their success, not yours!

That conservative return assumption of, say, 7 percent that is suggested to you in that little online retirement planning tool and that ignores uncertainty would project a value for our sample retirement plan participant that is worse than any historical period going back to 1926! Why would they do this? They can scare you into saving more so they get more fees! The more you save, the more they get in fees. They might sell you on the notion that they are just being conservative "to be safe," but the reality is that the conservative assumptions cost your lifestyle dearly and they profit from it at your expense.

What about that adviser who showed you a simulation that got you to 95 percent "success" (his, not yours!) to accumulate a $1 million retirement fund, and all it took to achieve this confidence level was tripling your annual savings? He probably said you had a "savings shortfall" or a "gap" in retirement funding. He probably even positioned it that you might want to even consider saving a bit more to avoid some of that 5 percent chance of "failure."

Did your friendly adviser also tell you that if it were 1929 and you followed his advice you would have ended up with an extra $1,500,000 above the $1 million you were targeting despite the crash of 1929 and the Great Depression? Is that how afraid you are of a depression and crash? Was that your goal? Are you really willing to triple your savings for the next 25 years and make all of the compromises to your lifestyle because you are that terrified of a depression and are willing to significantly compromise your lifestyle to have an EXTRA $1.5 million dollars stashed away beyond your goals if we go through a Great Depression?

My company creates the math engines and capital market research for thousands of financial advisers and their firms to run this type of analysis, and we try to get firms and their advisers to use them ethically. Recently, though, I was in a meeting where we were discussing the fact that a firm requested us to try to rig the mathematics to always get people scared into saving more so that the firm could get more fees and assets from their clients. That firm is no longer a client of ours because scaring people into needlessly sacrificing their only life IS NOT what our business is about. We fired them a client.

While the uncertainty is vast, and it is possible that you are not saving enough or may be spending too much, it is also possible that you are saving too much, spending too little, or taking more investment risk than is needed for what you personally value. We call this "needless sacrifice." This is the way math works. If it is possible to not be saving enough, it must also therefore be possible to be saving too much.

Uncertainty Is Manageable but Not Controllable

The preceding statement may appear as if it is a contradiction. You cannot control what the long-term results of the markets will be, nor can you control when high or low returns will happen. If you don't believe me, ask your adviser if he can control when a bull or bear market will occur. What you can do is tweak the choices in your lifestyle to constantly keep the odds tilted in your favor but avoid the needless sacrifice to your lifestyle of living your life now as if a depression already existed. If it comes, you may have to reduce your spending, so you should monitor the effect of the markets' continuous future uncertainty on your life. Instead of reducing spending, though, you have other choices that can work in poor markets. You might increase your portfolio risk, although mentally this is hard to do when a bear market has prices low, or compromise some other goal like a portion of an estate goal, delay buying the boat, and the like.

The financial product vendors would have you think that it is not possible to save too much money. However, as a rational being, you know that compromising your lifestyle by tripling what you save each year to accumulate 250 percent of your targeted retirement fund value in a crash of 1929 and Great Depression environment is probably too conservative and a needless sacrifice to your lifestyle. You could also wash used aluminum foil for reuse later if you really are that concerned about another depression. Think about how much you would save in your aluminum foil spending budget!

So, how do you take this vast uncertainty and make it manageable? First, while there is some remote chance of these wide extremes occurring, they are unlikely. Do you really care if there is a 2 percent chance of accumulating more than $7 million or a 20 percent chance of having more than $3 million? Certainly, you aren't going to live your life expecting these remote extremes to occur. More importantly, if your portfolio were producing results like that, wouldn't it make sense to change your plan? All of that extra wealth would allow you to safely take less investment risk, increase your spending, retire earlier, gift more to your favorite charities, and so on. All of these choices should be exposed to you long before your portfolio grows to such levels. So the reality is that it is highly unlikely that your portfolio would ever achieve those levels not just because the odds of it occurring are fairly low, but also, and more likely, because you would change what you are doing or planning if such strong results occurred. If you had an extra million or two lying around, wouldn't it change something in your life? Do you really think you would stick to the long-term plan you created 20 years ago just to see if it worked?

Likewise, if the markets are very unkind and we have another crash of 1929 with the ensuing Great Depression, do you really think you would not alter your lifestyle a bit? Would you really continually spend your portfolio down to maintain what you planned on 20 years ago just to see if the odds were right? Would you still buy that boat, the new luxury car, and take the vacations you planned on when your neighbors are waiting in soup lines for food just to survive?

This is the problem with most online planning tools, many financial planners, and almost all of the simulation tools. They calculate outcomes that assume no matter what happens you will never change your plans. Is that really the way you want to live your life? Do you really want to ignore opportunities to improve your lifestyle? Do you really want to risk financial ruin for the sake of sticking to a plan you made 5, 10, or 20 years ago?

There is an easier way to strike a rational balance. You have X amount of resources and Y amount of goals. The markets are highly uncertain, and you have some chance of winning the market lottery, which would enable larger, sooner, or more goals. Likewise, the markets may be unkind, and there is a risk that it wouldn't be safe to leave the Y goals unchanged in the face of unfortunate timing or results.

The simulation techniques that are available (but typically not used in a manner where they provide any value to you) can help you actually figure out when you should change your Y goals because of what happened to your X resources. If we think about the vast range of outcomes that may occur, assuming no changes or response to what is happening in the markets, there is an area where we can calculate that things are "safe enough," meaning that there is neither too much uncertainty nor needless sacrifice. You can think of it like a pension plan. Some amount of current assets has you "underfunded" and some amount of assets would have you "overfunded" for a particular set of goals. In between, we would be "adequately funded." We would want this area to have the balance tipped sufficiently in our favor, enabling us to live the life we planned on, despite severe overall long-term market results or very unfortunate timing of market results. If we could calculate this range (and we can), we would then know if we should be spending more, increasing goals, taking less risk, or moving goals sooner or when we should prudently tweak goals downward, delay them a bit, or move up the risk scale a notch.

The markets of 2008 have many in Congress demanding more "guaranteed income" products like pensions or even insurance. Insurance companies are not benevolent donors of wealth. They design their products so that a majority of the buyers LOSE on them sufficiently for them to profit despite the small minority of winners on the product. But, if you measure if you are overfunded (needless sacrifice) or underfunded (too uncertain) and change your spending, savings, estate goal, timing of goals, and risk exposure, you can constantly keep your own personal defined benefit plan adequately funded.

The Comfort and Confidence Zone

All of the analysis shown in the tables in Appendix A is based on this critical notion of avoiding too much uncertainty and needless sacrifice. We call it the comfort zone, which represents a range of rational confidence because it continuously considers all of the future uncertainty of the markets as it relates to your resources and goals. It keeps the odds tilted in your favor, considering bad timing of bull and bear markets or bad overall results, yet identifies when you are needlessly compromising your lifestyle and when continuing with an old plan without adjustment is too risky. Used correctly, the comfort and confidence zone can continuously and confidently guide you through the best choices about how to live your life without needless sacrifice or unnecessary investment risk.

To simplify the thousands of simulated returns and make them uncomplicated enough to understand in these terms is easy. It takes those thousands upon thousands of potential results to rationally assess your confidence, and we can reduce those results to a simple scale that we need to keep in balance. If the scale is in balance, the choices about what we are planning for our goals and overall exposure to the risk of the markets keeps the odds tilted sufficiently in our favor so we can be comfortable, as in Figure 3.4.

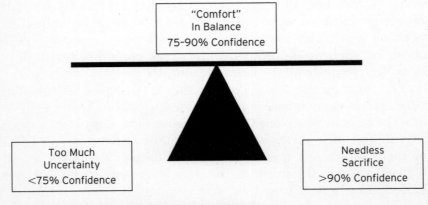

Figure 3.4   The Comfort Zone and Ranges of Confidence

This is not meant to imply that we have eliminated any chance of needing to make adjustments in the future. It merely means that, without paying attention to what is going on in the markets, you could still likely survive the worst historical markets like the crash of 1929 and the Great Depression without adjusting your goals. We wouldn't recommend ignoring the effect of that kind of a market on your resources, but in planning your life priorities in a balanced, rational fashion, it should be conservative enough and enable you to avoid needless sacrifice to your lifestyle.

All of the prices to a person's lifestyle of the excess retirement plan expenses illustrated in the tables in Appendix A are based on having this rational, comfortable balance. In essence, they provide examples of what the lifestyle price is with the burden of excess fees within your retirement plan and within this comfort and confidence zone.

It is possible that the simulations of market results may expose that you are indeed living your life as if the crash of 1929 were happening now and the Great Depression is about to follow. We call this "needless sacrifice" because these simulations are really far more severe than what we have ever experienced in the last 80 or so years. If a set of choices for your goals falls into the sacrifice zone (aka "overfunded"), you are needlessly sacrificing your lifestyle. You may be accepting more investment risk than is needed, saving more money than necessary, spending too little, or waiting too long for your goals and dreams. Such excess conservatism in how you are living your life can tip the scale out of balance as in Figure 3.5.

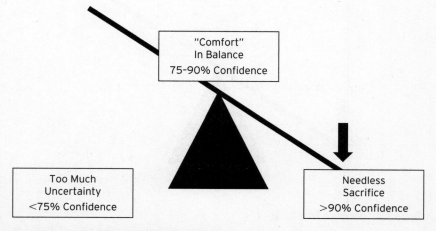

Figure 3.5   The Impact of Needless Sacrifice

Finally, your ideal dreams and goals and your desire to avoid as much investment risk as possible might combine into something that is asking more of the markets than they are likely to produce. The scale again tips out of balance as shown in Figure 3.6, suggesting you should consider delaying and/or altering some goals, perhaps saving more, or taking a bit more investment risk in attempting to achieve a bit more investment return. Without such adjustments, your plan would be too uncertain, or underfunded.

For all of the complicated jargon that can come out of investment simulations, the main question that you should be concerned about is: Are you in balance? Are you avoiding too much uncertainty? Are you avoiding needless sacrifice to your lifestyle?

As we mentioned at the beginning of this chapter, Appendix A presents a series of tables that will give you examples of the price of excessive retirement plan fees, in terms of one's lifestyle, while maintaining this balance. These are only examples, and if you want to find out what the real cost is to your life, you can use a free trial of the simulation tools we offer financial advisers (at www.wealthcarecapital .com) or call our toll-free number (1-866-261-0849) and use the code word Rip-off, and our staff will be happy to analyze it for you for free.

To get an idea of what your excess retirement plan fees are costing you, the tables in Appendix A lay out various ages, rates of saving, retirement income desires, asset allocations, and the like.

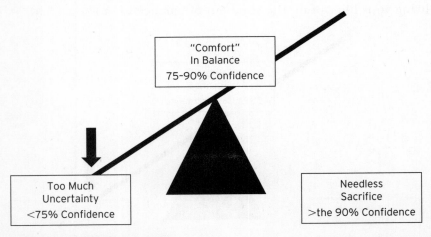

Figure 3.6   Too Much Uncertainty

You can probably find a table that is reasonably similar to your circumstances and discover the corresponding price to your lifestyle of the excess fees you are paying.

Remember, even if you are in a very small company and your employer needs to pass on all or most of the cost of your plan, if you are paying more than 0.75 percent a year in expenses, it is probably excessive. If your expenses are 1.25 percent, look at the tables that show the effect of an excess fee of 0.50 percent. If your current retirement plan expenses are 1.75 percent, look at the tables that show the effect of an excess 1 percent. If you would like to improve your retirement plan and avoid the effect of these excess fees to your lifestyle, then move on to the next chapter, and we will show you how you can easily start the process to fix your broken retirement plan. If you don't sort out your retirement plan expenses, no one else is likely to do it, and you will end up paying the price in terms of the lifestyle you can live.

4

Complaining Without Sounding Like a Complainer

When you finally experience Retirement Plan Sticker Shock (when the new fee disclosures go into effect sometime in 2012 and 2013) you would expect your employer to take some action to fix your needlessly expensive retirement plan. Unfortunately, since the employer is rarely paying any of the costs, they can be quite indifferent. If your costs are more than 0.75 percent a year, your plan needs to be fixed. (Chapter 8 will show you why you shouldn't need to pay any more.) Perhaps you found the price to your lifestyle in the tables in Appendix A and determined that it is worth fixing this problem. But you aren't in charge of selecting the vendor of your retirement plan for your company, and the company isn't paying these fees, the participants are, so what can you do to get your company to take action?

First, you probably do not want to be viewed as a complainer. Second, you cannot assume that whoever is in charge of selecting your retirement plan vendor is necessarily aware of these expenses or knows where he or she can go to find the lower-cost alternatives. Your company may be larger and may have a benefits department, and you will need their help if you are going to resolve the problem. Remember, whoever in your company selected your retirement plan vendor probably has some pride in the work he or she did to create it, so it is likely this person will be a bit defensive. Also, please keep in mind that most retirement plans have the revenue-sharing kickbacks we discussed in Chapter 2 and your employer was probably misled and sold on the premise that these kickbacks were supposedly a benefit to participants. The chances are very high that the person or people in your company who are responsible for your retirement plan are unaware these side deals are confiscating money from their retirement savings, too!

You Can Determine Your Retirement Plan

You will also need to understand how retirement plans are sold to employers if you are going to effectively solve the problem. For example, the top 10 providers of 401(k) plans, in terms of number of companies or plan sponsors, account for more than 300,000 plans or more than half of all 401(k) plans. At some point, maybe several years ago, your company probably didn't have a 401(k) plan. An insurance agent or broker probably sold the executives in your company on the notion that they should offer a 401(k) plan to be competitive. This agent or broker most likely also told the decision maker that offering such a plan would cost the company nothing or practically nothing, so it made sense to give the option to employees. In all probability, the agent or broker probably put together a proposal that included a selection of overpriced funds or variable annuities (the proposal didn't say these were overpriced) that showed your employer that the company expense for administering the plan would be somewhere from $10,000 a year all the way down to zero if the plan were large enough in terms of assets. The agent or broker also may have encouraged a matching contribution.

So the person you need to talk to about your retirement plan may well think the plan is in good shape even if it is not. This person could well believe that there is a wide selection of funds available, which is a good thing (despite the available funds being mostly excessively expensive ones). The cost of administration charged to the company is probably zero by now (because it has been bundled and skimmed out of other excessive expenses). By the way, it is possible that the cost of administration is charged against the earnings in your account, so it might be that the company has never paid for any of the cost of the plan. Other employees aren't complaining about the retirement plan (despite their Retirement Plan Sticker Shock). The "powers that be" probably feel that they have done a good job.

Yet your new fee disclosure shows your personal retirement plan expenses are 1.0 percent, 1.5 percent, or 2.0 percent a year or more, totaling several hundred of even several thousand dollars a year. These costs are far more than are needed, but the last person who will tell your employer the costs are too high is the insurance agent or broker who sold the plan to the company—an agent or broker who is getting a commission of 0.30 to 0.90 percent a year on your retirement assets or perhaps even more every year. Even if your employer questions the retirement plan salesperson about the expenses, this agent or broker likely will come up with some story about the great services he or she offers (like annual seminars where you get all that personal attention—NOT!), their brilliant fund selection (that in reality gambles on underperforming the benchmarks), and how what is important is the return net after fees, not the total fees paid. What the agent or broker won't say is that the brilliant fund selection is always in retrospect (past performance, which is not an indication of future results), and he clearly will not be able to explain why lower-cost alternatives are simply not offered (the reason these alternatives are not offered is that the agent or broker can't get paid his or her 0.30 to 0.90 percent on assets for showing up at a meeting once a year to sell the overpriced funds).

Here are the facts:

- Expenses are 100 percent certain, but past performance is not necessarily an indication of future results.
- Plan administration (the record-keeping fees) is not a cost that is tied to the plan assets; it is based on the number of participants. It is a bookkeeping function in which there are several independent vendors not tied to financial products that provide the retirement plan web site, record keeping, participant statements, and various employer services such as testing, compliance, and government form filings. For those independent firms that do not conflict themselves with side deals from the investment-product vendors, the cost shouldn't be any more than $35 a year per participant with an annual minimum of about $1,750 to $2,000 a year for the *whole company*.
- Globally diversified portfolios can be assembled from low-cost funds that do not have material investment minimums, redemption fees, deferred sales charges, or commissions. Our recommended portfolios can be found in Chapter 8, but

you can see that nearly everyone's risk tolerance and reward objective can be met with these portfolios of funds with expenses ranging from 0.10 to 0.14 percent a year.

- Personalized custom advice and monitoring should be available as an option by choice, instead of charged against everyone, along with management of the portfolios for no more than 0.30 to 0.65 percent a year charged *only* to those who select it.
- Custodial costs can be covered by several vendors for no more than 0.06 percent a year. Custodial costs are the book-keeping charges by banks or brokerages to keep track of how many shares of what securities the plan owns, and collect dividends, invest contributions, process withdrawals, and the like.
- A self-directed brokerage account option should be offered for all those who wish to play the game of gambling their retirement by outsmarting the markets. The additional cost of this option should be borne *only by the participants who select it*, and the only extra costs should be limited to the commissions (usually $12.95 or less) and excess fund fees (usually 0.50 percent or more) that they choose to pay when they select this option. Sometimes these accounts are also used when the participant has a personal advisor that is managing all of their assets and they use the brokerage account to increase the overall household tax efficiency.

Let's take a look at what the real total expenses should be, based on what is available in the market. Say your company has 100 employees participating in a 401(k) plan. Also assume that the average participant has a 401(k) balance of $35,000, which means the total plan assets are $3,500,000. Remember, either the company or the employees may bear the expenses, depending on how the company elects to structure the plan. Therefore, we will examine the total overall costs covering both the employer and employee perspective.

Record keeping/administration/testing/filings @ $35 a participant	$3,500
Custody @ 0.06 percent a year on $3,500,000	$2,100
Investment expenses @ 0.14% on assets (most expensive portfolio)	$4,900
TOTAL	$10,500
TOTAL as percent of assets	0.30%

How do I know these expenses are realistic? I know this because the 0.30 percent example above is more than our little company with only 40 participants and $2,000,000 in plan assets is paying. If we can have a plan with expenses this low, why can't you?

Don't tell me it is because of "other services." We have a powerful web site that tracks our performance with daily valuations and details every single transaction. Participants can have 100 percent of their investments invested in a self-directed brokerage account if they want to play that game, and only they bear their own additional commission costs. There are 13 funds to select from, in addition to the 1,500 no-load funds in the self-directed brokerage account—covering all macro asset classes, from large- and small-cap stocks to foreign stocks, real estate, short- and long-term bonds, cash, and so on. Participants receive quarterly statements that actually disclose the real fees they are paying. Six predesigned, professionally constructed portfolios are available to cover nearly everyone's time horizon and risk tolerance and if the participant chooses to select them, they pay only an additional 0.30 percent expense, also fully disclosed. And, if any participant wants a personally designed, managed, monitored, and continuously revised Wealthcare plan covering all of their life goals and assets, it is available for only that additional portfolio cost of 0.35 percent a year, keeping the maximum possible cost at 0.75 percent a year or less. How does this stack up against your 401(k)? If we can do this, so can your company!

Assuming the company pays for nothing and charges back all expenses to employees, the typical employee with a $35,000 balance would be paying about $105.50 a year, or 0.30 percent. In our company, the employer is paying for the record-keeping and custody fees, which is only $2,600 a year for our entire company versus the $9,000 extra our previous vendor was charging under a bundled revenue-sharing structure. The participant is paying only the investment expense between 0.10 percent and 0.14 percent, depending on the selected portfolio.

What about the advice? Each participant in our company can get personal advice with a Securities and Exchange Commission (SEC)-registered adviser acting as a fiduciary, instead of a broker or insurance salesman, for free. If a participant wants the investment adviser to continuously manage and monitor the portfolio and personal Wealthcare plan that is based on the participant's own goals and priorities, the participant can optionally select to hire the adviser to provide this service for 0.35 percent, charged only to those participants who select it. Doing so would raise the total expense to the employee participant to a maximum of 0.65 percent a year if the company is paying for nothing. If the company is paying for administrative costs, the participant is paying less than 0.55 percent with custom, personalized continuous life goal-relative advice even while using the most expensive portfolio that is continuously, professionally managed.

How do these expenses compare to what you are paying now? Do you have any alternatives in your current plan that could reduce your expenses to these levels while maintaining global diversification across major asset classes? Some of the custodians that are not conflicted—unlike the primary vendors with their army of salesmen—offer more than 33,000 different funds from which to select, probably all of the funds in your current plan, PLUS the lower-cost alternatives generally available that you can't currently access because the lower-cost alternatives don't offer the conflicted revenue sharing kickbacks.

What Do You Do with These Numbers?

Step 1 in getting your employer to look at this is a nonthreatening handwritten note to your benefits/human resources/payroll department. You need to address it to whatever area or person in your company has the most responsibility for your retirement plan. If your company is very small, it might even be to your chief executive officer or chief financial officer.

In your note, you do not want to focus on the fact that the expenses are too high. What you merely want to do is establish that you have seen what the total expenses are for you, and you wonder if there is any way some of the lower-cost alternatives can be made available. Handling it in this manner will potentially trigger your employer to contact the retirement-plan vendor.

Something like the sample message that follows is a good way to start:

To: Human Resources Dept.

From: MY NAME

Re: My 401(k)

Dear NAME:

Thank you so much for providing me the information I requested about our 401(k) plan. It was very helpful in my retirement-planning efforts.

One thing that I discovered in my personal situation that I thought I would share with you is that the funds I previously selected had annual expenses of _____ percent. I ran across the enclosed book, and it shows that any company can offer funds with expenses ranging from 0.10 percent a year to 0.14 percent a year. Reducing my expenses to those levels would save me a lot of money over time. Plus, of all of the alternatives we offer in our plan, none of them are close to these expenses, and many are 4 to 10 times the expense. I thought I'd share a copy of the book with you in hopes you might be able to find a way to offer some of these lower expense alternatives, too.

Thanks again!

Sincerely,

My Name

Put yourself in the shoes of the person who receives this note. This isn't a letter of complaint—it is a "thank you note." You are even giving the person a gift of this book. This human resources (HR) person likely will not be offended and may even send you a thank you note back for sending the book. However, the HR person probably won't read the book. He or she will most likely assume everything is fine because the vendor they selected told him or her that the fees were reasonable and he or she had confidence in the original decision to use that vendor. Also, he or she will probably mistakenly think that the cost to the company of offering lower cost funds is going to be very high, because those funds don't offer the revenue-sharing kickbacks the current expensive funds have because that is what the salesmen had said in the past.

You are but one voice in the company, and the odds are that NONE of your associates had done their homework on the expenses in the past. But, with the new fee disclosure coming around the corner, your coworkers are going to be experiencing Retirement Plan Sticker Shock too. Still it isn't likely that they are going to take action in an unstable job market. They don't want to be viewed as making waves, so despite being upset about the cost, they don't really know the price to their life of that cost (unless they read this book) or what a fair price is, or how to approach the employer in a positive, proactive manner.

There is a small chance that whomever you sent the book to will read it, research the truth behind all of the conflicted side deals, and actually start the work to offer the lowest-cost alternatives that will benefit everyone in the company. The odds of that are low.

I would suggest that, about 30 days after delivering the book, you send a follow-up e-mail to the person to whom you sent it, simply asking her if she enjoyed the book. If the HR person indicates she read it but checked with the vendor, and those lower-cost options aren't available in your plan, you will need to move on to the next chapter. If her response is that she hasn't gotten around to reading the book yet but plans to do so soon, you may want to follow up just one more time in another 60 days or so.

Remember, if your expenses are too high in your retirement plan, the odds are that you are in a smaller company, and these smaller companies are the ones where employees are harmed the most by the excess fees. These smaller companies simply are not large enough to have a full-time, dedicated staff in place to spend the time to do the homework and get past all of the salespeople to find the best alternatives. In all likelihood, the HR staff really is trying to do the best they can with the time available from their other responsibilities to devote to the company's retirement plan. YOU NEED TO REMEMBER THIS when you are interacting with the HR representative. While you might know the truth and have done the homework, it is reasonable for this person to assume that since no one else has mentioned it, and the time she spent on it was obviously her best attempt, the assumption will be that there really isn't a problem.

You also need to remember this is the retirement plan for the HR representative, too. You might have an opportunity to even meet with this person. I'd suggest taking some sticky notes to flag sections of this book you want to point out to her. I'd also be prepared to go over your own expenses and highlight the sections of this book that explain what lower-cost options are available in the market place.

But in the end, you will probably need some additional help. The next chapter covers how you can recruit allies to your cause of saving your own and your coworkers' retirements. This is how you can be the hero!

5

Rallying Your Troops–Just One Coworker Can Help

Y ou did your homework. Your expenses are excessive in your retirement plan and you know it. The price to your lifestyle is material. You told the "powers that be" and even gave them this book. Yet, nothing happened. Do not be surprised about this.

Human nature is an interesting thing. When the people in charge initially hear from you, they are starting with the assumption they have done a great job and that only one person in the company even is questioning the expenses. And those in charge are right. They did the best job they could, and odds are that you are the ONLY associate in the company who has mentioned a word about it. It is a good thing you handled it in a professional manner.

Yet you know (and could very well be the only person in the company who knows) that you could easily lower your expenses by 0.50 to 1.00 percent a year or more if the company would just spend a few hours to work on it. You also know saving the excess expenses could buy you years of extra retirement, enable you to spend thousands more a year, take far less investment risk, and so on, without jeopardizing your retirement.

An interesting aspect of human nature is the added weight we give to recent events (like performance records, we can't go back in time to actually earn that track record!). Maybe the cause of this goes back deep into our evolution? For example, perhaps we have this trait because it helped us to survive by first looking for water in the last place we found it. Yet part of our nature is to also discount the significance of single random observations. Just because we experience one driver cutting us off on our commute home from work, we do not materially alter our driving habits going forward in anticipation of many other motorists doing so. We assume that "driver" was an idiot, was not attentive, or was distracted. Yet if we were cut off three times on the way home one night, we might change the assumption from that "driver" to a new, more expansive conceptual assumption that "drivers" in this town are generally rude, aggressive, or not attentive.

These same human traits apply with your friends in human resources (HR). They will likely assume that your inquiry about fees is a single random event and will discount it just like they discount being cut off once on their commute home. However, their assumption about employees of the company in general may turn into this broader concept of many employees having concerns if they experience just a few more observations. This is particularly true IF it happens near the same point in time, just as you might do if you experienced three bad drivers in one night on your commute home.

So the person in HR basically ignored your homework and feedback because of her assumption. What is interesting is how her assumption completely flips to the reverse if she receives just two or three more similar observations from other employees. The HR person will change her perspective from the dismissive "only one person had a concern" to the perspective of "I've already heard from three people about this, so there must be many more." If two more people in your company did their homework and sent the book to the same person (this is critical) and that person is someone with the power to effect change (it must be), then the assumption this person makes flips from you being the only one concerned about it to wondering "how many more are concerned since I've already heard from three people."

To fix your retirement plan, you are likely going to need some help because of the assumption the "powers that be" will make about your lone comment. You need to get at least one, and probably no more than four, to help you in your cause to improve your lives.

These other employees—your helpers—won't need to buy the book, but it wouldn't hurt if they did and personally forwarded an extra copy on to the "powers that be." It isn't necessary, though. We didn't write this book to sell a million copies and we want to make it easy for you to accomplish your goals. The main point is to get the message to the decision makers that others are aware of the fees they are paying and that they know there are far lower cost options available that offer even better service.

But before this can happen, you will need to recruit your troops. You probably will not want to go into detail about your personal circumstances and information with your coworkers. That is understandable, and it isn't necessary in order to accomplish your objective. You will, however, need one, two, maybe up to four of your coworkers to get concerned enough to trigger an inquiry to the right person in your company who has some influence over the decision. There are a couple of options as to how you can accomplish this.

Water Cooler/Lunch Room/Happy Hour with Peers

A great way to start the conversation with your associates in these environments is to simply say, "Have you guys seen how much we are paying in our retirement plan?" Continue with, "I picked up this book that explains how to figure out the impact of these fees to your lifestyle, shows you what fair prices are for plans like ours and, contacted (NAME) in human resources."

Then, to get their response going, you can say, "I don't know what you are paying, but when I found out, I frankly had Retirement Plan Sticker Shock. I also found out that there are options out there that could reduce our costs by half without costing our employer one penny. This book I've read showed me that I'll have to work ____ years longer or save $____ more a year, just to make up for these extra needless fees!"

At this point in the conversation, you need to wait and see who cares enough about their future and their lifestyle to be concerned about it. There will be plenty of skeptics who say things like their broker charges them more than the retirement plan, or that their brilliant market timing is what is more important, that they picked some incredible fund, or that the nice person in human resources wouldn't select a plan with excessive fees. These people are not candidates to help you fix the problem, so don't waste any more time on them. Their complacency is why everyone is happy despite getting burned with massive, needless expense.

However, you might find a few people who are objective enough to want to learn about the facts. These folks may say something like, "Does that extra fee really make that much of a difference?" Or "How did you figure out the extra fees impacted you that much?" Or, even better, "I'll be damned if I'm going to work ____ years longer just to make up for needless fees!"

These are your targets for recruiting your troops. If you know these associates well enough, you might not be uncomfortable showing them the research you did, but it isn't necessary in most cases. While your troops might want your copy of this book to figure out their own individual expenses, it really isn't needed since you have already identified the excess expenses. All they really need to know is what they can do to help in the cause of lowering the expenses that every employee in your company is paying.

The best way to position this issue with the potential recruits is to say, "What have you got to lose by getting the company to look for a better deal on our plan?" Tell them you have already shown the "powers that be" the excessive expenses, and all this person needs is a little nudge to get her to look into more cost-effective options.

Alternatively, if you are lucky enough to get more than three troops, then have a different one of them send an e-mail to the appropriate person each Wednesday for a month with a link to this book's web site (www.retirementripoff.com) that says, "I thought you might find this of interest because I'm sure you are as concerned about our retirement plan expenses as I am." It is necessary to change the phrasing a bit each week so the recipient doesn't think it is spam or get annoyed by the repetition. If you don't use e-mail in your company, print out the page from the web site and have your troops send it in interoffice mail with a handwritten note.

How's that for easy? After you and your troops send this book several times and after your contact gets either a book, e-mail, or handwritten note every week for a month, there is a good chance that she will change her viewpoint.

Subordinates and Immediate Superiors

You may have someone who reports to you who hopefully respects your opinion. You might be this person's supervisor or manager.

Also, you may have a supervisor or manager to whom you report. Depending on how close the relationship is, these are good candidates to add to the cause.

If you supervise staff, you may be able to bring up these excessive expenses and encourage the staff to help in the cause. Have one or more of them e-mail you or send a note asking about the expenses and forward it to the person you contacted originally. A nice way to get their attention on this is to say something like, "I'm forwarding you this message from one of my staff about our retirement plan expenses because I wonder if this might be a human resources issue or perhaps a risk to the company if it is not handled appropriately. Please provide me some guidance as to the best way to handle this because I completely understand the employee's perspective."

If you have a good relationship with your supervisor, she can be a great ally in your cause. It may not be over the water cooler, in the lunch room, or at happy hour, but the next time you have a positive meeting with your manager, you might ask if you can bring up an unrelated topic about which you have a "great deal of personal concern."

Unless your supervisor does not have time for you—and if that's the case, wait until she does—she is likely to say, "Sure! What's on your mind?" It is important that you handle this appropriately. You don't want to be viewed as a complainer, nor do you want to get the person you contacted in HR/benefits in trouble.

If you have your manager's attention, remember that she probably carries more credibility with the HR/benefits department than you do, and getting your boss on your side is very valuable. She might view this as an opportunity to move up in the company and will have you to thank for it. So use your supervisor appropriately to help your cause. This might help you move up, too!

When dealing with your management, you will need to have more ammunition than your own research or this book. Fortuately, there is a ton of information available, and your knowledge of it will, at a minimum, impress your supervisor.

Start out by saying something like, "I know this isn't really my responsibility or even yours for that matter, but I feel an ethical obligation to share something I am concerned about with management." This statement will get 100 percent of your supervisor's attention. You have a 95 percent chance she will forget about what was preoccupying her and will truly listen to what you have to say. When your manager says, "Please, tell me about it," you will need to strike quickly, briefly, and succinctly without attacking your potential friend in HR/benefits.

You can respond with, "I'm sure you are aware of the congressional investigations about excessive fees in 401(k) plans and the study from the Government Accountability Office and the new fee disclosure rules that are going (or have gone) into effect for plan years ending starting in 2012." Then continue with, "In my case, I am personally paying $____ a year for my retirement plan. I researched it some, found a book on the topic, and forwarded a copy to Jerri in HR. It showed that I am easily paying an excess __ percent a year on my assets. I think Jerri is too busy with other things to focus on this. While I'd personally like to have a more cost-efficient retirement plan, what concerns me more is that the company might be at risk from the Labor Department if nothing is done about this."

Unless your supervisor is a complete idiot, she will pay attention to this and will contact the person in HR/benefits that you originally contacted (and possibly her supervisor, too). Again, look at the wording. You positioned the issue not as a complaint but as a concern for the company, and the company is legitimately at risk. There is an opportunity for both you and your supervisor to become heroes, and that can't be a bad thing.

After assembling your troops, be it peers, subordinates, or supervisors, there is still a chance that nothing will get done about your company's retirement plan problem. It might be because you targeted the wrong person in HR/benefits/payroll. If she was not the type of person who was going to do anything about it in the first place, despite the help of your troops, the problem might not get fixed.

Or maybe you are in a very small company and the chief executive officer/chief financial officer/owner is more worried about immediate business issues than what you are paying in your retirement plan. It is important to your future lifestyle and your career that you are empathetic to their situation. Don't let that stop you. The next chapter outlines what is needed when your troops, subordinates, and supervisors are ignored. It is more drastic, but it may be necessary in the face of such disregard for the facts by "the powers that be."

6

What Happens If My Employer Ignores Us?

If you and your troops targeted the wrong person and that person was not in a position to effect a change in your retirement plan, you might need to retry your efforts with your troops, targeting someone more senior in the organization. If, after a couple of attempts, you still do not see any action, this is your last resort.

Pension plans, profit sharing plans, 401(k) plans, 403(b) plans, and 457 plans are all regulated by the U.S. Department of Labor. The Labor Department enforces the myriad of rules that were born and continue to expand from a 1974 piece of legislation known as the **E**mployee **R**etirement **I**ncome **S**ecurity **A**ct (ERISA). The laws derived from this act are intended to protect employees' retirement funds. It is important to note that there are exceptions from compliance with ERISA for some 403(b) and 457 plans. Many sponsors of these plans falsely assume they are not subject to ERISA rules, but there is a complex array of detailed guidelines required to obtain such exception.

Regardless, among the many provisions of the ERISA legislation are definitions for who is a "fiduciary" for a retirement plan and the type of conduct that constitutes actions of a "prudent fiduciary."

There are provisions that prevent "self-dealing" by fiduciaries and requirements that the assets of a retirement plan be handled in a manner for the "sole benefit of participants."

Fiduciaries are also required to make sure that investments are "diversified" and that they "avoid any investment risk *unless it is clearly prudent* to do otherwise."

Finally, there is even a provision that covers expenses. Unfortunately, it was worded rather weakly, and how it has been interpreted in actual cases has not provided much protection for employees or the security of their retirement income. The provision relating to expenses only states that "expenses must be reasonable." Even this loose statement is offered further wiggle room by the addition of a provision saying "reasonable expenses relative to the overall services being provided."

You and I might interpret "reasonable" in very different ways. Go back to the expense ratios for the funds your plan has available. See if your plan offered a large-cap stock or S&P 500 Index Fund, regardless of whether you happen to own it. What was the expense ratio? Was it 0.25 percent a year? How about 0.30 percent or 0.50 percent? Was it 0.07 percent a year? THAT is the expense ratio of the Fidelity Spartan S&P 500 Index Fund (symbol FSMAX). This fund has no sales load, no redemption fees, and no 12b-1 fees. It does have a $100,000 initial investment minimum, but that minimum is for your WHOLE COMPANY and not for individual employees. Even a company with only $500,000 in assets in their 401(k) would probably have $100,000 in large-cap stocks and could meet the minimum. There is another S&P 500 Index Fund offered by the Teachers Insurance and Annuity Association–College Retirement Equities Fund (TIAA-CREF) that has expenses of 0.08 percent and total domestic equity index funds offered that have expenses of only 0.10 percent a year with company-wide investment minimums of only $10,000, and some other institutional share classes of funds available to retirement plans that have expenses in this range. These expense keep getting lower and lower while many retirement plan expenses have actually been increasing.

What Is Reasonable?

What are the expenses for the S&P 500 Index Fund or large-cap index fund in your retirement plan? Is it "reasonable" to pay three to six times as much for the same thing?

Paying $75,000 for a Camry?

We are not talking about the difference between a Lexus and a Camry. We are talking about paying $75,000 for a Camry when you can get the exact same car for around $21,000! That doesn't seem "reasonable" to me, and it probably doesn't seem reasonable to you, either.

If you really want to get steamed, look at your fund selections for "International Stocks," and find the lowest-cost offering. In my broken 401(k) plan, I was paying 1.06 percent a year. Now international investing does cost a bit more, but there are international index funds that are available with no loads, no minimums, no 12b-1fees, and no redemption fees for 0.15 percent a year or even less. Why would you pay 0.91 percent a year more (seven times as much) for the same thing? Is *that* reasonable?

Think about this! If you eventually accumulate $500,000 in your 401(k), that extra 0.91 percent a year in expense would be enough for you to make the payments on a Camry!

While no rational person could legitimately argue that this is reasonable, there are two loopholes that are used to justify how much of your money is confiscated out of your retirement fund by these expenses.

Somehow, the case law has in practice come to measure "reasonable" not relative to what the same offering is available for in the marketplace, but instead it is measured by what the average expense is across the millions of plans that are overpaying.

If I challenged the Principal Group for charging me seven times as much in expenses for owning the same thing, all their attorneys would have to do is go to Morningstar.com and show that the "category average" for "Foreign Large Blend" funds is 1.55 percent a year, and therefore their 1.06 percent a year is "reasonable." The ERISA standard for expenses has been interpreted so that your employer (a fiduciary) *does not have to find the lowest expenses*, only that they are *reasonable* under this lame interpretation. So much for the Employee Retirement Income Security Act protecting your retirement! When it comes to expenses, **ERISA should stand for "Employees Ripped-off Increasingly by Suspicious Accounting."**

I mentioned earlier that my company provides mathematical engines and capital market research for the financial services industry. One of the services we offer is a rating system for funds that exposes aspects that the popular stargazing methods do not. Believe it or not, the popular ratings systems out there, for all practical purposes, do not measure some of the very basic concerns anyone should be looking at when considering funds for retirement.

For example, in the popular rating systems in the market, the prudent fiduciary standard of diversification is essentially ignored, and, in fact, *to get a high rating, it almost requires that the fund being rated is not well diversified.*

Since expense is a certainty for the future, but past performance is not necessarily an indication of future results, you would think that expense would be part of the popular rating systems, but in most, it is not. The only impact where excess expenses normally would show up is if they are so extreme that they severely impact the short-term (i.e., three- to five-year) performance. With many funds making wild bets and thus not very diversified, an extra 1 to 2 percent of expense doesn't hit the radar in the ranking system over the short three- to five-year periods being measured. Hey, it's only your retirement we are talking about, right?

One would also think that the risk of underperforming would be part of the measurement of ranking. If one or two months of some lucky returns made a three- or five-year return very high, but the fund had below-market returns in many or most months, you would think this generally poor performance would show up in the rankings, but once again, it is usually ignored.

These are obvious basic measurements that are easy to calculate, yet many of the popular, so-called "objective" ratings systems ignore these basics in their rankings that any truly prudent fiduciary would consider. Obviously, risk and return need to be measured as well, but with past performance not necessarily an indication of future results, shouldn't an investor have a bit more to go on?

I'll tell you a little secret. We came up with a grading system that exposes all of these factors, and what you will discover is **that there are no free lunches out there**. Just like the popular systems that automatically slap five stars on any fund that happens to randomly fall in the top 10 percent for risk-adjusted return, we set a standard to be a grade of "D" if the fund's expenses are more than 50 percent higher than the lowest 10 percent of expense ratios. A total of 63 percent (more than 9,000 funds) of all of the 14,300 funds available in our database are charging at least 50 percent higher expenses or more. **A total of 3,307 funds earned an F because they were charging expenses 300 percent OR MORE** greater than the lowest 10 percent of funds. Some of these F-rated funds in our system were five-star funds in the popular, "objective" systems! So much for expenses being part of the typical rating system!

If you would like to look up your funds on this retirement grading scale, go to Fundgrades.com to see how your funds look from a retirement perspective. This will help you to see whether you are making a big gamble by not being diversified, taking a big risk of underperforming, taking needless investment risk, or paying excess expenses.

What this discussion of the fund-ranking systems means to you, though, is that lawsuits are not a good option for you, not just because bringing a lawsuit against your employer would not do much for your career, but also because the loose interpretation of what constitutes a "reasonable" expense has too many loopholes in it for you to win. Besides, all you really want is to have your retirement plan fixed, you don't want your friend in human resources (HR)/benefits to get in trouble.

The other loophole that makes it even more difficult to win a case is this notion of "expenses in the context of the overall services being provided." Most plans that have less than $5 to $10 million in assets are sold to your employer by either an insurance agent or a broker. In many cases, they might not be doing a whole lot for the commissions they are earning on your retirement fund. On small plans of less than $1 million in total investment assets, it isn't uncommon for the agent or broker to earn 0.30 to 0.90 percent each year on your assets. What do they do for this?

While some of these agents or brokers offer to provide personal consultation and advice to participants, more likely than not they "help" the employer figure out which funds to offer in your retirement plan and give a speech once or twice a year. Now, do you perceive a conflict of interest in this? The agents or brokers are paid more in commissions for offering more expensive funds. And, even if they are not paid directly for the funds used, there is an indirect benefit of making the plan an easier sale to the employer if they recommend funds that offer those kickbacks (revenue sharing) because the cost of administration and record keeping to the company will be lower.

If your friend in HR/benefits asks the retirement plan salesperson (again, usually an insurance agent or broker) if the company could offer one of these far less expensive funds (i.e., a Camry for a Camry price), the agent or broker has an easy defense to protect his or her commissions. He or she will say either, "We don't offer that fund on our platform" or perhaps, "We could offer it, but your administration expenses will be a lot higher."

Remember, the total cost for administration, recording keeping, government filings, statements, web site, and the like should be no more than $50 a year per employee and can easily be as little as $30 a year with an annual company-wide minimum of $1,500 to $2,000. But these agents and brokers need to get their commissions, so what they do is package the administration cost to be much higher and use expensive funds with kickbacks to bring the costs back in line. **My company's plan, before we fixed it, was being charged more than $500 a year per participant for administration**. That is 10 to 20 times the maximum amount it should—*and actually does*—cost the provider. If, instead of offering expensive funds, we went to only the lowest-cost fund options, either the company or the participants would have to pick up this additional administration cost, according to our salesperson.

These agents and brokers earn their commission somewhere, and this is the bait-and-switch method employed to protect it. And how is this used to help justify the notion of reasonable expenses? Well, their conflicted suggestions (many will not admit to being a fiduciary, but your employer may be counting on them for "advice" regardless) for offering expensive funds to you is supposedly a "service" that is part of that "expenses relative to the total services provided."

More likely than not, you too have been to speeches these agents or brokers offer once a year or so. They will tell you the virtues of maximizing your retirement plan contributions (even to the point of needless sacrifice to your lifestyle), show you how their (expensive) funds have higher star ratings, talk about asset allocation, and how "the risk of stocks lowers with time" and your retirement should be a long-term investment.

It is possible that your agent or broker is spending fewer than 10 hours a year working on your plan, and a lot of that time is used to sell people on buying excessively expensive funds, not on providing the objective fiduciary type of advice that you both expect and deserve.

If you are truly interested in finding out the commission your company's agent or broker is paid, you can request a copy of the Form 5500 from your employer that will likely disclose this information. The employer is obligated to provide it to you if you request it, but the employer has the right to charge you a fee to photocopy it for you. So much for disclosure.

At the top of page 2 of Schedule A in Form 5500, you will find out who was paid a commission, how much that commission was, and what they were paid in additional fees on top of the commission. Since we have fixed our plan and eliminated the middleman salesman, my company's plan doesn't show any expense. In our prior plan years ago before we fixed it, it showed our salesperson was making about $4,000 a year for basically showing up once a year to give a speech. Nice work if you can get it! His commissions and fees were about 0.40 percent, based on the value of the plan at the beginning of the 2005 tax year. The following year with most of the money having left the high-cost products early in the year, the commissions went from nearly $4,000 in the 2005 tax year to $163. For the 2008 plan year and thereafter it will be zero. **As the employer, this is the economic equivalent of making an additional $4,000 contribution to our employees' retirement**.

This agent or broker may be (as ours was) the nicest guy. He is just trying to earn a living, too. But neither the company nor the employees should be paying for "advice" that is conflicted or be paying for it if they were not using his services (like me and many others). And companies and employees should clearly have the option to avoid the expense if they are not using the "service."

This is why in some circumstances you and your troops may need to take more drastic action. The agent or broker who sold your employer on your retirement plan has an advantage over all of you. If the people in HR/benefits pay attention to your inquiries, their first step will be to contact their retirement plan sales agent or broker. The *agent or broker* has a lot of experience in evading fee disclosure and spinning the story so he can avoid losing or reducing his commissions. The more drastic action in the face of this conflicted agent or broker (who is going to do everything he can to convince your employer things are not broken) is instead to actually contact the Labor Department. They are waiting for your call.

In all likelihood, based on studies from the Government Accountability Office (GAO), Boston College, and AARP it would be reasonable to assume that perhaps more than half of all retirement plans are charging participants excessive fees based on what is available in the marketplace. Yet, according to the GAO study, the Labor Department received only 10 complaints in 2005.[*] This just shows how well these vendors (and sometimes employers) had been hiding the fees from participants. The new fee disclosures that are coming into effect should change this.

Contact the Labor Department

Having received only 10 complaints about retirement plan fees in 2005, the Labor Department is literally waiting for your call. So, here's the number: 1-866-4-USA-DOL or go to www.dol.gov.

Before you place the call, be prepared. The information you will need is not extensive (other than the familiarity with the key terms of ERISA we outlined in this chapter), but it will help if you have it handy when you contact them. First, you will need your employer's Employer Identification Number (EIN). This is on your W-2 form you get at tax time, it may be on your payroll stub, or, better yet, you can get the number from the Summary Annual Report your employer must deliver to you each year.

The next step you will need to be prepared for is the case you wish to make. It is best to phrase these issues in Labor Department jargon so they will take you seriously and know how to respond. You also need to have factual information that presents a strong case, regardless of whether it personally applies to you. The easiest case to make is to show the excessive fees you and your associates are paying for a Camry.

When the first person answers at the Labor Department (you may be on hold for a while, because they are obviously taking calls on many things other than retirement plan fee complaints), simply state, "I would like to complain about the excessive fees in my retirement plan." In all likelihood, you will be transferred to another individual.

When you get to the right person, restate that you are calling to complain about the excessive fees in your retirement plan and you "do not think they meet the ERISA standard of being reasonable relative to the services being offered."

---

[*]U.S. Government Accountability Office, "Private Pensions: Changes Needed to Provide 401(k) Plan Participants and the Department of Labor Better Information on Fees," GAO-07-2, 1 November 2006, p. 21.

You may be asked why you think this. If so, tell them that fees charged for index funds are ____ to ____ times (e.g., three to seven times) what other plans have available, and the services your plan offers are less than what smaller companies provide at far less cost. Then tell them you have contacted your employer about this and that several other associates in your company have done so as well, but the employer has not done anything about it, to your knowledge, and you would like to seek "whistle-blower" protection of your identity to protect you from any possible retaliation from your employer.

The Labor Department may ask for a lot of personal information about you. Provide it ONLY if you are given the assurance that your employer will not know you are the one who turned them in. If the person says they cannot provide you with that protection, ask to speak to a supervisor and repeat the process.

Remember, this step is intended only as a last resort. You and your troops should exhaust several attempts within your company before you take this step. But, if it is needed, do not be afraid to use it, as long as you are guaranteed protection by the Labor Department for having them research your company's retirement plan. The reality is that an investigation may be triggered, and it will take a lot of time. The Labor Department may start with merely a letter that only mentions an investigation about the fees in your company's plan. This, however, will trigger actions by your employer to seek out the lower-cost alternatives available in the market, so by the time any serious investigation takes place, your retirement plan could very likely be fixed.

Finally, don't give up. You might be employed for the next 10, 20, or more years, so in the first 6 months to a year, if all of these steps do not repair your retirement plan, keep up the effort with your troops. Rally a few more. Eventually, you can avoid the retirement rip-off.

But when you do get your retirement plan fixed, it will be all for nothing if you don't use it to improve your life. The next chapter will show you how to maximize the dividend you receive by repairing your broken retirement plan.

7

Now That My Retirement Plan Is Fixed, How Can I Make the Most of My Life?

If you look at the tables in Appendix A that show you the various prices to your lifestyle of excessive retirement plan fees, you may realize that there are several choices you can make in using your fixed retirement plan to improve your lifestyle.

Which options might you choose? Do you reduce equity exposure and portfolio risk so that you can sleep better at night? Do you reduce your savings to buy that new sports car you have always dreamed of or to send your child to private school? Do you retire earlier? Travel more in retirement? The choices are endless. A few are outlined in the introduction, discussed in Chapter 1 and Appendix A gives additional examples.

More Bait and Switch

Watch the television ads from various financial services firms. Many of them talk about "making the most of your life" and "achieving your dreams," but the question you should ask is whether the advertising is just an attempt to draw you in or is it actually WHAT they deliver? Odds are that these ads are only an attempt to draw you in, because I have witnessed *very few advisers who actually deliver* on the promise of *what their firms are advertising*.

As a 20-plus-year veteran of the financial services industry, I will tell you some secrets that the financial services industry does not want exposed:

- Many advisers care more about the PRODUCTS they can put into your portfolio than how you can use your portfolio to achieve your dreams and goals.
- Experts in the home office at major firms provide guidance to their "advisers" (salespeople), but a nonexpert salesperson is normally who is ultimately responsible for what is recommended to you. What is recommended frequently makes more sense to the adviser than for the client (if the advice is objectively evaluated).
- Discussion by the adviser about your personal goals is frequently used only to package the advice into a more effective sales pitch for a portfolio they want to sell you. Often, there are more rational choices the adviser has ignored that could improve *both your portfolio AND your lifestyle.*

The financial services industry will deny this. Yet, the facts are on my side. Forget about the 30,000-plus advisers we have serviced in one form or another to validate our observation. Forget about our repeated attempts to get them to focus on actually delivering advice about making the most of your life since that is what their firms are advertising, and that it is possible to actually deliver that. Forget about the "advisers" who completely evade the risk of underperforming the markets when they attempt to justify their high-cost portfolio recommendations. Forget about the hundreds of rational and reasonably objective advisers who understand the contradictions, yet they still want to "add the sizzle to your portfolio," because they think you won't pay them anything "if they don't play the game."

You may be one of the lucky clients who has an adviser who is focused on your valued goals and is dedicated to helping you reach them. You may already be working with a Certified Wealthcare Analyst™ or an adviser who has adopted a somewhat similar process. If so, you may already be on the road to making the most of your life. Chances are, though, that your advisory relationship is something like one of the following:

- Maybe you deal with a bank brokerage that just happens to recommend funds it also manages. How is that for objective?

- Maybe you deal with a discount brokerage firm that provides you with great personal service and recommends its own funds.
- Maybe you deal with a no-load fund company that provides you with exceptional personalized service and consistently recommends its own funds.
- Maybe you deal with a full-service firm that recommends only investments it does not manage, but still plays the game with your portfolio of accepting the real risk of underperformance in the hope of possibly (but likely marginally) superior results.
- Maybe your adviser attempts to identify your tolerance for risk and proceeds to position you in a portfolio that is likely to experience it!
- Maybe your adviser regularly monitors your performance and recommends new investments AFTER they have performed poorly. (The smart guy we hired got dumb, but here's a better smart guy based on his five-year record—SO WHY DIDN'T THEY RECOMMEND HIM BEFORE WE HIRED THE GUY WHO BECAME DUMB?)

The reality is that Wall Street is the biggest casino in the world, and many advisers are paid for convincing you to play the game. They are good at it. They make money whether you win or not, just as real casinos do in poker games.

There are some fee-based advisors who will spin their gambling game by saying, "My interests are aligned with yours, because if your portfolio grows, my fees grow, but if your portfolio goes down, my fees go down." What if *your* interest is spending your portfolio to finance your retirement? Is the fee structure tied to the portfolio value aligned with your interests? The real interest many advisers have is to create an air of objectivity but sell you on taking risks you have the choice to avoid, and getting you to sacrifice your lifestyle to maximize how much is invested or being "played." If that doesn't sound like a casino, what does?

If I sound angry and frustrated, it is only because I am. I'm sure that there is a large market of gambling investors out there who want to play the games Wall Street is promoting. However, there probably is also a fairly large market of people who just want someone they can trust. Someone who will listen to what they are trying to achieve. Someone who is objective and not paid based on selling conflicted investment selections. Someone who can objectively advise them on the best choices for making the most of their lives. Someone who is an empathetic, objective listener and not an aggressive, conflicted talker.

Unfortunately, the industry has few of these types of people because such skills contradict the coercion skills needed to sell you. Instead of empathetic, objective listeners, by and large the industry is populated with aggressive, conflicted talkers. Their brains just are not wired to deliver the services about your dreams and goals their firms shamelessly advertise.

The standard solution offered by the industry is their portfolio of products—NOT your goals, your dreams, or the best choices among them.

How can you tell if your adviser is one of the few who MIGHT actually deliver?

- **If your adviser asks you your tolerance for risk WITHOUT asking if you prefer to take LESS risk, the adviser is a gambler, gambling with YOUR life, and not someone who will make the most of your dreams.**
- **If your adviser asks you how much more you might be willing to save, WITHOUT also asking how much you would like to reduce your savings, the adviser is focused on his pocket, NOT yours.**
- **If your adviser never asked you whether you might be willing to delay retirement a year if it meant taking less investment risk, the adviser is selling you, not advising you.**

Think about these few simple issues. To "make the most of your life" and "achieve your dreams," wouldn't you—and your adviser—by necessity need to understand your position on risk, savings, and retirement and the relative priorities about the choices among them based on what you value? The real reason most advisers do not ask about your life or your dreams is that what **you want** *conflicts* with *the Wall Street casino profiting from your gaming activities.*

Of course, there are advisers out there who do care about those specific issues and will ask you about saving less and taking less risk and all of these questions that matter to you. You may be able to find them simply by asking these types of questions and learning whether they are thinking about you and what you want to accomplish instead of about themselves or their products. Ask your friends, relatives, and coworkers about their experiences with advisers and whether any of them have been asked about whether they would like to save less or take less investment risk. The answer will be revealing.

The Benefits of Stopping the Retirement Rip-off!

In the introduction, we outlined a short list of the choices that would be available to you if you were to get your retirement plan fixed.

- Save less money?
- Plan on retiring earlier?
- Work fewer hours?
- Add a travel budget to your plan for retirement?
- Take less investment risk so that market gyrations still let you sleep at night?
- Take the vacation of your dreams?
- Leave a bequest to your church or school?
- Buy the new sports car you have always dreamed about?
- Pay off credit card bills?
- Send your child to a private school?
- Build an addition on your house?
- Help your elderly parents improve their lifestyle?
- Upgrade the way you pursue your hobby?
- Buy a vacation home?

This is just a short list of options. You may have other goals in mind to pursue if you had the resources to do so. The tables in Appendix A show you examples of some of these alternatives. But to make the most of your life, you probably need some help in analyzing the choices because there are so many options and all of them have impacts—some major and some minor; it all depends.

For example, say that you have already accumulated $500,000 in your 401(k), you are three years away from retirement, you are saving $5,000 a year, and your 401(k) is just meant to supplement your retirement income above Social Security. Do you really think that the $15,000 you plan on saving over the next three years will make any difference? Contributing that amount over the next three years has only a 1 percent chance of making a difference (see Figure 7.1).

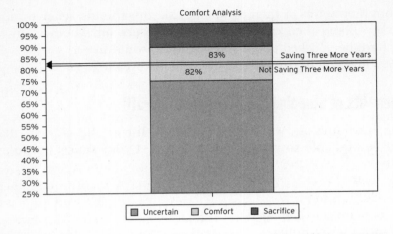

Zone	Plan Name	Simulation Method	Comfort Level	Status
1 ☐	**Saving Three More Years**	Monte Carlo	83%	Comfort
	Comfort – Sufficient confidence without undue sacrifice, changes to goals likely to be minor and manageable.			
2 ☐	**Not Saving Three More Years**	Monte Carlo	82%	Comfort
	Comfort – Sufficient confidence without undue sacrifice, changes to goals likely to be minor and manageable.			

	Saving Three More Years	Not Saving Three More Years
Retirement Age		
Client	65	65
Spouse	65	65
Retirement Need		
Client	$48,000	$48,000
Target End Value		
Today's Dollars	$0	$0
Actual Dollars	$0	$0
Avg. Annual Savings		
Client	$5,000	$0
Spouse	$0	$0
Default Inflation Rate	3%	3%
Investment Adjustment	−0.75%	−0.75%
Median Return	9.04%	9.04%
Risk		
Std. Deviation**	15.14%	15.14%
Downside (95%-tile)**	−12.96%	−12.96%

Figure 7.1   Comfort Analysis of Savings for the Next Three Years before Retirement

However, for a person who has only $50,000 in a retirement plan and is 20 years away from retirement, not making the $5,000-a-year contribution has a huge impact. Even discontinuing the contributions to the retirement plan for the next three years has a significant impact. This impact is illustrated in the savings example shown in Figure 7.2.

With so many options, the choices you have may seem overwhelming. There are a myriad of possible other choices. Maybe you would reduce savings a bit, increase risk a notch, but retire a little sooner. There are endless nuances and combinations and as long as the advice you are getting is from a vendor of products, these choices—about YOUR life—will in many cases be ignored.

I wish I could tell you that the answer for making the most of your life is simple. Well, it *is* simple if you know how. But it takes an empathetic, objective listener to deliver that advice. It takes someone who is not conflicted and is paid for delivering *that* service instead of being paid for selling you on investments or paying ridiculous fees. Why does the industry tie fees to investments if they are giving you advice? Couldn't you implement the portfolio yourself but still get the advice? Ask if your adviser is willing to do that!

The choices you have are vast. The solution is easy if you have the right person with the right motivation servicing you. If you call our toll-free line, you can get a current recommendation for free from such an empathetic, objective listener. It is best to block off about an hour and to have your spouse/partner available as well. Just call 1-866-261-0849 and tell them you have the code word *Rip-off*, and they will create a free recommendation based on your newly repaired retirement plan and any other resources and goals you may have.

The Only Thing Constant Is Change

Remember in Chapter 3 how, if all we did was randomize actual historical returns, our sample middle-class participant had a 96 percent chance of accumulating a retirement fund of anywhere from $134,000 to $25 million? That means there is a 4 percent chance (or 1 in 25) that it would be outside of this range! Of course, as we mentioned, you would change your lifestyle long before either of these extremes presented themselves, so they are purely theoretical.

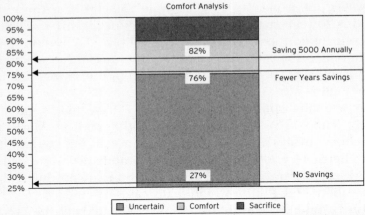

	Zone	Plan Name	Simulation Method	Comfort Level	Status
1	☐	**Saving 5000 Annually**	Monte Carlo	82%	Comfort
	Comfort – Sufficient confidence without undue sacrifice, changes to goals likely to be minor and manageable.				
2	◼	**No Savings**	Monte Carlo	27%	Uncertain
	Uncertain – Confidence is too low, significant changes to goals may be necessary now and into the future. You may want to adjust your plan to achieve a comfort level between 75 and 90 percent.				
3	☐	**Fewer Years Savings**	Monte Carlo	76%	Comfort
	Comfort – Sufficient confidence without undue sacrifice, changes to goals likely to be minor and manageable.				

	Saving 5000 Annually	**Not Savings**	**Fewer Years Savings**
Retirement Age			
Client	65	65	65
Spouse	65	65	65
Retirement Need			
Client	$36,000	$36,000	$36,000
Target End Value			
Today's Dollars	$0	$0	$0
Actual Dollars	$0	$0	$0
Avg. Annual Savings			
Client	$5,000	$0	$4,286
Spouse	$0	$0	$0
Default Inflation Rate	3%	3%	3%
Investment Adjustment	−0.75%	−0.75%	−0.75%
Median Return	8.24%	8.24%	8.24%
Risk			
Std. Deviation**	12.17%	12.17%	12.17%
Downside (95%-tile)**	−9.92%	−9.92%	−9.92%

Figure 7.2   Comfort Analysis of Saving $ 5,000 a Year, Saving for Fewer Years, and Saving Nothing

But, since no one can control what the markets might do and the range of uncertainty is so vast even assuming that you just blindly stick with your plan regardless of what is going on, **maybe you should frequently pay attention to this uncertainty**.

The markets from 2008 should be an ample reminder to you that the markets will misbehave. Your financial adviser cannot predict what your portfolio will be worth over the next year, yet alone the next 30 or 40 years. Whatever plan your adviser shows you, regardless of the initial confidence level, the reality is that it is almost certain that things will not go according to plan.

The markets will almost certainly misbehave, and your personal goals and priorities, no matter how well defined or how detailed the analysis, will also almost certainly change. This means that the typical adviser's approach of designing a long-term plan and providing you the coaching to **"stick with it for the long term" is in contradiction to reality of both the markets and your life**.

This is where the typical adviser in the industry will fall short. When you experience a severe bear market (which is bound to happen at some point in your life, and could occur at any time even though we have just experienced a severe bear market), instead of suggesting solutions that tweak your lifestyle choices to shift the odds back in your favor, the typical adviser will instead do everything in his power to coerce you to "stick with your long-term plan." He will use guilt, if needed. He will remind you of the maximum risk you said you could tolerate. He will pull out articles from "experts" demonstrating that the *average* bear market lasts only 12 months (that means many of them last LONGER).

What he is unlikely to do is tell you the choices you have, based on what you personally value, to make some adjustments to your plan that would move you back toward that comfortable balance *despite* the depreciation in your portfolios.

The reverse is true, as well. If you are lucky and end up with some very strong markets, the adviser will be fat and happy, because his clients are, as well. But instead of advising you about the choices you have to take some investment risk off the table (because you can now afford to do so) or telling you to spend some more money (because you can now afford to), he will likely pat himself on the back for the lucky bull market in which he just happened to be around for the ride.

Instead of providing advice about what makes the most sense for your life BECAUSE of what has been happening in the markets, many advisers only report WHAT happened. **There is a big difference between being an adviser and being a reporter**.

A reporter shows you what happened. He might even explain his theory about why what happened . . . ummm . . . happened. But the fact is, NO ONE **can change what happened**. So while looking at your returns relative to benchmarks might be interesting information, IT CANNOT BE CHANGED. IT HAS ALREADY HAPPENED.

This is part of the game Wall Street plays in its casino. Like the casinos do, Wall Street and its investment product vendors show advertisements about achieving your dreams. Once they get you to the table, though, they stop measuring your dreams and goals and only provide you with a win/loss statement of what happened. They call this a "performance report." You will observe that the major things you are trying to achieve are not part of such a report. There is no retirement income goal being monitored or measured. Your desired retirement age isn't there, either. Nor is your travel budget, your new sports car, or your bequest to your church or other charity.

This performance report will show you that relative to all of the other gamers in the Wall Street casino (either the market "benchmarks" or peer group ranks of funds and managers) where your results fell. The adviser may advise you to bet on a different horse since yours has been losing (the adviser won't take blame for this). Or, if your luck happened to be better than the other gamblers, the adviser will take credit for picking these winning "horses" (funds or money managers).

But these advisers won't tell you that it is time for you to take risk off the table or spend more money because it makes sense to do so for what you are trying to achieve. These advisers won't tell you that it might be a good idea to plan on compromising some of your lower-priority goals, or delay some of them for a while *because* of what happened in the markets.

But advisers should do all of these things if THAT is what you as a customer are seeking advice about from them. Their firms' ads sure make it sound like that is what the advisers will do. That is why I call it a bait and switch.

The Markets Are Not the Only Things that Are Uncertain

Besides the uncertainty of the markets' behavior in how it might affect the lifestyle you are planning on, over your lifetime your life goals and priorities will no doubt change as well. This is just one more reason why any financial planner's projection of how much money you might accumulate is useless. It is always based on numerous assumptions. There are assumptions about the behavior of the markets. Assumptions about how much you will save and what tax rates will be. There are assumptions about inflation and assumptions about the goals you wish to achieve. Some may even include some assumptions about your priorities (although this is rare).

Do you know anyone who used to love their job, but their company was acquired, and now they do nothing but complain about how the culture has changed? Do you think that they might prioritize early retirement more in the face of this change?

Do you know anyone who has taken up a new hobby in the last 10 years? Scuba diving? Flying? Photography? Woodworking? Gambling? All of these hobbies take money that would have never been accounted for in their lives and planning prior to the person actually engaging in the new activity.

What about the uncertainty of health? Do you know anyone who has been economically and, more importantly, emotionally affected by cancer? Heart disease? A car accident? Drug or alcohol addiction? Divorce? All of these are real uncertainties that might affect the choices and priorities you make in your life, despite all the insurance the broker sells you for some of these things.

The reality is that your life is just as uncertain as the markets. Frankly, to many people, this uncertainty and how one can influence it by the choices they make is what makes life worth living. To others, this uncertainty is a crippling fear that causes them to needlessly sacrifice the only life they do have.

If you live your life in crippling terror of everything that can go wrong, you won't benefit by fixing your retirement plan, because the list of other things that can go wrong is as endless as the expenses that might occur. If you like playing the Wall Street casino game of worrying more about beating other players instead of making the most of your life, who cares if your retirement plan is too expensive, because there will be an endless stream of new funds with which you can "play."

But if you are sick of the games, if you really want to strike a rational balance of the best choices in your life, if you wish to capitalize on the choices you have to improve your life, then I hope you take the steps outlined in this book to make your goals a reality.

8

Resources, Investment Selection, Asset Allocation, Tools, and Advice

Investment Selection

This morning, as I sat down to write this chapter, there was a promotion on CNBC announcing the appearance of a mutual fund manager who was rated "Five Stars" with a five-year compound return of more than 35 percent (this Chapter was written several years ago). CNBC said it was definitely something I should listen to since this manager was an expert. What a great track record! He must be brilliant! Surely he will be my ticket to easy street!

Hold on a second. Before I get too excited about this unique opportunity, didn't I hear that past performance is not necessarily an indication of future results? Doesn't this sound familiar? This oft-cited phrase comes from a requirement of the Financial Industry Regulatory Authority (FINRA, formerly the National Association of Securities Dealers [NASD]). FINRA is the self-regulatory organization (not a government agency) that supposedly protects investors by making sure member firms abide by certain standards that protect the reputation of the securities-peddling industry. All broker/dealers are members of the FINRA. Thus, their primary regulators are themselves. These broker/dealers are not necessarily fiduciaries acting in your best interests, although the recent Dodd/Frank Financial Reform Bill requires a study be done to examine whether they should be fiduciaries. But, currently, they are not necessarily acting as fiduciary advisers. They are required to disclose to you that they are salespeople, not advisers, despite the misleading titles they give their employees (if you look at the fine print in your brokerage agreements, you will find this disclosure of their myriads of conflicts). There are numerous rules that the industry—broker/dealers—has come up with to "protect" investors, and the brokers/dealers all agree to abide by these rules so they can continue peddling securities.

The statement, "Past performance is not necessarily an indication of future results," is required by FINRA for those who sell securities and show performance records. Think about the statement. *If it is true, and you were an objective adviser instead of a salesman, why would you show past* performance? If it isn't an indication of future results, the record is meaningless. Hmmm. Yet everyone is showing you their record. Sound like the casinos again?

As the CEO of a business, I get calls from "financial advisers" (securities peddlers) all the time. They normally go into how they have some fund, stock, partnership, or the like, with a great track record that I should invest in. The conversation goes something like this:

"Mr. Loeper, George Salesman here with Fly-by-Night Brokerage. The last time we spoke *(note: usually we haven't spoken before, but it is more effective in their pitch to say that we have)*, you said you would be interested in great investment ideas, and I have one for you today. The Acme Fund has a 10-year record of superior risk-adjusted returns relative to the S&P 500, and the same management team has been and is still in place."

At this point, my response goes something like this, "Are you saying that past performance is an indication of future results?"

Now, most product peddlers know that even their own industry would consider it a violation of regulations to imply that past performance is an indication of future results, so they normally respond with something like, "There are no guarantees about any investment, but this team does have a great long-term record."

Now, to me, this sure sounds like they are at least implying that the performance record might be an indication of future results. When I have pushed them on this and asked, "Is past performance an indication of future results?," they dutifully respond, "Not necessarily."

And I respond, "Then why should I care about it?"

They normally retort with something like, "While past performance is not necessarily an indication of future results, certainly you would want to work with a team that has a great long-term record. What else would you have to go on? We don't invest based on hunches around here; we need proven records!"

Can you perceive the contradiction in his statement? Flipped around outside of the salesman's spin on it, he is saying, "Track records are not reliable for choosing superior investments, but what you should pick are investments based on those unreliable track records."

We did a simple little study on this (there have been numerous academic and industry articles on the topic as well). As of the end of the first quarter of 2007, 54 percent of the 6,000 mutual funds that had been around since at least the first quarter of 2000 **materially underperformed** their best-fit benchmark for the trailing three years (we eliminated funds that did not remotely fit any benchmark). That means that over half of the mutual funds performed well below their benchmarks over the past three years.

We then went back to the first quarter of 2003 and found the top 5 percent of these 6,000 funds rated on their relative return to their best-fit benchmark. These top-rated funds all outperformed their benchmark by at least 50 percent of the volatility of the benchmark as of the end of the first quarter of 2003. However, when we looked at these funds four years later, 54 percent of those top-rated funds *also materially underperformed* their benchmark for the trailing three years—THE SAME PERCENTAGE AS ALL FUNDS!

What does this show us? The fact that the top-rated funds were among the best in 2003 not only was no indication the funds would perform well in future years, but these top-rated funds underperformed just as often as all of the funds—low-rated or high-rated—that we tested. The track record had no apparent connection with how the fund would perform in later years. This is why FINRA requires the statement about past performance not being an indication of future results.

The Risk of Underperforming Is Higher than the Chance of Outperforming

Every month we publish updated information for the grading distribution of all funds for the last three years. (See: www.fundgrades .com/GradeDistribution.aspx.) As of April 30, 2011, 77.08 percent of all funds had a return grade between C+ and C−, or somewhere close to the benchmark. Only 4.98 percent of all funds had return grades of B− or better. That's about a one-in-20 chance of having a return materially better than the benchmark. But, 17.94 percent of all funds had a return grade of D+ or worse, meaning they materially underperformed the benchmark. This means (at least for this most recent three-year period) that if you are making an active bet on trying to pick winners, that most of the time (about 0.75) you'll end up near the benchmark return, about 5 percent of the time you will pick a real winner, and about 18 percent of the time you would pick a real loser. The odds of picking a loser versus a winner are really stacked against you. The risk of picking a real loser is about three and a half times the hope of picking a real winner. Add on the certainty of expenses and this is just not a rational gamble. It might be fun and the bragging rights we get for those rare winners are emotionally rewarding, but it is very, very unlikely that you or any advisor are going to beat these odds.

But track records—no matter how unreliable—do make compelling sales pitches. Human nature wants to extrapolate what will happen (future tense) from what has *happened* (observe this is past tense) even if there is no evidence that the past is any indication of what is to come.

The reality is that there is no free lunch that IS predictable. A track record is what happened to someone else's money, NOT YOURS, and IS NOT an indication of future results. It is an effective sales tool, though, since it preys on our innate desire to project forward past observations despite the disclosure that says we should ignore it.

If track records are useless, are there data elements that are more predictive? Perhaps. Certainly, one would want to evaluate whether a fund under consideration for purchase is diversified or is making big, unpredictable bets with your money. We measure this by calculating a statistic called the *correlation coefficient*. Without getting into the detailed mathematics of this statistic, in essence it measures how directionally similar the performance is between two sets of returns, such as a fund versus a benchmark. That is, if one return goes up, will the other return also rise? If so, then the returns may be said to be correlated.

Another data element that is more predictive of results is the subject of this book—expenses related to an investment. Expenses have surprising (or maybe not so surprising) relationships to results. If you think about this, it makes sense because the expenses that are coming from your investment are a 100 percent certainty (unlike track records supposedly demonstrating skill, but also luck, on the part of fund managers). As a group, funds with high expense ratios are much less likely to perform at or above average than lower-expense-ratio funds. Likewise, a far smaller percentage of the low-expense-ratio funds end up with terrible performance than their higher-priced competitors. Obviously, this impact of expenses should not be ignored.

Risk and return records are not an indication of future results, but they probably should at least be observed so long as we do not excessively value the data. There is a means of evaluating these statistics relative to the best-fit benchmark by combining this with correlation. Unfortunately, most of the rating services simply slap their ratings on a particular fund *relative to other "similar" funds*, without paying attention to the benchmark. The effect is that most rating systems ignore the risk relative to the benchmark or even the right benchmark, and **in fact the best way to get a high return rating for a fund is to have the fund misclassified into the wrong category**.

An example of how misleading these "peer group and universe ranks" can be might make this effect more obvious. One of the star-gazing rating systems out there would classify a total market index fund (owns large, small, value, and growth stocks) as "large-cap blend" thereby throwing the fund into the same "universe" or "peer group" as the system would use to classify an S&P 500 index fund that owns only large-cap stocks. The two funds don't own the same stocks, but they are both index funds. Because the total market index fund owns small-cap stocks and recently they have been doing well, the fund gets rated a 4 for large-cap blend versus 3 for the S&P 500 index fund. Fifteen years ago the total market index fund would have been rated a 2 instead of a 4, because the small-cap stocks it owns underperformed. One fund isn't better than the other. They are different. The best way to get a good return rating and stargazing grade is to be misclassified into the wrong peer group!

One other data element or measure that one should consider in evaluating potential investments is "luck" in terms of frequency of consistently not screwing up. We call this "material underperformance risk," and we can measure it by looking at the best-fit benchmark for the fund we want to examine, reducing the benchmark by a reasonable (like the lowest 10 percent) expense ratio, and then seeing the percentage of the months where the fund underperformed by more than the reasonable expense. Clearly, if a fund more often than not underperforms by more than this reasonable expense, yet has a good long-term return grade, this combination of factors might suggest that one or two high-performing months have "saved" the long-term record.

Fundgrades.com

You can look up these grades as well as an overall grade that combines them all at Fundgrades.com. I will not tell you that this is predictive of a particular fund's future performance. However, using the overall grades here probably isn't as bad as looking at track records. Funds are graded on an A+ through F grade relative to the most appropriate benchmark (no misleading misclassification into peer groups) for both an overall grade and an examination of each of the criteria discussed previously that we know expose some useful information.

While this grading system isn't predictive of which funds will be star performers, it might help you avoid some senseless risks. For example, nearly 75 percent of the honor roll funds from the Fundgrades.com grading routine, as determined based on 2003 data, ended up being rated average or above based on data through 2007. Likewise, 65 to 85 percent of the funds graded as D+ through F based on 2003 data remained below average when tested again in 2007.

While resources like Morningstar, Yahoo!, Google Finance, Lipper, and the like may provide you with a lot of interesting data, be careful about how much weight you give it. Peer groups can be very misleading for many reasons. Track records are not predictive, and it is impossible to discern whether the "great track records" boasted by a few funds were caused by skill or luck. Finally, even if you found someone with skill, you never know whether the "secret" of the method might be discovered by others, thus eliminating the advantage.

Asset Allocation

The main thing is to keep the main thing the main thing. Asset allocation is a main thing. I've written a number of white papers for the industry on the topic (go to Wealthcarecapital.com and click on the "Whitepapers" link) that you can review if you would like to learn more about this topic than we can cover here.

What's the main thing about asset allocation? The bottom line is the key drivers are going to be your allocation—of your investments—to stocks, bonds, and cash AND how well you are diversified in your selections for these asset classes. This element of diversification is the most misunderstood.

I've met people who think they are diversified in their portfolios because they bought the same sets of funds from three different brokerage firms. Diversification is based on what you own. If you do not own everything in the benchmark, in proportion to the weighting in the benchmark, then you are not completely diversified. In essence, you are making a bet. This is why index funds are so popular among objectivists that don't want to be sold. With many index funds (properly selected), you are getting a complete portfolio that is not making any bets against the benchmark. You have to be careful about this, though, because more and more index funds are created for the exact opposite purpose. Instead of being an inexpensive way to get a broadly diversified portfolio, many new index funds and exchange-traded funds (ETFs) are designed to focus on a nondiversified piece of the market like an industry or sector, market capitalization segment, or value or growth style.

Thus, the securities-peddling industry has taken these relatively pure, cost-effective, and unbiased vehicles and packaged them into all kinds of products and services that defeat their purpose. There are advisers that will attempt to time the market and shift the weights in your allocation around in hopes of timing things correctly (while exposing you to the risk of timing everything incorrectly—a risk that you could have avoided).

There are portfolios of indexes that are not diversified at all, making huge bets on small-cap, micro, or value stocks, bets that subject you to risks you have the choice to avoid. All of these approaches are just a means of continuing to get you to play the Wall Street casino game.

The securities peddlers have even created and defined new, "better" indices that "outperform" the old ones based on "long-term track records." Don't buy this for a minute. It is hype. If it sounds too good to be true, it probably is, and it is likely going to cost you a lot of your hard-earned savings to find that out.

Think about the 54 percent of the mutual funds that materially (not just by a little, but by a lot) underperformed their best-fit benchmark, as we mentioned earlier, in our 2007 study. This is a little more than the advantage a casino has over you in roulette. Roulette is one of the biggest "take" table games in the casino, which means it has the worst odds for the players. Yet this is the same result as the entire mutual fund industry. The industry nonetheless seems to be able to spin it (pun intended) so you keep playing the game despite the disadvantage.

There were a couple of studies done by Brinson, Hood, and Beebower that are often misquoted by the industry. What the studies showed was that more than 90 percent of the *variance* in investment returns is explained by your allocation to stocks, bonds, and cash. This means that less than 10 percent of the *variance* is explained by real estate, foreign, small-cap, growth, value, alternative investments, and so on. The way the industry usually misstates these studies, though, is to misquote them by saying, "More than 90 percent of your *returns are due* to asset allocation" (*subtext:* the way our firm defines asset allocation). Observe that they replaced "*variance is explained by*" with "*returns are due to*," which is a big deal if you understand the difference. You will also observe that they do not normally disclose that the 90-plus percent was based on stocks, bonds, and cash. Instead, they will use this study to show why you need 10 percent in small-cap value and 10 percent in small-cap growth—which, if you buy their mystical pie slices, is the exact same as 20 percent in small-cap blend. The more pie slices the better, though! The better for the salesman and not the investor. The growth and value pieces of the whole **are not** diversified. By definition, these securities peddlers, by splitting the whole into a variety of parts, are eliminating pieces of the more diversified whole.

Those pieces perform differently at different times. Everyone was selling an overweighting to the high-performing growth piece in the 1990s (which then blew up in the three-year bear market starting in 2000), and now these same securities peddlers are all pushing "value tilted" or "fundamentally weighted" portfolios that—you guessed it—currently have GREAT TRACK RECORDS! That is, they had great records until the heavy weighting to financial stocks blew up in 2008.

The odds of you or anyone outsmarting the markets are literally the same as winning a bet at the worst odds in any of a casino's table games. But many are tempted. The difference is that in the Wall Street casino, they are tempted to play that game and make the bet with their retirement assets, not with a $500 entertainment budget.

Forget the hype. Don't take any more investment risk than makes sense for what you are trying to achieve. What follows is an easy-to-use, do-it-yourself scoring model that shows you—based on your time horizon, risk tolerance, and liquidity needs—how to select a somewhat reasonable asset allocation. We designed it for retirement plans that want to offer participants an easy way to select a reasonable asset allocation since your asset allocation is one of the "main things."

Questionnaire

INSTRUCTIONS: *Complete these eight questions, total the POINT VALUE scores from questions 1 and 2 for your TIME HORIZON score, and questions 3 through 8 for your RISK TOLERANCE score, and find the intersection of these scores on the scoring model.*

Time Horizon Section
QUESTION #1. Do you expect to begin withdrawing money (or borrowing) from your portfolio account within the next 10 years? If so, how soon?

CHECK ONE Answer:

	Answers	Point Value
____	No	15
____	Yes, within the next 2 years	0
____	Yes, within the next 3–5 years	5
____	Yes, within the next 6–7 years	7
____	Yes, but not for at least 8–9 years	10

ENTER THE POINT VALUE FOR YOUR ANSWER: ____

QUESTION #2. If and when you begin withdrawing (or borrowing) from your portfolio account, over what period of time will the withdrawals last?

	Answers	Point Value
____	I will withdraw the entire account balance, all at once, for a specific goal	0
____	Over a 1–3-year period, depleting most or all of the account	1
____	Over a 4–7-year period, depleting most or all of the account	3

(Continued)

	Answers	Point Value
____	For more than 7 years, depleting most or all of the account	5
____	When I begin withdrawals, I expect to produce a continuous income stream without depleting the account	16
____	I never plan to make withdrawals from this account	20

ENTER THE POINT VALUE FOR YOUR ANSWER: ____

ADD THE TOTAL POINT VALUE OF QUESTIONS #1 and #2 combined and ENTER HERE: ____
THIS IS YOUR TIME HORIZON SCORE TO BE USED LATER

Risk Tolerance Section

QUESTION #3. Inflation impacts the effective spending power of your money over time.

To design an appropriate portfolio for you, we need to understand your attitude about the trade-off between preserving spending power versus growing your assets *after* the effects of inflation.

Portfolios that are likely to preserve or increase spending power over long periods of time, though, have higher volatility over shorter time periods.

Which best describes your attitude about accepting short-term risk relative to long-term growth?

	Answers	Point Value
____	Long-term maximum growth, in excess of inflation, is my primary objective even though the short-term risk will be very high.	15
____	Long-term growth, in excess of inflation, is my primary objective, but I am NOT willing to accept extreme short-term risk.	12
____	I desire a moderate balance between growth, in excess of inflation, and short-term risk.	6
____	My primary objective is to avoid short-term risk, even though it is likely that there will be little or no long-term growth in excess of inflation.	0

ENTER THE POINT VALUE FOR YOUR ANSWER: ____

QUESTION #4. Investments that are likely to produce higher long-term average returns are also likely to have a greater chance of losing money. Also, for these types of investments, the magnitude of extreme losses increases as well. The following table demonstrates this trade-off between average return, the likelihood of losing money in any ONE YEAR, AND how extreme declines may be. Please select the portfolio that best balances these trade-offs between risk and return for you.

	Answers	Point Value
____	PORTFOLIO A	20
____	PORTFOLIO B	18
____	PORTFOLIO C	12
____	PORTFOLIO D	8
____	PORTFOLIO E	5
____	PORTFOLIO F	−20

ENTER THE POINT VALUE FOR YOUR ANSWER: ____

	Potential Average Return	Chance of Losing Money In Any ONE Year	Worst Year of 75 Years	Worst Year of 30 Years
Portfolio A	12.5%	1 In 3	−46%	−24%
Portfolio B	12.0%	1 in 4	−41%	−21%
Portfolio C	11.3%	1 in 5	−37%	−18%
Portfolio D	10.0%	1 in 6	−28%	−12%
Portfolio E	9.0%	1 in 7	−22%	−8%
Portfolio F	7.8%	1 in 8	−15%	−3%

QUESTION #5. Based on the information from the previous question, there is obviously a trade-off between risk and return. Which of the following best describes your attitude about this decision in balancing your desire to seek returns relative to the risk you can tolerate?

	Answers	Point Value
____	My primary goal is preservation of principal and risk avoidance. I will accept lower returns in an effort to avoid investment risk.	0
____	I want to avoid risk, but will accept a relatively small amount to achieve a slightly higher return.	5
____	I can tolerate a moderate amount of risk in an effort to achieve a moderate amount of growth.	10
____	I want to achieve potentially high returns, and I am willing to accept the high amount of risk associated with this goal.	15

ENTER THE POINT VALUE FOR YOUR ANSWER: ____

QUESTION #6. To achieve your investment objectives, it is important that you continue with your strategy even in periods of severe short-term price swings (volatility) as well as prolonged down markets. If your portfolio fell by 20 percent over a short period, assuming you still had several years before you needed the money, how do you think you would respond?

	Answers	Point Value
____	I would not make any changes since I anticipated this sort of volatility.	15
____	I would want to reconsider my portfolio allocation, but if the overall market decline for portfolios like mine were similar, I would likely stick to my strategy.	10
____	I would want to reconsider my portfolio allocation and cautiously adjust my portfolio toward more conservative investments over time.	5
____	I would immediately move my investments to very safe and conservative alternatives.	0

ENTER THE POINT VALUE FOR YOUR ANSWER: ____

QUESTION #7. The graph that follows shows a hypothetical potential range of returns over any 12-month period of six model portfolio allocations. Please note that the highest median potential returns also have the greatest potential losses.

Which of these portfolios would you prefer to hold?

	Answers	Point Value
____	PORTFOLIO F	−20
____	PORTFOLIO E	5
____	PORTFOLIO D	8
____	PORTFOLIO C	12
____	PORTFOLIO B	18
____	PORTFOLIO A	20

ENTER THE POINT VALUE FOR YOUR ANSWER: ____

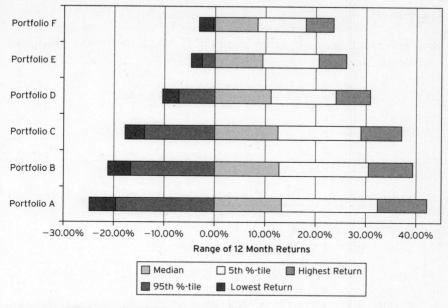

Range of 12-Month Returns Model Portfolio Allocations

QUESTION #8. To summarize your objectives, which of the following statements best describes your overall attitude between the trade-off between short-term risk and the possibility of achieving your long-term investment goal?

	Answers	Point Value
____	I can accept short-term losses to maximize the potential I will achieve my long-term investment goals.	15
____	I am equally concerned with avoiding short-term losses and meeting my long-term investment goals.	8
____	Avoiding short-term losses is more important to me than achieving my long-term investment goals.	5

ENTER THE POINT VALUE FOR YOUR ANSWER: ____

Scoring

Risk Tolerance Scoring: Enter the POINT VALUES for the following questions:

Question #	Point Value
#8	_____
#7	_____
#6	_____
#5	_____
#4	_____
#3	_____

YOUR TOTAL RISK SCORE: ___
(add the point values of questions #3 – #8)

Enter Your TIME HORIZON SCORE (sum of point values from questions #1 and #2) from page 100:
YOUR TIME HORIZON SCORE: ___

Find the Roman numeral that is at the intersection of your time horizon and risk scores.

Risk Tolerance		Time Horizon Score (Sum of #1 and #2)			
Score		>7	7–12	13–20	<20
<	10	I	I	I	I
11	– 20	I	I	II	II
21	– 35	I	II	II	III
36	– 50	I	II	III	III
51	– 65	I	III	IV	IV
66	– 80	I	IV	IV	V
80	– 100	I	V	VI	VI

Portfolio#	I	II	III	IV	V	VI
Asset Allocation	Risk Averse	Balance Income	Balanced	Balanced Growth	Growth	Aggressive Growth
Domestic Stocks	26	39	53	71	77	85
Foreign stocks	4	6	7	9	13	15
Total stock exposure	30	45	60	80	90	100
Treasury Bonds	60	50	37	18	10	0
Cash equivalents	10	5	3	2	0	0

Scoring Model and Model Portfolios

The scoring model and model portfolios are designed to help investors choose portfolios based on their time horizon and tolerance for risk. It does not include personal goals, priorities, or other assets, and really the only way to determine the right allocation for you is to consider these other variables. So, the answer you get from this questionnaire, while probably being better than what you would get with a lifecycle or target date fund is missing the goals you personally value. If you don't know where to turn to figure that out, feel free to speak with one of our Wealthcare specialists to help you make better decisions about how your personal goals, choices, and priorities fit into your overall financial situation. There is no charge for this service unless you later wish to have us continuously advise you about these choices in the future. Our toll-free line is (1-866-261-0849). Just use the code word *Rip-off* to get your free analysis.

However, if you wish to use the scoring model, here is an example of how it works:

Assume **YOUR TIME HORIZON Score was 15**. That would mean you would be working with the Time Horizon column of **13–20** because your score of 15 falls between **13 and 20**:

Risk Tolerance		Time Horizon Score (Sum of #1 and #2)			
Score		>7	7–12	13–20	< 20
<	10	I	I	I	I
11 —	20	I	I	II	II
21 —	35	I	II	II	III
36 —	50	I	II	**III**	III
51 —	65	I	III	IV	IV
66 —	80	I	IV	IV	V
80 —	100	I	V	VI	VI

Now, let's **assume your RISK TOLERANCE Score was 42**. That would mean you would be working with the risk tolerance row of **36–50** because 42 falls between **36 and 50**.

The correct model for these scores, based on the responses, would be Portfolio **III—Balanced**. It is the model that falls at the *intersection of the risk tolerance row and time horizon column*. Where do your scores place you?

With all these people trying to beat the "market" and the odds of picking a winner worse than the typical roulette table odds, why do people play the game? Are you really a patient long-term investor like the industry tells you that you should be?

As we mentioned earlier, it only makes sense to assume the risk level that makes sense for what you are trying to achieve. Even if you can tolerate more risk, why take it if it isn't needed for you to achieve what you personally value? The best way to determine this is to go through the Wealthcare process with someone who is not a commissioned salesperson but instead is an objective adviser.

So, while asset allocation is *a* main thing, your goals and priorities are still THE main thing. The reality is that it appears all the fiddling around with large, medium, and small pie slices is not really going to make any difference in your results. All the pieces and breakdowns of such an asset allocation will sound impressive and complicated, though.

For example, take a look at these two materially different allocations, and think about how hard it would be to actually perceive a difference between them based on the results over an 80-year investing lifetime.

	Aggressive Portfolio	More Conservative
Allocation:	60% Large/40% Small	55% Large/25% Small 18% Bonds/2% Cash
Number of years in the last 80 years that performed:		
Less than −30%:	3 (1930, 1931, 1937)	2 (1931, 1937)
Less than −1.55%:	20	19
Greater than +15%:	38	38
Between +15% and −1.55%:	22	23

Think about this whenever you talk to one of those advisers who boasts about his magical asset allocation based on a 5-, 10-, or even 20-year record. The reality is that the markets themselves drive the majority of the results achieved, and small shifts in the pieces did not then—and are not now—going to have a predictably significant impact.

Unless you have too much money or your goals are extremely modest (maybe you have a goal shortage?), you can probably be best served by having a low-cost portfolio allocation that captures the market results instead of trying to bet on beating them.

We have six model portfolios ranging from a low-risk (Risk Averse) portfolio with only 30 percent in stocks to a 100 percent stock portfolio (Aggressive Growth) that are all efficient and very inexpensive to construct. They are:

Six Model Portfolios

I. **Risk Averse**, low-risk portfolio with income emphasis

II. **Balanced Income**, moderate-risk blend of growth and income with income bias

III. **Balanced**, moderate risk with a balance between growth and income

IV. **Balanced Growth**, moderately high-risk blend of growth and income with growth bias

V. **Growth**, high risk with growth emphasis

VI. **Aggressive Growth**, very high risk focused on growth

Portfolio#	I	II	III	IV	V	VI
Asset Allocation	Risk Averse	Balanced Income	Balanced	Balanced Growth	Growth	Aggressive Growth
Domestic Stocks	26	39	53	71	77	85
Foreign Stocks	4	6	7	9	13	15
Total Stock Exposure	30	45	60	80	90	100
Treasury Bonds	60	50	37	18	10	0
Cash equivalents	10	5	3	2	0	0

Nearly anyone's financial goals can be met with one of these models, as shown in Figure 8.1. They are inexpensive and easy to construct; very tax efficient (if done correctly due to the low turnover); and are not making bets against the markets, gambling on styles, or taking irrational risks.

"Age"-Based Investing, "Life Cycle," and "Target Date" Funds

We discussed these briefly in Chapter 2 in addressing their fees and some of their problems, but for those that skipped that Chapter, I wanted to just put a reminder in this chapter to protect you.

Be careful whenever you are investing based on someone else's rule of thumb. There are a myriad of "easy" ways to determine your allocation, but they almost always will end up being the wrong choice for you at some time in your life. Conventional wisdom says

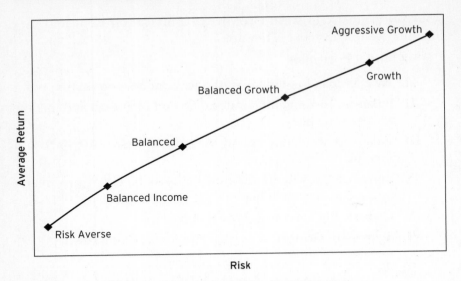

Figure 8.1   Theoretical Risk versus Return for Wealthcare Portfolio Allocations

that if you are younger, you should have more in stocks. In many cases this might make sense, but that does not mean it always will. What if you are terrified of market risk, and you have a large inheritance coming later in life that you can use to confidently fund your goals? WHY would you expose yourself to needless investment risk merely because Suze Orman says you are young and therefore should own more stocks?

Life cycle or target funds are very similar. You choose a date now (better hope it doesn't change), and the fund automatically lowers your equity exposure over time as you approach that fixed date. It doesn't matter whether the automatic changes make sense for what you are trying to achieve. It doesn't matter that the fund will change the allocation at potentially the wrong time for your goals based on what is going on in the markets; the fund simply will change the allocation based on the passing of time in the calendar without regard to whether it makes sense for you.

This *is not* how to make the most of your life, and the problems created by using such simple strategies—strategies that are ignoring goals you are personally trying to achieve and the reasons you value those goals—will likely cost your lifestyle far more than your excessive retirement plan fees.

Life-Relative Allocation

The time to decrease your equity exposure and risk is when you can *afford* to do so for what you are trying to achieve. It might have to do with the passing of time, but a decrease in equity exposure might be indicated far sooner if you happen to have a "lucky" bull market result that occurs over a period of just a few short years. Such a market could enable you to confidently fund all those goals you personally value with far less equity exposure, not because of the passing of time but precisely because of what happened in the markets. Life cycle and target funds completely ignore this possibility and will continue exposing you to excessive risk you do not need to take.

The inverse can happen as well. Sometimes those past "wins" in the market lottery might have you rationally reducing your equity exposure over time, but if a particularly bad bear market occurs, it might make sense, even if you are older, to move up the risk scale a notch or two in order to maintain confidence in achieving the goals you value. Target date funds, life cycle funds, and age-based allocations would have you doing the exact opposite. Just when it makes sense to increase your equity allocation a bit for the goals you are funding due to market changes, they all would have you reducing your equity exposure without regard to the markets or your goals.

Many financial advisers wrongly accuse our company of "passive" management. It is understandable, because from their *market-relative gambling game* perspective, we are passive. We are not making timing or style bets. We do not attempt to forecast what the markets will do, and we always assume they are uncertain. We don't mislead people into thinking they will "beat the market" with us by using our track records of superior risk-adjusted performance without regard to future performance. The portfolios we recommend use passive indices, because these indices are inexpensive and tax efficient—two certainties we think one should capitalize on, if possible. We just don't take the risk of materially underperforming the strategic allocation that makes sense for your goals in hopes of *maybe* outperforming, but also *maybe* underperforming.

That doesn't mean your allocation won't change. We continuously manage the appropriate allocation for what you are trying to achieve. If you think about it, we actually provide far more customized services for clients. The Wall Street gamers, if they think the market is headed for a rally, will increase the equity exposure in all of their clients' portfolios regardless of whether that makes sense for their clients' goals. Sometimes such bets will pay off, and they will look like geniuses, but sometimes such gambles won't, and they will come up with excuses.

But you are a lot different than everyone else, and your allocation should be matched to what you are trying to achieve. We always assume the markets are constantly uncertain. We assume risk is always present. Wouldn't it make sense that for some clients, who may have been initially positioned very conservatively because of modest goals, we might advise them to increase their stock allocation a bit if their goals become less modest or the markets produced poor results that lowered their available resources?

At the same time, while we are advising those clients to move up a notch on the risk scale, might it not make sense that some clients might have other unplanned resources become available that perhaps would enable them to move down the risk scale a bit? **Neither** of these outcomes happens in the market-relative casino on Wall Street. Increasing or decreasing equity exposure in that game isn't based on either of these client-specific circumstances that might be present. Therefore, in the market-relative game, there are always some clients having their main investment decision of strategic asset allocation handled exactly the opposite of how it should be.

So we actively manage a client's strategic exposure as it matches their unique goals and changing market conditions and what that means to the client's confidence of exceeding their goals. To this end, we have two sets of specific portfolios that are very cost efficient. One set is constructed of low-cost index funds for use in retirement plans, and the other is a portfolio of exchange-traded funds (ETFs) that can be more tax efficient than mutual funds for taxable accounts. Both sets of portfolios own essentially the same securities in the same proportion, weighted the same.

The retirement plan portfolios are constructed as shown in Figures 8.2, 8.3, and 8.4.

You will observe that most of the expense ratios for these funds are 0.25 percent a year or less, and, of course, when you assemble those funds together, your portfolio expenses will be in that neighborhood as well. This is probably between one half and one tenth the amount in expenses you are paying now. You might also notice the optional 55-basis-point management fee. This optional fee is charged only to those investors who voluntarily choose to have us continuously rebalance their portfolio and help them, on an ongoing basis, to choose when they should change models based on *their* goals, priorities, and the markets. Even with that level of personalized, continuous, life-relative advice, you see that all of the portfolios charge less than 0.70 percent in expenses each year for the management, advising, quarterly goal, and portfolio monitoring services offered. This is our company's 401(k), and if our company can offer this high level of service with low expenses to our employees, your company could, too! In fact, this portfolio sheet could be useful to you in your effort to fix your retirement plan. Look at the S&P 500 Index Fund expense for Fidelity Spartan. It is 10 basis points. Is your plan's S&P 500 Index Fund charging double, triple, or quadruple that expense for the SAME THING?

Of course, these are just the total investment expenses. Our company's 401(k) has administration costs as well. There are plenty of vendors out there competing to provide the necessary services of record keeping, statements, web site, government form filings, and so on. Services like these fall into the administration category and will be disclosed only in the Summary Annual Report mentioned in Chapter 2. In our company's case, we found a vendor that charges $35 a year per participant with an annual $1,750 company-wide minimum. There are several vendors in that price range; if your benefits person would like us to refer one to you, have them call our toll-free line (1-866-261-0849) and use the code word *Rip-off*. With a total plan balance of about $2,000,000 for our plan, this administration cost is about 0.09 percent a year. Our company pays that for participants, but companies could pass this on to participants if necessary.

Finally, there is a custody charge that is 0.06 percent a year because our balance is over $1 million. Our plan administrator absorbs this cost for plans with under $1 million in assets, but in our case, since we are more than $1 million, this adds an annual additional cost of $1,200 FOR THE ENTIRE PLAN, not per participant. Our company pays this cost for employees as well, but it could be charged against participant balances if the company chose to do so. Custody service charges are paid to a bank trust company for keeping track of the securities, collecting dividends, and the like.

Sample Asset Allocations Utilizing Benchmark Unmanaged Indices

Data shown for sample asset allocations reflects risk characteristics and performance of underlying indices, rebalanced monthly and is for risk/return analysis purposes only.

Please see accompanying page for further important disclosure information regarding this analysis.

Data Updated Through March 31, 2011

Aggressive Growth Allocation

(data start date: January 1, 1981)

Asset Class Allocation Indices	Asset Weighting
U.S. Equity (Wilshire 5000 Index)	85.00%
Int'l Equity (MSCI EAFE - Europe, Australia, Far East)	15.00%
Fixed Income (Citigroup 7-10 Year Treasury)	0.00%
Cash (T-Bill - 3 Month Yield)	0.00%

Annualized Performance - Net of 0.70% per annum in Advisory and Mutual Fund Expenses					
1 Year	3 Year	5 Year	10 Year	20 Year	Since Inception
15.82%	2.24%	2.41%	4.13%	7.95%	9.93%
Model Portfolio Standard Deviation (since inception January 1, 1981)					15.26%

Performance Statistics - Since Inception		
Highest 1 Month Return	12.42%	Lowest 1 Month Return -21.52%
Highest 3 Month Return	27.64%	Lowest 3 Month Return -32.13%
Highest 12 Month Return	59.93%	Lowest 12 Month Return -44.60%

The index asset allocation returns reflected cannot be directly owned by a retirement plan participant. Cost of implementation with index and money market mutual funds with blended expense ratios of .15% is assumed and a plan advisory fee of .55%

Growth Allocation

(data start date: January 1, 1981)

Asset Class Allocation Indices	Asset Weighting
U.S. Equity (Wilshire 5000 Index)	77.00%
Int'l Equity (MSCI EAFE - Europe, Australia, Far East)	13.00%
Fixed Income (Citigroup 7-10 Year Treasury)	10.00%
Cash (T-Bill - 3 Month Yield)	0.00%

Annualized Performance - Net of 0.70% per annum in Advisory and Mutual Fund Expenses					
1 Year	3 Year	5 Year	10 Year	20 Year	Since Inception
15.17%	2.73%	3.00%	4.42%	7.96%	9.91%
Model Portfolio Standard Deviation (since inception January 1, 1981)					13.83%

Performance Statistics - Since Inception		
Highest 1 Month Return	11.29%	Lowest 1 Month Return -18.95%
Highest 3 Month Return	24.48%	Lowest 3 Month Return -28.73%
Highest 12 Month Return	56.96%	Lowest 12 Month Return -40.54%

The index asset allocation returns reflected cannot be directly owned by a retirement plan participant. Cost of implementation with index and money market mutual funds with blended expense ratios of .15% is assumed and a plan advisory fee of .55%

Balanced Growth Allocation

(data start date: January 1, 1981)

Asset Class Allocation Indices	Asset Weighting
U.S. Equity (Wilshire 5000 Index)	71.00%
Int'l Equity (MSCI EAFE - Europe, Australia, Far East)	9.00%
Fixed Income (Citigroup 7-10 Year Treasury)	18.00%
Cash (T-Bill - 3 Month Yield)	2.00%

Annualized Performance - Net of 0.70% per annum in Advisory and Mutual Fund Expenses					
1 Year	3 Year	5 Year	10 Year	20 Year	Since Inception
14.42%	3.18%	3.47%	4.54%	7.91%	9.78%
Model Portfolio Standard Deviation (since inception January 1, 1981)					12.47%

Performance Statistics - Since Inception		
Highest 1 Month Return	10.20%	Lowest 1 Month Return -16.64%
Highest 3 Month Return	22.05%	Lowest 3 Month Return -25.25%
Highest 12 Month Return	54.16%	Lowest 12 Month Return -36.18%

The index asset allocation returns reflected cannot be directly owned by a retirement plan participant. Cost of implementation with index and money market mutual funds with blended expense ratios of .15% is assumed and a plan advisory fee of .55%

Balanced Allocation

(data start date: January 1, 1981)

Asset Class Allocation Indices	Asset Weighting
U.S. Equity (Wilshire 5000 Index)	53.00%
Int'l Equity (MSCI EAFE - Europe, Australia, Far East)	7.00%
Fixed Income (Citigroup 7-10 Year Treasury)	37.00%
Cash (T-Bill - 3 Month Yield)	3.00%

Annualized Performance - Net of 0.70% per annum in Advisory and Mutual Fund Expenses					
1 Year	3 Year	5 Year	10 Year	20 Year	Since Inception
12.64%	3.65%	4.35%	4.89%	7.68%	9.54%
Model Portfolio Standard Deviation (since inception January 1, 1981)					9.82%

Performance Statistics - Since Inception			
Highest 1 Month Return	8.36%	Lowest 1 Month Return	-11.36%
Highest 3 Month Return	20.62%	Lowest 3 Month Return	-18.05%
Highest 12 Month Return	47.40%	Lowest 12 Month Return	-27.11%

The index asset allocation returns reflected cannot be directly owned by a retirement plan participant. Cost of implementation with index and money market mutual funds with blended expense ratios of .15% is assumed and a plan advisory fee of .55%

Balanced Income Allocation

(data start date: January 1, 1981)

Asset Class Allocation Indices	Asset Weighting
U.S. Equity (Wilshire 5000 Index)	39.00%
Int'l Equity (MSCI EAFE - Europe, Australia, Far East)	6.00%
Fixed Income (Citigroup 7-10 Year Treasury)	50.00%
Cash (T-Bill - 3 Month Yield)	5.00%

Annualized Performance - Net of 0.70% per annum in Advisory and Mutual Fund Expenses					
1 Year	3 Year	5 Year	10 Year	20 Year	Since Inception
11.05%	3.74%	4.82%	5.01%	7.36%	9.23%
Model Portfolio Standard Deviation (since inception January 1, 1981)					8.08%

Performance Statistics - Since Inception			
Highest 1 Month Return	7.48%	Lowest 1 Month Return	-8.77%
Highest 3 Month Return	19.20%	Lowest 3 Month Return	-12.47%
Highest 12 Month Return	41.96%	Lowest 12 Month Return	-19.79%

The index asset allocation returns reflected cannot be directly owned by a retirement plan participant. Cost of implementation with index and money market mutual funds with blended expense ratios of .15% is assumed and a plan advisory fee of .55%

Risk Averse Allocation

(data start date: January 1, 1981)

Asset Class Allocation Indices	Asset Weighting
U.S. Equity (Wilshire 5000 Index)	26.00%
Int'l Equity (MSCI EAFE - Europe, Australia, Far East)	4.00%
Fixed Income (Citigroup 7-10 Year Treasury)	60.00%
Cash (T-Bill - 3 Month Yield)	10.00%

Annualized Performance - Net of 0.70% per annum in Advisory and Mutual Fund Expenses					
1 Year	3 Year	5 Year	10 Year	20 Year	Since Inception
9.19%	3.61%	5.05%	4.89%	6.88%	8.73%
Model Portfolio Standard Deviation (since inception January 1, 1981)					6.65%

Performance Statistics - Since Inception			
Highest 1 Month Return	6.57%	Lowest 1 Month Return	-6.20%
Highest 3 Month Return	17.55%	Lowest 3 Month Return	-7.94%
Highest 12 Month Return	36.23%	Lowest 12 Month Return	-11.98%

The index asset allocation returns reflected cannot be directly owned by a retirement plan participant. Cost of implementation with index and money market mutual funds with blended expense ratios of .15% is assumed and a plan advisory fee of .55%

THE RETURN DATA IN THIS ANALYSIS IS NOT AN ADVISOR PERFORMANCE TRACK RECORD AND ANY REPRESENTATION VERBAL OR WRITTEN TO THE CONTRARY IS FALSE. PAST PERFORMANCE IS NOT AN INDICATION OF FUTURE RESULTS. NO INVESTOR CAN INVEST DIRECTLY IN AN UNMANAGED INDEX.

Figure 8.2   Wealthcare Capital Management Retirement Plan Model Portfolio Asset Allocations

IMPORTANT DISCLOSURES

FINANCEWARE, INC. DBA WEALTHCARE CAPITAL MANAGEMENT ("WCM") IS A REGISTERED INVESTMENT ADVISER AND COMPILED THE PERFORMANCE DATA IN THIS ANALYSIS WHICH HAS NOT BEEN VERIFIED INDEPENDENTLY. THE ASSET CLASS PERFORMANCE INFORMATION PRESENTED HERE REPRESENTS CALCULATED RESULTS FROM JANUARY 1, 1981 THROUGH MARCH 31, 2011 USING MONTHLY REBALANCING. THE TIME PERIODS SELECTED WERE BASED ON THE DATA AVAILABILITY OF REPRESENTATIVE ASSET CLASS INDICES. THE BLENDED PERFORMANCE OF THE SAMPLE ASSET ALLOCATIONS ARE DERIVED FROM UNDERLYING UNMANAGED INDICES' MONTHLY RETUN DATA, **NOT FROM ACTUAL CLIENT OR FIRM ACCOUNTS OR ANY INDEX MUTUAL OR MONEY MARKET FUNDS RECOMMENDED BY WCM.**

CALCULATED ALLOCATION PERFORMANCE IS PREPARED FOR THE SOLE PURPOSE OF SHOWING THE RISK AND RETURN CHARACTERISTICS OF DIFFERENT WEIGHTINGS OF EQUITIES, FIXED INCOME AND CASH ON AN UNMANAGED ASSET ALLOCATION. CALCULATIONS WERE MADE USING A COMPUTER PROGRAM THAT STARTS WITH THE FIRST DAY OF THE GIVEN TIME PERIOD AND EVALUATES THE WEIGHTED AVERAGE PERFORMANCE OF THE INDICATED INDICES BASED ON THE TARGET WEIGHTING FOR EACH ASSET CLASS ALLOCATION ASSUMING MONTHLY REBALANCING.

NO INVESTOR CAN INVEST DIRECTLY IN A PASSIVE INDEX. AS SUCH, WCM RECOMMENDS PASSIVE INDEX MUTUAL FUNDS AS PROXIES FOR AN UNDERLYING PASSIVE INDEX. RETIREMENT PLAN PARTICIPANTS SHOULD BE AWARE THAT YOU CANNOT ACHIEVE THE RETURNS SHOWN BECAUSE AN ACTUAL ACCOUNT WILL INCUR OPERATING AND MANAGEMENT EXPENSES FROM THE INDEX MUTUAL FUND SELECTED AND POSSIBLY ADVISORY, CUSTODIAL, RECORDKEEPING AND OTHER RETIREMENT PLAN EXPENSES (DEPENDING ON IF A PLAN SPONSOR CHOOSES TO PASS SOME OR ALL OF THOSE NON-FUND EXPENSES ONTO ITS PLAN PARTICIPANTS). THE PASSIVE INDEX MUTUAL FUNDS THAT WCM RECOMMENDS TO ITS ADVISED RETIREMENT PLAN CLIENTS HAVE WEIGHTED AVERAGE FUND PORTFOLIO EXPENSES THAT VARY BY ASSET CLASS WEIGHTINGS WHICH, AS OF THIS ANALYSIS DATE, VARIED FROM 0.10% to 0.15% PER ANNUM, WHILE THE MAXIMUM ADVISORY FEE CHARGED FOR A WCM ADVISED PLAN (WITH IN PERSON LOCATION SERVICES) IS 0.55% PER ANNUM, BILLED QUARTERLY IN ADVANCE. THE RETURNS SHOWN ABOVE REFLECT THE DEDUCTION OF AN ESTIMATED BLENDED MUTUAL FUND EXPENSE RATIO OF .15% COMBINED WITH AN ADVISORY FEE OF 0.55% PER ANNUM BILLED MONTHLY IN ARREARS. OTHER PLAN EXPENSES MAY ALSO APPLY TO FURTHER REDUCE THE NET RETURN.

NOT ALL PLANS ADVISED BY WCM HAVE AVAILABLE AS FUND OPTIONS WCM's PREFERRED PASSIVE INDEX MUTUAL FUNDS. BASED ON PLAN DESIGN AND THE PLAN VENDOR RETIREMENT PLATFORM, PLAN SPONSORS MAY SELECT, INDEPENDENT OF WCM's ADVISORY SERVICES, NON-PREFERRED PASSIVE INDEX AND ACTIVELY MANAGED MUTUAL FUNDS. THEREFORE, INDEX FUNDS RECOMMENDED IN SOME OF WCM's ADVISED RETIREMENT PLANS MAY HAVE HIGHER INTERNAL FUND EXPENSES THAN THOSE NOTED IN THESE DISCLOSURES. COSTS FOR PLAN ADMINISTRATION, CUSTODY AND OTHER PLAN EXPENSES CAN VARY WIDELY BASED ON A RETIREMENT PLANS AGGREGATE DOLLAR VALUE, NUMBER OF PARTICIPANTS AND OTHER FACTORS SET BY VENDORS (UNAFFILIATED WITH WCM) THAT PLAN SPONSORS CHOOSE TO ENGAGE FOR THOSE SERVICES.

ADDITIONALLY, THE PASSIVE INDEX MUTUAL FUNDS THAT WCM SELECTS AS ASSET CLASS PROXIES INCUR SOME DEGREE OF PERFORMANCE TRACKING ERROR, FAVORABLE OR UNFAVORABLE, COMPARED TO THE UNMANAGED INDEX IT WAS SELECTED TO SERVE AS AN ASSET CLASS PROXY FOR. IN SOME WCM ADVISED PLANS, ONE OR MORE ASSET CLASSES MAY HAVE LIMITED CHOICES DUE TO THE FUND'S EXPENSE COST EFFECTIVENESS, TRACKING ERROR HISTORY AND STATED TARGET PERFORMANCE BENCHMARKS, AND AS SUCH, WCM WILL RECOMMEND FROM THOSE AVAILABLE CHOICES THE FUNDS THAT WCM BELIEVES ARE, OVERALL, THE BEST ASSET CLASS SURROGATE INVESTMENT OPTIONS AVAILABLE FOR THAT PARTICULAR RETIREMENT PLAN.

THE RETURN DATA SHOWN DOES NOT REPRESENT ACTUAL ACCOUNT PERFORMANCE AND SHOULD NOT BE INTERPRETED AS AN INDICATION OF SUCH PERFORMANCE. ASSET CLASS RETURN PERFORMANCE DOES NOT REPRESENT THE IMPACT THAT MATERIAL ECONOMIC AND MARKET FACTORS MIGHT HAVE ON AN INVESTOR'S DECISION MAKING PROCESS IF THE INVESTOR WAS ACTUALLY INVESTED IN THE MARKET. THE CALCULATION OF PERFORMANCE DIFFERS FROM ACTUAL PARTICIPANT ACCOUNT PERFORMANCE BECAUSE THE INVESTMENT STRATEGY MAY BE ADJUSTED BY A PARTICIPANT AT ANY TIME FOR ANY REASON. THE RESULTS OF THE UNMANAGED INDEX ASSET CLASS ALLOCATIONS REFLECT THE REINVESTMENT OF DIVIDENDS AND OTHER DISTRIBUTIONS. AS WITH ANY INVESTMENT STRATEGY, THERE IS POTENTIAL FOR PROFIT AS WELL AS POSSIBILITY OF LOSSES.

THE GROSS RETURN INFORMATION FOR UNMANAGED INDICES USED IN THE ASSET ALLOCATIONS BEFORE DEDUCTION OF EXPENSES REPRESENTATIVE OF THOSE IN AN ADVISED WCM RETIREMENT PLAN SHOWN IN THIS ANALYSIS ARE FROM THIRD PARTY SOURCES BELIEVED TO BE RELIABLE BUT NOT VERIFIED INDEPENDENTLY BY WCM. THOSE THIRD PARTY SOURCES COLLECTED DATA FROM FINANCIAL INSTITUTIONS AND RELATED TYPES OF ENTITIES THAT CREATED THE INDICES AND PUBLISH THE INDICES' VALUES PERIODICALLY, AND FROM SUCH VALUES THIRD PARTY SOURCES CALCULATE PERFORMANCE INFORMATION USED IN THIS REPORT.

INVESTORS REVIEWING THIS INFORMATION SHOULD RECOGNIZE THAT PAST PERFORMANCE HAS NO RELATION TO FUTURE RESULTS.

Figure 8.3 Disclosures for Wealthcare Portfolio Allocations

How Do We Know that Fees More Than 0.75 Percent Are Too High?

Well, we know this because even our small company is paying less. Look through the expenses starting with the model portfolios. Let's look at the WORST CASE EXPENSE with the EMPLOYER PAYING NOTHING and full customized quarterly consultations and continuous advice for EVERY participant:

	Annual Expense	Annual Expense
Most expensive portfolio expense ratio:	0.1472%	0.1472%
Personalized management, monitoring, and consultation:	0.5500%	0.2750%
(Optional)	(All participants)	(Half of participants)
Administration, record keeping, web site, government filings, testing:	0.0900%	0.0900%
Custody (holding the securities in trust):	0.0600%	0.0600%
TOTAL:	0.8472%	0.5722%

This is the MOST you should pay, and with it you should expect a great deal of personalized consultation and service. Most participants that are getting the continuous personalized consultations could construct the model portfolios for a total cost of only 0.30 percent, if they knew what the right model was for their goals and priorities. If they know the answer and can manage the allocation themselves, save the advisory fees. If not, it might be worth the price to the lifestyle you will ultimately obtain by receiving this advice. Now, most companies absorb some or all of the administration and custody costs, as our company does. If your company would be willing to pay the $3,000 a year as ours does for those services, your expenses (your total costs) would drop by 0.15 percent to no more than 0.6972 percent a year for the most expensive portfolio and 0.65 percent for the least expensive one, including quarterly continuous advice and consultation.

Finally, if you didn't want the optional continuous monitoring, life goal advice, portfolio management, quarterly consultations, and so on, you could create your own portfolios from these funds

Retirement Plan - Fund Information Summary

Asset Class	Symbol	Description	Annual Expense Ratio	Annualized Fund Returns - Net of Assumed Advisory Fees Through 3/31/2011			
				1 Year	3 Year	5 Year	10 Year
Domestic Total Market Equity	FSTMX	**Fidelity Spartan Total Market Index Fund - Investor Class**	**0.10%**	**16.94%**	**3.05%**	**2.56%**	**3.90%**
		Benchmark - Dow Jones US Total Stock Market Index	*NA*	17.73%	3.69%	3.18%	4.56%
Large Cap Equity Blend	FUSEX [1]	**Fidelity Spartan 500 Index Fund - Investor Class**	**0.10%**	**14.92%**	**1.77%**	**2.02%**	**2.64%**
		Benchmark - S&P 500 Index	*NA*	15.65%	2.35%	2.62%	3.29%
Large Cap Equity Growth	VIGRX	**Vanguard Growth Index Fund - Investor Shares**	**0.28%**	**16.43%**	**4.08%**	**3.58%**	**3.19%**
		*Benchmark - Blended Large Cap Growth Index**	*NA*	17.34%	4.86%	4.34%	3.93%
		*(*S&P 500/Barra Growth Index (through 5/16/2003), MSCI US Prime Market Growth Index thereafter)*					
Large Cap Equity Value	VIVAX	**Vanguard Value Index Fund - Investor Shares**	**0.26%**	**14.57%**	**0.40%**	**1.13%**	**2.81%**
		*Benchmark - Blended Large Cap Value Index**	*NA*	15.44%	1.01%	1.78%	3.49%
		*(*S&P 500/Barra Value Index (through 5/16/2003), MSCI US Prime Market Value Index thereafter)*					
Mid-Cap Equity Blend	NMPAX	**Columbia Mid Cap Index Fund - Class Z**	**0.25%**	**25.97%**	**9.30%**	**5.40%**	**8.58%**
		Benchmark - S&P Midcap 400 Index	*NA*	26.95%	10.00%	6.07%	9.36%
Small Cap Equity Blend	NAESX	**Vanguard Small-Cap Index Fund - Investor Shares**	**0.28%**	**26.04%**	**9.40%**	**4.17%**	**8.26%**
		*Benchmark - Blended Small-Cap Equity Index**	*NA*	26.87%	10.00%	4.76%	8.76%
		*(*Russell 2000 Index through 5/16/2003, MSCI US Small-Cap 1750 thereafter)*					
Foreign Large Cap Equity Blend	FSIIX	**Fidelity Spartan International Index Fund - Investor Shares**	**0.10%**	**9.81%**	**-3.40%**	**0.84%**	**4.78%**
		Benchmark - Morgan Stanley EAFE Index (Europe, Australia, Far East)	*NA*	10.55%	-2.86%	1.47%	5.56%
Specialty - Real Estate	VGSIX	**Vanguard REIT Index Fund - Investor Shares**	**0.26%**	**23.52%**	**2.39%**	**1.28%**	**10.72%**
		*Benchmark - Blended MSCI US REIT Index**	*NA*	24.28%	2.83%	1.79%	11.35%
		*(*MSCI US REIT Index adjusted to include 2% cash position through 4/30/2009, MSCI US REIT Index thereafter)*					

116

Category	Ticker	Fund / Benchmark	Expense Ratio				
Short-Term Bond	VBISX	**Vanguard Short-Term Bond Index Fund - Investor Shares**	**0.22%**	**2.28%**	**2.96%**	**4.40%**	**3.71%**
		Barclays Capital U.S. 1-5 Year Government/Credit Float Adjusted Index*	*NA*	3.13%	3.71%	5.09%	4.58%
		(*Barclays Capital U.S. 1-5 Year Government/Credit Bond Index through December 31, 2009; Barclays Capital U.S. 1-5 Year Government/Credit Float Adjusted Index thereafter.)					
Intermediate Bond	DFIGX	**DFA Intermediate Government Fixed Income Portfolio**	**0.15%**	**4.57%**	**4.16%**	**5.96%**	**5.36%**
		Benchmark - Barclays Capital US Government Bond Index	*NA*	4.28%	3.66%	5.63%	5.15%
Long-Term Bond	VBLTX	**Vanguard Long-Term Bond Index Fund**	**0.22%**	**7.61%**	**5.68%**	**6.01%**	**6.19%**
		Barclays Capital U.S. Long Government/Credit Float Adjusted Index*	*NA*	8.45%	6.50%	6.65%	6.82%
		(*Barclays Capital U.S. Long Government/Credit Bond Index through 12/31/09; Barclays Capital U.S. Long Government/Credit Float Adjusted Index thereafter.)					
Money Market	VMMXX	**Vanguard Prime Money Market Fund**	**0.23%**	**-0.48%**	**0.25%**	**1.89%**	**1.70%**
		Benchmark - Money Market Funds Average (Derived from Lipper data)	*NA*	0.00%	0.47%	1.98%	1.74%
Money Market	FGRXX [2]	**Fidelity US Government Reserves**	**0.28%**	**-0.53%**	**0.09%**	**1.73%**	**1.61%**
		Benchmark - U.S. Gov't Money Market Funds Average (Derived from Lipper data)	*NA*	0.00%	0.36%	1.89%	1.72%

1 Fidelity Spartan S&P 500 Index Fund - Advantage Class (FUSVX) may be substituted for Fidelity Spartan S&P 500 Index Fund - Investor Class (FUSEX) when prudent for plans that exceed certain minimum investment requirements.

2 The Fund Manager for Fidelity US Government Reserves Fund (FGRXX) does not list a benchmark for the fund. An average of all Government Money Market Funds performance data is believed to be an accurate benchmark by Financeware, Inc. d/b/a Wealthcare Capital Management ("WCM") and is utilized by other fund managers operating a fund with a similar strategy.

IMPORTANT DISCLOSURES

All performance results have been compiled by WCM but have not been independently verified. All fund performance is net of each fund's expense ratio and assumed advisory fees, while benchmark unmanaged index data is gross of expenses and cannot be invested in directly by a plan participant. The data is sourced from the respective fund manager's website, Standard & Poor's or Thomson Reuters and is believed to be accurate but is not guaranteed as accurate by WCM. All fund returns are net of an estimated maximum potential 0.55% annual retirement plan advisory fee charged by WCM and deducted from annualized return data for the time periods indicated, which may or may not be allocated to a plan participant's account in any specific WCM-advised retirement plan. Retirement plans, and often plan participant accounts, incur additional non-advisory expenses related to custodial, plan administrator and recordkeeping services. These expenses are not reflected in the performance data listed above, but some or all of such fees may be deducted from participants' plan balances in any specific retirement plan. The returns calculated above assume the plan participant has made no account contributions or withdrawals over the return periods shown.

Plan participants reviewing this information should recognize that past performance is not an indication of future results. As with any investment, there is potential for profit as well as the possibility of losses. The above is intended as an overview of the funds available to WCM-advised plan participants and is for general comparison purposes only. Plan participants should review the individual fund's prospectus prior to making an investment decision. Each fund's materials can usually be found on the fund website or through a link on the plan administrator's website. It should not be assumed that all account holdings will correspond directly to any comparative indices.

Figure 8.4   Wealthcare Retirement Plan Suggested Funds

(just copy the portfolio allocations in your investment selection and make sure you rebalance), and your total expenses would be between about 0.10 percent and 0.14 percent.

THIS is why I'm asking you to pay attention to your expenses: To understand what you are paying. To encourage your employer to look for better alternatives like I did for my associates. Have your employer call me if they don't know where to start. It isn't hard to fix a broken retirement plan and make it much better.

If you are paying 0.75 to 3.0 percent a year or more, the price to your lifestyle is huge. Look at the tables in Appendix A and decide whether a little effort on your part might be worth thousands of dollars or years of a better retirement. This is a RIP-OFF that YOU can fix.

Using the Appendix A Tables to Estimate the Price of Excess Fees in Your Life

We have calculated the "In Balance" and confidently supported lifestyle for 401(k) participants at various ages, current retirement plan balances, savings rates, and broad asset allocation at fair total expenses. Based on that "In Balance" **base case** at fair fee levels of 0.75 percent a year TOTAL EXPENSE, we then calculated the price to your lifestyle of an excess 0.50 percent a year in TOTAL 401(k) expenses and of an excess 1.00 percent yearly in TOTAL 401(k) expenses.

For each scenario we then calculated the following PRICES to your LIFESTYLE of these EXCESS expenses in your 401(k):

"Additional Annual Savings Needed"

This is the additional amount you would need to save EACH YEAR until age 65 to make up for the additional excess expenses you are paying.

"Delay Retirement by This Many Years"

This is how many additional years you would need to work BEYOND age 65 to make up for the additional excess expenses you are paying.

"Reduce Annual Retirement Income By"

This is how much you would need to reduce your annual retirement spending in today's spending power (i.e., inflation adjusted) to make up for the additional excess expenses you are paying.

"Increased Risk of Outliving Resources"

As we discussed earlier, it may not make sense to needlessly sacrifice your life for a remote risk you can adapt to if unfortunate market results or timing of those results occur. All base case plans are based on accepting this rational balance of sufficiently high confidence, yet avoiding needless sacrifice. Thus, all have some risk of outliving resources if unfortunate markets occur and nothing is done about it. The "Increased Risk of Outliving Resources" shows how much that risk increases due to EXCESS FEES. For example, if the results are 120 percent, the risk of outliving your money is 2.2 TIMES the risk at lower fee levels. If the results are 55 percent, the price to the excess fees is 1.55 TIMES the risk at lower fee levels.

"Reduction to Age 65 Portfolio Values"

This is the price of excess fees to the size of your retirement fund at age 65 based on a "likely more than" number and "likely less than" number. You can think of it simply as a range of how much more money you could have at retirement if you were paying more reasonable fees. The "likely more than" number is the value that 95 percent of the simulations exceeded under the lower cost base case. Thus, there is a very high chance that your excess fees will cost you at least that amount. The "likely less than" number is the 5 percentile result, which means you have less than a 1 in 20 chance of your excess fees costing you more than that figure.

Using the Tables—An Example

First, find the closest combination of your *current* age and *current* retirement account balance based on the heading of the top of each page.

TOTAL ANNUAL SAVINGS:	$2,500		$5,000	
Allocation: 80% Stock/20% Bonds:				
Base Comfortable "In Balance" Case:				
Maximum Fair Total Expense:	0.75%		0.75%	
Retirement Income @ Age 65	$17,600		$17,600	
Age 65 Range of Portfolio Values:	$206,292 to $2,313,620		$206,292 to $2,313,620	
EXCESS EXPENSE:	0.50%	1.00%	0.50%	1.00%
	(1.25% total)	(1.75% total)	(1.25% total)	(1.75% total)
PRICE TO LIFESTYLE OF EXCESS EXPENSE:				
Additional Annual Savings Needed:	$800	$1,800	$800	$1,800
Delay Retirement by This Many Years:	3	7	3	7
Reduce Annual Retirement Income by:	$3,100	$5,700	$3,100	$5,700
Increased Risk of Outliving Resources:	54%	100%	54%	100%
Reduction to Age 65 Portfolio Values:				
Likely More Than:	$29,893	$56,041	$29,893	$56,041
Likely Less Than:	$331,976	$631,328	$331,976	$631,328

Figure 8.5   Age 25 with Current 401(k) Balance of $25,000

Next, find the *column* below that heading that most closely matches your CURRENT total contribution to your retirement plan including BOTH your deferral AND your employer match.

Then, find the section with the asset allocation that most closely matches your long-term planned strategic *allocation.*

Finally, find the column that most closely matches your *excess (or total)* expenses.

As Figure 8.5 highlights, we have a 25-year-old who has around $25,000 in his or her retirement plan whose combined salary deferrals and employer matches are near $2,500 a year with an asset allocation that is near 80 percent stocks and 20 percent bonds and who is paying an excess fee of 0.50 percent a year (or 1.25 percent total).

The Price of Excess Fees

For this person, we can see that **the price to his or her lifestyle of these excess expenses** versus the base case with more reasonable fees would require *one* of the following to make up for the fees:

Additional annual savings needed:	$800 a year
Delay retirement by this many years:	3 years past age 65
Reduce annual retirement income by:	$3,100 a year (versus base of $17,600)
Increased risk of outliving resources:	54% (or 1.54 TIMES the risk)
Reduction to age 65 portfolio values:	$29,893–$331,976

9

How Much Is That Guarantee in the Window?

"The fact that a great many people believe something is no guarantee of its truth."

—W. Somerset Maugham

Guaranteed income for life! This is the marketing cry of the insurance industry, and emotionally it has a lot of appeal. The soothing comfort implied is so enticing that there are actually proposals from the Obama administration to encourage Americans to buy annuities with their retirement savings (see: "Retiree Annuities May Be Promoted by Obama Aides," Bloomberg, January 8, 2010). I guess this is what happens when the government owns an insurance company.

Even the *Wall Street Journal* has fallen prey to this marketing ploy as exemplified in the story "Locking in Future Income," that appeared on December 9, 2009. In this story about variable annuities, the *WSJ* does a reasonable job of disclosing the "very steep fees" (the price of the guarantee? . . . not really as you will learn) and that you can't get the guaranteed amount in a lump sum. They also warn about the complexity of these products and offer a summary of additional warnings. But, a favorable message about the value of the guarantees in the "timing" section of the article stated: "If, for instance, the market falls sharply just after you buy and your underlying funds take a dive, the guarantee could prove quite valuable."

Let's examine this "quite valuable" benefit the *WSJ* article highlighted. What happens if the markets fall sharply just after you buy? This is after all one of the two main things you are trying to protect yourself from by buying an annuity (the other is the risk of outliving your wealth).

The example the article used was a 60 year old who put $100,000 in a variable annuity in 2000 just as the bear market at the beginning of the decade started. Fortunately, the annuity had an annual "guarantee" of 5 percent growth per year for the benefit base. As of October 31, 2009, this means the benefit base (not available in a lump sum) would entitle the annuity buyer to an annual lifetime income of $7,500 because of the guarantee that protected his benefit base. That $7,500 annual benefit is based on a 5 percent payout rate for the annuitant who is now 69 years old and a benefit base that has grown to $150,000 (according to the article). At normal life expectancy (50/50 odds), the annuitant would receive $120,000 in annuity payments for tying up $100,000 for 26 years. Care to calculate the internal rate of return (IRR) on that? The consumer (and most agents that sell these things) would believe they were getting a 5 percent return because of how the insurance company promotes the 5 percent guaranteed increase to the benefit base and the 5 percent payout rate. In reality though, this is the equivalent of getting a 1.84 percent return for the first 10 years and zero for the next 16 years. Does this sound like a good deal to you? Sure doesn't seem anywhere close to 5 percent.

To clear the fog of the confusing contract language, let's just back test all of these cash flows historically. We have a 60 year old who invests in a simple 60/40 portfolio (60 percent domestic equities, 37 percent government bonds, and 3 percent cash) and pays an advisor a 1 percent annual advisory fee. Each year we will calculate and tax his investments assuming moderate Virginia state income taxes and current Federal tax rates. We will assume annual rebalancing plus 20 percent annual turnover and 80 percent of capital gains being realized as long term. Also, we will withdraw the same $7,500 a year (but in our case net after tax and after expenses) starting at age 69 and continuing to death at normal life expectancy.

Going back to 1926, there were 697 26-year periods for us to back test based on monthly data. If this investor started in September, 1929 right before the Crash of 1929 and the ensuing Great Depression, he would have ended up with $42,241 left over versus ZERO in the annuity at normal life expectancy. In fact, in EVERY ONE of the historical periods, the annuity guarantee that the *WSJ* called "quite valuable" cost the investor at least $42,241 or more. At the 90th percentile outcome, the guarantee cost the investor $250,089. At the 75th percentile, the guarantee of the annuity cost the investor a whopping $339,068, more than three times the initial investment. There was a 50 percent chance the guarantee would cost the investor an incredible $441,896!

But, these ending values of what is leftover in the portfolio are not all profit for the insurance company. That's because there is a 50 percent chance the investor will live past normal life expectancy. Before we examine the effect of the value of the lifetime income guarantee though, objectively think about this example and what the insurance company is coercing agents to sell. Half of all of the clients sold this product will end up dying before normal life expectancy and if the Crash of 1929 and the Great Depression were to start the month following each of their initial investments, the annuity would cost all of them AT LEAST 42 percent of their initial investment; MORE if they die before normal life expectancy or if the markets aren't as bad as the Great Depression.

As would be expected though, the insurance company actuaries have designed the product to have very favorable odds for them to profit. Insurance companies are not benevolent donors of wealth. There is a risk that many of the annuitants (about half) will live past normal life expectancy and the insurance company needs the "premiums" of the other half of the annuitants who lose out on this bet to insure against this longevity risk they are taking with the other half. Do not assume that the actuaries haven't figured out how to still profit on this risk.

The 60 year old in our example has a 71 percent chance of being dead by age 90 (you may wish to find a better way of articulating this). Running the same historical back test for the 637 31-year periods back to 1926, we find that the simple balanced portfolio STILL exceeded the cash flow from the annuity in every historical period. In the worst historical period starting with the 1929 Crash, the guarantee of the annuity cost the investor $14,758. Starting in December 1926 (the 95 percentile outcome), the guarantee of the annuity cost the investor $213,447. Starting in June of 1926 (the 87th percentile outcome), the guarantee of the annuity cost the investor $403,385. Remember, the investor only has a 29 percent chance of living this long.

Extending the life expectancy to age 97 (less than a 10 percent chance of the investor living this long) we see where the risk is for the insurance company (note … this is sarcasm). Of the 553 38-year historical back tests going back to 1926, there were TWO of the 553 periods where the balanced portfolio would have run out of money. The cost of the annuity guarantee, IF the investor lives to age 97 (less than 1 in 10 chance of this) had a 95 percent chance of costing the investor more than $238,561. Remember, he only invested $100,000 in the first place!

A one-in-10 chance of outliving your money is still scary … or so the insurance company would like to have their agents and annuitant victims believe. There is essentially no chance (at least from actuarial tables less than a 1-in-1,000 chance) of the annuitant living to 111. Back testing the balanced portfolio back to 1926 once again sheds light on how conservative actuaries are in ensuring profits for the insurance company at the expense of their customers.

There were 385 52-year periods for us to test going back to 1926. In about 2 percent of those (seven to be exact), the investor would have run out of money IF he or she lived to 111. If he started in July 1929 (the 95th percentile outcome), just a few months before the 1929 Crash and the Great Depression, and he lived to age 111, the cost of the guarantee of the annuity would have been $230,526.

Understanding the combination of how unlikely the perfect storm of remote odds are can be daunting because we have uncertain market returns, uncertain timing of returns that can impact the wealth, and uncertain mortality. Our company has the rights to a patent to assess these risks together using Monte Carlo simulation so we can come to one simple probability of the odds of whether or not the annuity guarantee has value.

Out of 1,000 random lifetimes with simulated random returns even more extreme than have been historically observed, in 997 of the outcomes the annuity had a negative relative value to the simple balanced portfolio. There was a 90 percent chance the annuity guarantee would cost the investor more than $149,000 (about 1.5

times the initial investment) and a 75 percent chance it would cost more than $243,000.

Does this sound "quite valuable" to you? Think about the other factors on top of this. The cash flows we modeled for spendable income were net after taxes and fees versus the annuity that would likely have some portion of the payment being taxed at ordinary income rates. The annuity has essentially zero liquidity where the balanced portfolio offered flexibility to adjust future income withdrawals if there was an unexpected immediate cash need. Now the agents will tell you that there is "some" liquidity in the annuity ... for example that you can make withdrawals of up to 10 percent of the contract value. But you normally you cannot cash in the whole thing at once (true liquidity), at least not the "benefit base" values that have all of those guarantees. Of course, we are also assuming the insurance company financially survives a Great Depression environment and can honor its promise to pay.

Stealing Your Bucket List from You

The sales efforts behind these products are specifically designed to prey on your emotions. Agents are misled by the insurance company and wholesalers into believing that every one of these annuities they sell is "helping" people to "secure a guaranteed income for life." How Noble! NOT!

The agents can get so brainwashed after hearing this for years that they lose all objectivity in evaluating the use of these products. (It doesn't help their objectivity that the agents normally make between 4 and 8 percent of the initial investment when they sell one of these things, often with some sort of ongoing trail commission to boot!)

For example, last year I had an encounter with an agent that had become so programmed by the insurance industry that he refused to evaluate the decision objectively. He insisted that the annuity he was selling was really a good deal for the consumer. While conceptually he acknowledged that the insurance company sold the product to make money, somehow his clients were still benefitting. So, I had him give me an example of a client situation where the annuity would benefit the client.

The illustration tool he used allowed the annuity terms to be back tested for any ONE specific historical time period of his choosing. The first illustration he ran was supposed to convince me of the value of the guarantee, so he selected a historical period with terrible market returns. I ran the cash flows the annuity guaranteed in the illustration, and tested them against the capital markets in every historical period, not just ONE of the worst. In 90 percent of the hundreds of historical time periods, the capital markets would have exceeded the income the annuity guaranteed, even if the client lived to 100. Knowing that half the clients that he sold these things to would not live past normal life expectancy, he didn't appreciate me showing that the guarantee for them wouldn't be worth anything in 98 percent of the historical periods. He didn't like these answers. In essence, somewhere between 90 and 98 percent of his clients were likely to be harmed by this product.

He then came back to me with an argument that basically said that the guarantee is only for protection against really bad markets, and the annuity offered upside in stronger markets that would produce more income than the guarantee. To demonstrate this, he ran some more illustrations that had higher market returns that "capitalized" on the "step up" feature of the annuity, which would increase the annuity cash flows at various times as new high-water marks are achieved. He was confident that this higher income would prove to me the value of annuity.

But, the expense drag of the annuity made this impossible to compare favorably to the capital markets with just the advisor's 1 percent fee, and portfolio expenses of 0.12 percent for index funds. The annuity had all those expenses, plus another 1.12 percent in annuity expenses. Why that is so hard for him to understand is beyond me. I showed him that if the client lived to 100, there was only a 50 percent chance the annuity would meet the projected cash flows while without the drag of the annuity expenses, the capital markets would have exceeded those cash flows in 88 percent of the historical periods. He didn't like this either.

Grasping at straws, he then ran another illustration for a historical time period with much stronger returns. The income stream from the annuity continued to increase based on the time period he selected with strong markets. But, obviously the expense drag of the annuity would once again lower the odds of the client actually receiving those increases. There was only a 26 percent historical chance the annuity would produce these higher annuity payments. Without the drag of the annuity expenses, living to age 95, there was a 50 percent chance the markets would have exceeded what the annuity only had a 26 percent chance of exceeding. That's almost double the odds of a higher income.

We had this exchange via e-mail, sending one another various reports and commentary. We finally got together in person for a meeting to discuss this. Despite all of the evidence I provided, despite the logic of the insurance company's motive to profit, despite the fact that all I was doing was running the same historical analysis for all of the historical periods instead of just one "cherry picked" historical period as was the case in each of his illustrations, he came back to me with a very simple answer. He said, "I don't trust the math."

All I can say to this is to quote Justin Hayward who said, *"There's none so blind as those who will not see."*

Emotions and Reason

Emotions drive a lot of our decisions. And financial product manufacturers exploit both the emotions of clients and advisors to mislead them into making bad decisions. These products benefit only agents, the insurance company, and a TINY percentage of the buyers. The odds are stacked HUGELY against the buyer. That is why they don't show the odds. Instead, they use emotional scare tactics, like "What if the markets go through another huge decline? The guarantee of the annuity will protect you!" How comforting (and misleading) is that when they completely evade the odds?

Then they claim, "Plus you will participate and get higher income if the markets produce strong returns!" which implies that you can emotionally have your cake and eat it too.

Finally, to address some of the concerns of giving up your assets to an insurance company for the rest of your life so they can give it back to you in small pieces, they'll say, "there are withdrawal features that permit you to make withdrawals of the greater of 10 percent of the contract value or any amount over your initial investment." Emotionally, this pitch has a lot of appeal. A guaranteed income for life ... guaranteed 5 percent returns even if the markets lose money, increases in income if the markets are strong, liquidity if you need it for something unexpected. What a great emotional (and misleading) pitch! The only thing they are evading is the reason side of this, that the odds of you being able to do better than any of the "features" of the product without the expense burden of the product are HUGE. Or, in other terms, the odds that this product will harm you are likely to be in the 85 to 98 percent range because of the extra CERTAIN burden of expenses. If they rationally disclosed this, they wouldn't sell many of them, which is why they don't disclose it.

Let me share with you one emotional reason the often limited liquidity (or significant penalty for getting liquidity) is a risk that you have with locking up your money in an annuity. The insurance companies and agents won't talk about this emotionally (and remote) concerning situation. But, think about this in your own life before you stroke the check and sign the application the salesman has convinced you to buy.

What if sometime down the road, perhaps not all that late in life, like 75, or 80, when you are still physically able to pursue dreams; you discover that you have some disease where you only have a year to live. We've seen this happen to many clients. It isn't common, and the odds are fairly low of this happening. But, what if it did? What would you do? If you had your money tied up in an annuity, you wouldn't be able to get to most of your money to go through and scratch off your bucket list like clients that maintain constant liquidity could do. The insurance company is going to get a windfall, and in your last year of life, you will be constrained by assets locked up in a contract that was designed so you can't outlive your money, even if you lived to 95. But you're not going to live that long. And, you won't be able to live your last year like you wanted to, and could have, if it were not for the restrictions of the annuity.

I have yet to see one example of these products that make economic sense. Emotionally, they are appealing if only they are presented in a misleading manner. Please don't sacrifice your only life for a brainwashed agent's commission and an insurance company's profit.

Avoid Needless Risk

In the Wealthcare process we avoid needless risk so in reality it is unlikely we would recommend a portfolio with 60 percent equity exposure to the client if it wasn't needed to confidently fund their income need as was used in many of these historical examples.

Many advisors argue that the guarantees of the annuity "help" people in getting more comfortable in having higher equity exposure than they might otherwise be comfortable. I would argue that positioning people in portfolios that have higher risk based on a misleading value of a guarantee is providing no service to the client.

Lower risk portfolios than that 60 percent exposure we modeled against the guaranteed income illustration show that even with lower equity exposure, the client still was better off without the annuity. In fact, a Monte Carlo simulation with random returns and life spans actually showed the annuity guarantee costing the investor in 999 of 1,000 simulations if the portfolio had 45 percent equity exposure (our balanced income allocation) and 997 simulations for our 30 percent equity exposure (our risk-averse allocation), the same odds of the balanced portfolio.

Do the odds against the annuity having value sound like the kind of recommendations someone would give if they cared about their client? Does it help them to have more equity than they are comfortable with if the expenses make it almost certain they are going to lose?

BEFORE you buy one of these things, think through this *rationally* and *emotionally*. **In that order!**

10

Hidden Expenses in Government Union and Some 403(b) Plans

In 2011, government union battles with Governors in Wisconsin and Ohio made headlines for weeks. Massive protests by the Unions, legislators leaving town to prevent a quorum in an attempt to block a vote, and then lawsuits challenging the ultimate passage of legislation made for heated debates. I'm not going to comment on either political side of the debate. Instead, I'm going to focus on some things on which union members, legislators, Governors, and tax payers should all be able to agree. Could we agree that:

#1—Excessive fees should not be skimmed from government union and teachers' 403(b) retirement accounts.

#2—Participant fee disclosures for such plans should be the same as all ERISA plans.

#3—Excessive fees cost union members in the form of reduced benefits, and taxpayers in the form of additional contributions to make up for the drain of fees on plan assets.

#4—Union leaders should not be able to receive kickbacks from product vendors or obtain hidden union "dues" by skimming excess fees from retirement plan assets.

I believe the only people that would have problems with these premises would be:

- Politicians that receive political contributions from the product vendors skimming excess fees from these plans.
- Union leaders that have negotiated product contracts that hide kickbacks they receive by skimming hidden fees from members' retirement accounts.
- Expensive product vendors that are using their excessive fees to gain business by political favors through political contributions and kickbacks to the Unions.

The fee disclosure rules that are going into effect for everyone else's retirement plans beginning in 2012 will not apply to Government 457 plans and some (but not all) 403(b) plans. That is because the fee disclosures only will be required for plans that are subject to ERISA. Government 457 plans (like many police and firefighter union plans) are generally not subject to ERISA so it is likely that the excessive hidden fees will continue to escape scrutiny.

Likewise, some 403(b) plans for teachers unions can sometimes escape being subject to ERISA by following some complex structuring alternatives. These rules are too complicated to detail here and participants have no control over whether the plan will be subject to ERISA. Suffice it to say though that just as excessive fees have a huge lifestyle cost to retirement plan participants (for example, needing higher contributions to make up for the fees) the math applies to these plans as well.

Teacher Abuse

Some of the 403(b) plans that I have seen for teachers are absolutely egregious in how expensive the products are. I've seen plans that use variable annuities with expenses more than 3 percent annually, about 2.5 percent more than some of these large plans should cost. Such cost structures are not uncommon and just like in all other retirement plans, something has to give to make up for the excessive fees. Contributions will need to be larger (to provide the same retirement income benefit), or retirement benefits will have to be reduced (to make up for the fees that reduce how much is accumulated in a participant's individual retirement account) or the participant will have to work longer. That's just the way math works.

Now, I'm not privy to the retirement-plan specifics for the states generating the most media attention on these debates, but I can tell you that in some of the plans I've seen, neither the taxpayers NOR the union members would need to increase their contributions if they just eliminated the excessive fees in the retirement plan.

Take for example a theoretical state budget proposal to lower the cost of state employee benefits to taxpayers. When it comes to retirement-plan benefits, most state budget makers look at the cost of how much the state is contributing versus how much participants must contribute to their retirement-plan accounts.

Both sides rightfully get emotional about this. State budgets are under serious pressure and many have deep deficits they can no longer finance. Say for example that the state budget proposal has participants increasing their retirement plan contribution from 2 percent of income to 4 percent. That's double the amount! Participants feel as though they were promised a benefit and to them it feels as though the state is changing the rules of the game, right in the middle of the fourth inning. For a teacher making $50,000 a year, a 2 percent increase in her retirement plan contribution costs her $1,000 a year. For the state, that's a reduction of $1,000 a year in the cost of benefits for each teacher.

If the 403(b) plan for our teacher had excess fees of 2.5 percent, as many do, she is already paying an extra $1,000 a year if her retirement account balance is $40,000, she just doesn't see it. That's the problem with these product expenses. Since they come right out of the value of the shares, they are essentially hidden costs unless you dig up all of the expense ratios, mortality and expense charges, contract charges, and so on, and do the math to figure out what you are really paying.

Unlike your contributions to your account, you don't see these retirement plan expenses on your payroll stub. The unions don't pay these expenses (but the participants do) and in some cases the unions are conflicted because some receive kickbacks (think of these as extra hidden union dues) from product vendors with excessive fees. The states normally do not control which plans are offered since union leadership usually controls the product offerings. Thus the state and taxpayers aren't paying these fees (the participants are).

But for a 25-year-old teacher making $50,000 a year and working a 40-year career until retirement at age 65, a 2.5 percent excess fee equates to an additional contribution of more than $6,900 a year! That's nearly 14 percent of compensation! Instead of states changing the game on participants and requiring participants to double their contribution, how about the state cut its contribution by the same 2 percent of compensation as originally proposed, and instead of doubling the participant's contribution from 2 percent to 4 percent, REDUCE the participant's contribution to ZERO. If there were 2.5 percent in excess fees that were eliminated, the net effect to the participant would equate to an additional $4,900 annual contribution, even though both the state and the teacher are reducing their contributions by $1,000 each.

Even if the excess fees are only 1.5 percent (which is VERY common in 403(b) and 457 plans), both the state and teacher could still save $1,000 each per year in the form of reduced contributions and the net equivalent contribution to the teachers account would still equate to an INCREASE in contributions of $1,600 a year.

New Regulations, Old Conflicts

Some of the new financial regulations, particularly as they apply to registered investment advisers, should lessen the amount of political influence campaign contributions have on the use of various over-priced retirement-plan products. The new regulations require advisers and their firms to monitor political contributions and the Securities and Exchange Commission (SEC) will be examining the firm's procedures for making sure that government business isn't obtained through the use of political contributions.

My firm has never done business with government retirement plans because of the corruption that is so prevalent among lawmakers and unions using participants' retirement assets as a bargaining chip for their own gain. Their role should be to select the lowest cost and most diversified products for the participants whose interest they should serve. Instead, many do not care how much the participant pays and instead care only for how much the vendor will pay the union, or make in political contributions. The regulatory reform may fix some of the issues on political contributions, but the union conflicts will remain.

I've heard a rumor, though I have not been able to verify it so take this only as a rumor, that one large police and firefighter union received a NEW BUILDING by switching vendors from one expensive variable annuity product to another.

NEA and AARP

It wouldn't surprise me if that rumor was true based on what I've seen with unions and associations like the American Association of Retired Persons (AARP) and the National Education Association (NEA) promoting products as "benefits to members" when the primary consideration is how much the union or association gets paid for promoting the product to members.

A good example comes from the NEA. The NEA is a supposed "non-profit" and "non-partisan" organization with a 2002 to 2003 fiscal-year budget of $267 million and 565 employees. Much of their purpose is for lobbying. Clearly some of their revenues come from membership dues from their 2.7 million members. They also happen to sponsor a variable annuity that is used in numerous state 403(b) retirement plans for teachers and administrators. Guess what, the NEA effectively gets paid a commission for selling teachers a needlessly expensive retirement product. What a GREAT member "benefit"!

The following comes right from the NEA "Value Builder" web site:

> Security Distributors, Inc. and certain of its affiliates (collectively "Security Benefit") make the NEA Valuebuilder products available under this program pursuant to an agreement with NEA's wholly-owned subsidiary, **NEA's Member Benefits Corporation ("MBC")**. Security Benefit has the exclusive right to offer the NEA Valuebuilder products under the program, and MBC generally may not enter into arrangements with other providers of similar investment programs or otherwise promote to NEA members or their employers any investment products that compete with the NEA Valuebuilder products. MBC promotes the program to NEA members and their employers and provides certain services in connection with the program. **Security Benefit pays an annual fee to MBC based in part on the average assets invested in the NEA Valuebuilder products under the agreement. You may wish to take into account this agreement and arrangement, including any fees paid, when considering and evaluating any communications relating to the NEA Valuebuilder products.** (emphasis added)

> **The web address where this disclosure comes from is:**
> **www.neamb.com/home/1199_905.htm**

What this very creative fine print is essentially saying is that NEA has a conflict of interest because they get paid based on your assets through fees skimmed from your account values by Security Benefit, the product vendor.

This plan is HUGE, so you would think the fees would be competitive. They aren't even close. For example, there are a number of index funds in the program, which you would think would be cost effective. THEY ARE NOT. The index funds this plan uses have expense ratios that are about SIX TIMES as expensive as what is otherwise available. Why do you suppose that would be the case? Has the NEA never heard of Fidelity or Vanguard, which have index funds that track the same indices as the NEA product and cost **80 PERCENT LESS**? Or might it be that such low-cost funds don't have enough in expenses to pay the NEA its marketing fee? No need to speculate on the answer to this since the fine print disclosure essentially tells us that is the case. The answer why they are not using lower-cost options that are readily available IS BECAUSE THEY ARE SKIMMING FEES FROM MEMBERS' ACCOUNTS.

AARP plays a similar game with the products they endorse. They mislead the public into thinking they have shopped the world for the benefit of their members, but in reality what they have shopped for is products willing to pay significant kickbacks for getting the AARP endorsement.

Now you might be fans of what either of these organizations stand for and the issues they advance when they lobby legislators. If you do, then it would be appropriate for you to join as a paying member and even to make additional donations if you want to support the cause.

I personally think it is quite a different issue to have them mislead you into thinking they have a great retirement plan they have chosen as a "benefit" to their members and proceed to hide in fine print disclosures that they are on the take for peddling an overpriced product to you. They actually don't even disclose the product is overpriced, merely that you should "take into account" . . . "when considering and evaluating any communications relating to the NEA Valuebuilder products."

So regardless of whether you are a participant being asked by states to up your contribution, or a state trying to control budget deficits, there is one thing that is certain: Conflicted expensive product sales are costing both of you and this is one thing on which you should both agree.

11

Summary

Have you ever spent the time to have a yard sale? How much did that bring in for you? Do you spend time clipping coupons? Do you go out of your way to fill up your tank at lower-cost gas stations? Have you ever made a special trip to a store because of an item that was on sale? Have you spent time shopping around for lower mortgage rates for a purchase of a home or to refinance? Have you spent time searching online for better prices of a product you want to buy? Have you ever taken the time to get multiple bids from different contractors to do work on your home? Have you ever gone to more than one car dealer to see if you could get a better price on a car purchase?

You have probably at some point in your life done one or more of these things to save some money. But for some of you, fixing your retirement plan might save you more money than doing all of these things COMBINED. Yet, most people neglect applying the few hours of effort needed to reap these savings. Do yourself a favor the next time you are tempted to do one of the above and instead invest the time to eliminate needless costs from your retirement plan. Look back in the Appendix to see how much it will save you each year, how many more years of retirement you could enjoy, or how much more you could spend in retirement if you just take the steps needed to eliminate needless fees.

Control What Is Controllable

There are things that you can control with certainty (or effective certainty). Fees are 100 percent certain. Control them. Do not pay needless fees.

Taxes (although not tax rates) can be controlled as well, at least to the point of avoiding making decisions that would cause you to pay taxes you could have otherwise avoided.

You can control the risk of materially underperforming the markets with near certainty by indexing. Don't pay extra fees with 100 percent certainty to an advisor croupier for a hope of materially superior performance that comes with a risk of material underperformance. It is an irrational gamble.

While you cannot control the markets, you can control how much market risk you are subject to by your basic asset allocation. Don't take more risk than is necessary to confidently exceed your goals. If you can afford to take less risk, take less risk even if you can "tolerate" more, unless of course taking more risk confidently buys you goals you value more than avoiding risk.

Don't pay fees to an advisor whose purpose is to identify your maximum tolerance for risk (pain) and proceeds to position you in a portfolio designed to experience that risk, or an advisor who coerces you to sacrifice goals you value to achieve goals you do not value.

Do make the most of your one life. If you are paying an advisor fees, make sure it is for what YOU value. He should identify your ideal dreams and acceptable compromises, then craft continuous life-relative advice that helps you make the most of your life despite the continuous future uncertainty of the markets.

I hope you have enjoyed this book, and I sincerely you hope you take the time to improve your life. It is worth it. Let me know if you do. You can e-mail me at author@wealthcarecapital.com.

Appendix A

Lifestyle Prices of Excessive Retirement Plan Expenses

Age 25
Current 401(k) Balance: $25,000 141
Current 401(k) Balance: $75,000 143
Current 401(k) Balance: $150,000 145
Current 401(k) Balance: $250,000 147

Age 30
Current 401(k) Balance: $25,000 149
Current 401(k) Balance: $75,000 151
Current 401(k) Balance: $150,000 153
Current 401(k) Balance: $250,000 155

Age 35
Current 401(k) Balance: $25,000 157
Current 401(k) Balance: $75,000 159
Current 401(k) Balance: $150,000 161
Current 401(k) Balance: $250,000 163

Age 40
Current 401(k) Balance: $25,000 165
Current 401(k) Balance: $75,000 167
Current 401(k) Balance: $150,000 169
Current 401(k) Balance: $250,000 171

Age 45
Current 401(k) Balance: $25,000 173
Current 401(k) Balance: $75,000 175
Current 401(k) Balance: $150,000 177
Current 401(k) Balance: $250,000 179

Age 50
Current 401(k) Balance: $25,000 181
Current 401(k) Balance: $75,000 183
Current 401(k) Balance: $150,000 185
Current 401(k) Balance: $250,000 187

Age 55
Current 401(k) Balance: $25,000 189
Current 401(k) Balance: $75,000 191
Current 401(k) Balance: $150,000 193
Current 401(k) Balance: $250,000 195

Age 60
Current 401(k) Balance: $25,000 197
Current 401(k) Balance: $75,000 199
Current 401(k) Balance: $150,000 201
Current 401(k) Balance: $250,000 203

AGE 25 WITH CURRENT 401(K) BALANCE OF $25,000

Total Annual Savings	$2,500		$5,000	
Allocation: **80% Stock/20% Bonds**				
Base Comfortable "In Balance" Case:				
Maximum Fair Total Expense	0.75%		0.75%	
Retirement Income @ Age 65	$17,600		$29,100	
Age 65 Range of Portfolio Values	$206,292 to $2,313,620		$345,907 to $3,504,041	
EXCESS EXPENSE:	**0.50%** (1.25% total)	**1.00%** (1.75% total)	**0.50%** (1.25% total)	**1.00%** (1.75% total)
COST OF EXCESS EXPENSE				
Additional Annual Savings Needed	$800	$1,800	$1,300	$2,900
Delay Retirement by:	3 Years	7 Years	3 Years	6 Years
Reduce Annual Retirement Income by	$3,100	$5,700	$4,900	$9,200
Increased Risk of Outliving Resources	54%	100%	51%	99%
Reduction to Age 65 Portfolio Values:				
Likely More than:	$29,893	$26,148	$46,356	$39,929
Likely Less than:	$331,976	$331,976	$482,194	$895,018

Allocation: **60% Stock/40% Bonds**				
Base Comfortable "In Balance" Case:				
Maximum Fair Total Expense	0.75%		0.75%	
Retirement Income @ Age 65	$14,200		$23,500	
Age 65 Range of Portfolio Values	$192,515 to $1,343,585		$330,420 to $2,094,401	
EXCESS EXPENSE:	**0.50%** (1.25% total)	**1.00%** (1.75% total)	**0.50%** (1.25% total)	**1.00%** (1.75% total)
COST OF EXCESS EXPENSE				
Additional Annual Savings Needed	$900	$1,800	$1,300	$2,700
Delay Retirement by:	4 Years	7 Years	3 Years	6 Years
Reduce Annual Retirement Income by	$2,600	$4,700	$4,000	$7,400
Increased Risk of Outliving Resources	57%	121%	52%	116%
Reduction to Age 65 Portfolio Values:				
Likely More than:	$25,859	$21,481	$43,540	$35,002
Likely Less than:	$194,418	$194,418	$266,647	$516,334

Allocation: **45% Stock/55% Bonds**				
Base Comfortable "In Balance" Case:				
Maximum Fair Total Expense	0.75%		0.75%	
Retirement Income @ Age 65	$11,700		$19,800	
Age 65 Range of Portfolio Values	$181,072 to $903,914		$313,423 to $1,431,857	
EXCESS EXPENSE:	**0.50%** (1.25% total)	**1.00%** (1.75% total)	**0.50%** (1.25% total)	**1.00%** (1.75% total)
COST OF EXCESS EXPENSE				
Additional Annual Savings Needed	$800	$1,700	$1,300	$2,700
Delay Retirement by:	4 Years	7 Years	4 Years	7 Years
Reduce Annual Retirement Income by	$2,100	$3,800	$3,500	$6,300
Increased Risk of Outliving Resources	64%	144%	64%	144%
Reduction to Age 65 Portfolio Values:				
Likely More than:	$23,745	$20,382	$39,029	$32,002
Likely Less than:	$127,260	$127,260	$194,180	$360,522

Total annual savings is COMBINED annual employee AND employer contribution

AGE 25 WITH CURRENT 401(K) BALANCE OF $25,000

Total Annual Savings	$10,000		$15,000	
Allocation: **80% Stock/20% Bonds**				
Base Comfortable "In Balance" Case:				
Maximum Fair Total Expense	0.75%		0.75%	
Retirement Income @ Age 65	$51,700		$74,300	
Age 65 Range of Portfolio Values	$625,209 to $6,004,903		$904,512 to $8,437,812	
EXCESS EXPENSE:	**0.50%**	**1.00%**	**0.50%**	**1.00%**
	(1.25% total)	(1.75% total)	(1.25% total)	(1.75% total)
COST OF EXCESS EXPENSE				
Additional Annual Savings Needed	$2,300	$4,800	$3,200	$6,700
Delay Retirement by:	3 Years	6 Years	3 Years	6 Years
Reduce Annual Retirement Income by	$8,500	$15,600	$12,400	$22,000
Increased Risk of Outliving Resources	47%	93%	47%	93%
Reduction to Age 65 Portfolio Values:				
Likely More than:	$77,329	$61,982	$106,239	$94,047
Likely Less than:	$800,589	$800,589	$1,152,010	$2,089,466

Allocation: **60% Stock/40% Bonds**				
Base Comfortable "In Balance" Case:				
Maximum Fair Total Expense	0.75%		0.75%	
Retirement Income @ Age 65	$42,500		$61,200	
Age 65 Range of Portfolio Values	$604,462 to $3,655,605		$869,623 to $5,186,829	
EXCESS EXPENSE:	**0.50%**	**1.00%**	**0.50%**	**1.00%**
	(1.25% total)	(1.75% total)	(1.25% total)	(1.75% total)
COST OF EXCESS EXPENSE				
Additional Annual Savings Needed	$2,200	$4,800	$3,100	$6,700
Delay Retirement by:	3 Years	6 Years	3 Years	6 Years
Reduce Annual Retirement Income by	$6,900	$12,900	$10,000	$18,100
Increased Risk of Outliving Resources	51%	117%	51%	117%
Reduction to Age 65 Portfolio Values:				
Likely More than:	$76,130	$66,612	$107,075	$90,621
Likely Less than:	$471,163	$471,163	$667,727	$1,232,874

Allocation: **45% Stock/55% Bonds**				
Base Comfortable "In Balance" Case:				
Maximum Fair Total Expense	0.75%		0.75%	
Retirement Income @ Age 65	$35,800		$52,000	
Age 65 Range of Portfolio Values	$574,850 to $2,489,330		$828,360 to $3,544,292	
EXCESS EXPENSE:	**0.50%**	**1.00%**	**0.50%**	**1.00%**
	(1.25% total)	(1.75% total)	(1.25% total)	(1.75% total)
COST OF EXCESS EXPENSE				
Additional Annual Savings Needed	$2,200	$4,800	$3,300	$7,000
Delay Retirement by:	3 Years	6 Years	4 Years	6 Years
Reduce Annual Retirement Income by	$5,900	$10,800	$8,700	$15,700
Increased Risk of Outliving Resources	63%	144%	64%	147%
Reduction to Age 65 Portfolio Values:				
Likely More than:	$68,440	$59,131	$91,096	$89,375
Likely Less than:	$317,564	$317,564	$452,844	$825,680

Total annual savings is COMBINED annual employee AND employer contribution

AGE 25 WITH CURRENT 401(K) BALANCE OF $75,000

Total Annual Savings	$2,500		$5,000	
Allocation: **80% Stock/20% Bonds**				
Base Comfortable "In Balance" Case:				
Maximum Fair Total Expense	0.75%		0.75%	
Retirement Income @ Age 65	$29,300		$41,200	
Age 65 Range of Portfolio Values	$329,353 to $4,546,624		$480,207 to $5,757,768	
EXCESS EXPENSE:	**0.50%**	**1.00%**	**0.50%**	**1.00%**
	(1.25% total)	(1.75% total)	(1.25% total)	(1.75% total)
COST OF EXCESS EXPENSE				
Additional Annual Savings Needed	$1,400	$3,000	$1,900	$4,200
Delay Retirement by:	4 Years	7 Years	3 Years	7 Years
Reduce Annual Retirement Income by	$5,500	$10,100	$7,600	$13,800
Increased Risk of Outliving Resources	42%	101%	52%	99%
Reduction to Age 65 Portfolio Values:				
Likely More than:	$53,020	$42,748	$75,041	$63,894
Likely Less than:	$707,335	$707,335	$888,946	$1,636,250

Allocation: **60% Stock/40% Bonds**				
Base Comfortable "In Balance" Case:				
Maximum Fair Total Expense	0.75%		0.75%	
Retirement Income @ Age 65	$23,300		$33,000	
Age 65 Range of Portfolio Values	$305,795 to $2,591,061		$444,353 to $3,291,666	
EXCESS EXPENSE:	**0.50%**	**1.00%**	**0.50%**	**1.00%**
	(1.25% total)	(1.75% total)	(1.25% total)	(1.75% total)
COST OF EXCESS EXPENSE				
Additional Annual Savings Needed	$1,400	$3,000	$1,900	$4,100
Delay Retirement by:	4 Years	7 Years	4 Years	7 Years
Reduce Annual Retirement Income by	$4,500	$8,200	$5,900	$11,000
Increased Risk of Outliving Resources	58%	113%	57%	119%
Reduction to Age 65 Portfolio Values:				
Likely More than:	$47,757	$40,929	$63,119	$56,750
Likely Less than:	$409,231	$409,231	$490,228	$913,381

Allocation: **45% Stock/55% Bonds**				
Base Comfortable "In Balance" Case:				
Maximum Fair Total Expense	0.75%		0.75%	
Retirement Income @ Age 65	$19,000		$26,900	
Age 65 Range of Portfolio Values	$278,245 to $1,667,339		$409,541 to $2,162,271	
EXCESS EXPENSE:	**0.50%**	**1.00%**	**0.50%**	**1.00%**
	(1.25% total)	(1.75% total)	(1.25% total)	(1.75% total)
COST OF EXCESS EXPENSE				
Additional Annual Savings Needed	$1,400	$3,000	$1,800	$3,800
Delay Retirement by:	4 Years	8 Years	4 Years	7 Years
Reduce Annual Retirement Income by	$3,800	$6,800	$4,900	$9,000
Increased Risk of Outliving Resources	70%	147%	62%	144%
Reduction to Age 65 Portfolio Values:				
Likely More than:	$44,418	$36,235	$56,738	$48,353
Likely Less than:	$263,799	$263,799	$318,890	$587,846

Total annual savings is COMBINED annual employee AND employer contribution

AGE 25 WITH CURRENT 401(K) BALANCE OF $75,000

Total Annual Savings	$10,000		$15,000	
Allocation: **80% Stock/20% Bonds**				
Base Comfortable "In Balance" Case:				
Maximum Fair Total Expense	0.75%		0.75%	
Retirement Income @ Age 65	$64,600		$87,500	
Age 65 Range of Portfolio Values	$753,791 to $8,164,758		$1,037,477 to $10,511,880	
EXCESS EXPENSE:	**0.50%**	**1.00%**	**0.50%**	**1.00%**
	(1.25% total)	(1.75% total)	(1.25% total)	(1.75% total)
COST OF EXCESS EXPENSE				
Additional Annual Savings Needed	$3,000	$6,500	$3,900	$8,600
Delay Retirement by:	3 Years	6 Years	3 Years	6 Years
Reduce Annual Retirement Income by	$11,400	$20,700	$14,900	$27,600
Increased Risk of Outliving Resources	53%	99%	51%	98%
Reduction to Age 65 Portfolio Values:				
Likely More than:	$107,593	$84,269	$139,067	$119,787
Likely Less than:	$1,169,195	$1,169,195	$1,446,580	$2,685,055

Allocation: **60% Stock/40% Bonds**				
Base Comfortable "In Balance" Case:				
Maximum Fair Total Expense	0.75%		0.75%	
Retirement Income @ Age 65	$51,600		$70,700	
Age 65 Range of Portfolio Values	$714,150 to $4,783,691		$991,017 to $6,282,961	
EXCESS EXPENSE:	**0.50%**	**1.00%**	**0.50%**	**1.00%**
	(1.25% total)	(1.75% total)	(1.25% total)	(1.75% total)
COST OF EXCESS EXPENSE				
Additional Annual Savings Needed	$2,800	$6,200	$3,900	$8,100
Delay Retirement by:	3 Years	6 Years	3 Years	6 Years
Reduce Annual Retirement Income by	$8,900	$16,400	$12,200	$22,300
Increased Risk of Outliving Resources	51%	117%	52%	115%
Reduction to Age 65 Portfolio Values:				
Likely More than:	$89,603	$80,112	$130,620	$105,006
Likely Less than:	$678,143	$678,143	$799,942	$1,549,002

Allocation: **45% Stock/55% Bonds**				
Base Comfortable "In Balance" Case:				
Maximum Fair Total Expense	0.75%		0.75%	
Retirement Income @ Age 65	$42,900		$59,600	
Age 65 Range of Portfolio Values	$678,566 to $3,241,506		$940,026 to $4,295,328	
EXCESS EXPENSE:	**0.50%**	**1.00%**	**0.50%**	**1.00%**
	(1.25% total)	(1.75% total)	(1.25% total)	(1.75% total)
COST OF EXCESS EXPENSE				
Additional Annual Savings Needed	$2,600	$6,000	$3,900	$8,200
Delay Retirement by:	4 Years	7 Years	4 Years	7 Years
Reduce Annual Retirement Income by	$7,100	$13,500	$10,500	$19,000
Increased Risk of Outliving Resources	63%	143%	67%	145%
Reduction to Age 65 Portfolio Values:				
Likely More than:	$87,836	$76,165	$117,087	$96,004
Likely Less than:	$450,549	$450,549	$582,539	$1,081,567

Total annual savings is COMBINED annual employee AND employer contribution

AGE 25 WITH CURRENT 401(K) BALANCE OF $150,000

Total Annual Savings	$2,500		$5,000	
Allocation: **80% Stock/20% Bonds**				
Base Comfortable "In Balance" Case:				
Maximum Fair Total Expense	0.75%		0.75%	
Retirement Income @ Age 65	$47,400		$58,700	
Age 65 Range of Portfolio Values	$522,295 to $7,928,625		$658,584 to $9,093,127	
EXCESS EXPENSE:	**0.50%**	**1.00%**	**0.50%**	**1.00%**
	(1.25% total)	(1.75% total)	(1.25% total)	(1.75% total)
COST OF EXCESS EXPENSE				
Additional Annual Savings Needed	$2,400	$5,300	$2,800	$6,100
Delay Retirement by:	4 Years	8 Years	4 Years	7 Years
Reduce Annual Retirement Income by	$9,500	$17,300	$11,100	$20,200
Increased Risk of Outliving Resources	45%	99%	42%	101%
Reduction to Age 65 Portfolio Values:				
Likely More than:	$93,767	$78,091	$106,039	$85,496
Likely Less than:	$1,291,370	$1,291,370	$1,414,670	$2,627,181

Allocation: **60% Stock/40% Bonds**				
Base Comfortable "In Balance" Case:				
Maximum Fair Total Expense	0.75%		0.75%	
Retirement Income @ Age 65	$36,900		$46,600	
Age 65 Range of Portfolio Values	$478,335 to $4,325,362		$611,591 to $5,182,122	
EXCESS EXPENSE:	**0.50%**	**1.00%**	**0.50%**	**1.00%**
	(1.25% total)	(1.75% total)	(1.25% total)	(1.75% total)
COST OF EXCESS EXPENSE				
Additional Annual Savings Needed	$2,300	$4,900	$2,700	$6,000
Delay Retirement by:	4 Years	8 Years	4 Years	7 Years
Reduce Annual Retirement Income by	$7,400	$13,400	$8,900	$16,400
Increased Risk of Outliving Resources	63%	120%	58%	113%
Reduction to Age 65 Portfolio Values:				
Likely More than:	$82,356	$66,489	$95,515	$81,857
Likely Less than:	$701,692	$701,692	$818,463	$1,507,085

Allocation: **45% Stock/55% Bonds**				
Base Comfortable "In Balance" Case:				
Maximum Fair Total Expense	0.75%		0.75%	
Retirement Income @ Age 65	$29,900		$38,000	
Age 65 Range of Portfolio Values	$421,331 to $2,825,736		$556,489 to $3,334,679	
EXCESS EXPENSE:	**0.50%**	**1.00%**	**0.50%**	**1.00%**
	(1.25% total)	(1.75% total)	(1.25% total)	(1.75% total)
COST OF EXCESS EXPENSE				
Additional Annual Savings Needed	$2,200	$4,900	$2,800	$5,900
Delay Retirement by:	5 Years	9 Years	4 Years	8 Years
Reduce Annual Retirement Income by	$6,000	$11,100	$7,500	$13,600
Increased Risk of Outliving Resources	69%	153%	70%	147%
Reduction to Age 65 Portfolio Values:				
Likely More than:	$72,379	$59,038	$88,834	$72,470
Likely Less than:	$466,888	$466,888	$527,599	$965,695

Total annual savings is COMBINED annual employee AND employer contribution

AGE 25 WITH CURRENT 401(K) BALANCE OF $150,000

Total Annual Savings	$10,000		$15,000	
Allocation: **80% Stock/20% Bonds**				
Base Comfortable "In Balance" Case:				
Maximum Fair Total Expense	0.75%		0.75%	
Retirement Income @ Age 65	$82,500		$106,100	
Age 65 Range of Portfolio Values	$960,293 to $11,515,415		$1,237,144 to $13,881,116	
EXCESS EXPENSE:	**0.50%**	**1.00%**	**0.50%**	**1.00%**
	(1.25% total)	(1.75% total)	(1.25% total)	(1.75% total)
COST OF EXCESS EXPENSE				
Additional Annual Savings Needed	$3,800	$8,300	$4,900	$10,600
Delay Retirement by:	3 Years	7 Years	3 Years	7 Years
Reduce Annual Retirement Income by	$15,200	$27,600	$18,900	$34,600
Increased Risk of Outliving Resources	52%	100%	51%	95%
Reduction to Age 65 Portfolio Values:				
Likely More than:	$150,082	$127,788	$179,356	$156,890
Likely Less than:	$1,777,893	$1,777,893	$1,991,857	$3,787,973

Allocation: **60% Stock/40% Bonds**				
Base Comfortable "In Balance" Case:				
Maximum Fair Total Expense	0.75%		0.75%	
Retirement Income @ Age 65	$66,100		$85,200	
Age 65 Range of Portfolio Values	$888,584 to $6,583,211		$1,155,089 to $8,061,512	
EXCESS EXPENSE:	**0.50%**	**1.00%**	**0.50%**	**1.00%**
	(1.25% total)	(1.75% total)	(1.25% total)	(1.75% total)
COST OF EXCESS EXPENSE				
Additional Annual Savings Needed	$3,800	$8,200	$4,900	$10,600
Delay Retirement by:	4 Years	7 Years	4 Years	7 Years
Reduce Annual Retirement Income by	$11,900	$22,100	$15,600	$28,100
Increased Risk of Outliving Resources	58%	120%	57%	121%
Reduction to Age 65 Portfolio Values:				
Likely More than:	$126,237	$113,501	$155,155	$128,886
Likely Less than:	$980,457	$980,457	$1,166,509	$2,159,243

Allocation: **45% Stock/55% Bonds**				
Base Comfortable "In Balance" Case:				
Maximum Fair Total Expense	0.75%		0.75%	
Retirement Income @ Age 65	$53,900		$70,200	
Age 65 Range of Portfolio Values	$818,961 to $4,324,420		$1,086,434 to $5,423,481	
EXCESS EXPENSE:	**0.50%**	**1.00%**	**0.50%**	**1.00%**
	(1.25% total)	(1.75% total)	(1.25% total)	(1.75% total)
COST OF EXCESS EXPENSE				
Additional Annual Savings Needed	$3,600	$7,600	$4,500	$10,000
Delay Retirement by:	4 Years	7 Years	4 Years	7 Years
Reduce Annual Retirement Income by	$9,900	$18,000	$12,500	$22,600
Increased Risk of Outliving Resources	63%	146%	64%	144%
Reduction to Age 65 Portfolio Values:				
Likely More than:	$113,477	$96,706	$142,473	$122,291
Likely Less than:	$637,780	$637,780	$763,554	$1,414,700

Total annual savings is COMBINED annual employee AND employer contribution

AGE 25 WITH CURRENT 401(K) BALANCE OF $250,000

Total Annual Savings	$2,500		$5,000	
Allocation: **80% Stock/20% Bonds**				
Base Comfortable "In Balance" Case:				
Maximum Fair Total Expense	0.75%		0.75%	
Retirement Income @ Age 65	$71,300		$83,000	
Age 65 Range of Portfolio Values	$770,592 to $12,493,600		$910,292 to $13,620,231	
EXCESS EXPENSE:	**0.50%**	**1.00%**	**0.50%**	**1.00%**
	(1.25% total)	(1.75% total)	(1.25% total)	(1.75% total)
COST OF EXCESS EXPENSE				
Additional Annual Savings Needed	$3,900	$8,000	$4,200	$9,000
Delay Retirement by:	5 Years	8 Years	4 Years	8 Years
Reduce Annual Retirement Income by	$14,800	$26,600	$16,600	$30,400
Increased Risk of Outliving Resources	48%	98%	45%	99%
Reduction to Age 65 Portfolio Values:				
Likely More than:	$139,899	$117,191	$161,078	$126,456
Likely Less than:	$2,074,700	$2,074,700	$2,192,824	$4,048,204

Allocation: **60% Stock/40% Bonds**				
Base Comfortable "In Balance" Case:				
Maximum Fair Total Expense	0.75%		0.75%	
Retirement Income @ Age 65	$55,500		$65,000	
Age 65 Range of Portfolio Values	$695,289 to $6,803,729		$842,549 to $7,498,294	
EXCESS EXPENSE:	**0.50%**	**1.00%**	**0.50%**	**1.00%**
	(1.25% total)	(1.75% total)	(1.25% total)	(1.75% total)
COST OF EXCESS EXPENSE				
Additional Annual Savings Needed	$3,600	$7,600	$4,000	$8,500
Delay Retirement by:	5 Years	8 Years	4 Years	8 Years
Reduce Annual Retirement Income by	$11,800	$21,100	$13,000	$23,900
Increased Risk of Outliving Resources	60%	119%	60%	117%
Reduction to Age 65 Portfolio Values:				
Likely More than:	$125,646	$101,508	$143,720	$116,067
Likely Less than:	$1,133,117	$1,133,117	$1,206,522	$2,220,636

Allocation: **45% Stock/55% Bonds**				
Base Comfortable "In Balance" Case:				
Maximum Fair Total Expense	0.75%		0.75%	
Retirement Income @ Age 65	$44,500		$52,600	
Age 65 Range of Portfolio Values	$614,540 to $4,343,084		$741,933 to $4,875,627	
EXCESS EXPENSE:	**0.50%**	**1.00%**	**0.50%**	**1.00%**
	(1.25% total)	(1.75% total)	(1.25% total)	(1.75% total)
COST OF EXCESS EXPENSE				
Additional Annual Savings Needed	$3,500	$7,700	$4,000	$8,500
Delay Retirement by:	5 Years	9 Years	5 Years	8 Years
Reduce Annual Retirement Income by	$9,500	$17,000	$11,000	$19,300
Increased Risk of Outliving Resources	70%	150%	70%	152%
Reduction to Age 65 Portfolio Values:				
Likely More than:	$106,715	$92,165	$122,466	$100,139
Likely Less than:	$718,194	$718,194	$797,094	$1,478,844

Total annual savings is COMBINED annual employee AND employer contribution

AGE 25 WITH CURRENT 401(K) BALANCE OF $250,000

Total Annual Savings	$10,000		$15,000	
Allocation: **80% Stock/20% Bonds**				
Base Comfortable "In Balance" Case:				
Maximum Fair Total Expense	0.75%		0.75%	
Retirement Income @ Age 65	$106,300		$130,000	
Age 65 Range of Portfolio Values	$1,203,895 to $16,024,098		$1,507,347 to $18,444,190	
EXCESS EXPENSE:	**0.50%**	**1.00%**	**0.50%**	**1.00%**
	(1.25% total)	(1.75% total)	(1.25% total)	(1.75% total)
COST OF EXCESS EXPENSE				
Additional Annual Savings Needed	$5,200	$10,900	$6,100	$13,200
Delay Retirement by:	4 Years	7 Years	4 Years	7 Years
Reduce Annual Retirement Income by	$20,000	$36,400	$24,300	$44,000
Increased Risk of Outliving Resources	46%	101%	52%	101%
Reduction to Age 65 Portfolio Values:				
Likely More than:	$181,416	$162,690	$231,947	$206,453
Likely Less than:	$2,527,816	$2,527,816	$2,854,169	$5,231,528

Allocation: **60% Stock/40% Bonds**				
Base Comfortable "In Balance" Case:				
Maximum Fair Total Expense	0.75%		0.75%	
Retirement Income @ Age 65	$84,200		$103,800	
Age 65 Range of Portfolio Values	$1,113,314 to $9,106,001		$1,386,429 to $10,514,590	
EXCESS EXPENSE:	**0.50%**	**1.00%**	**0.50%**	**1.00%**
	(1.25% total)	(1.75% total)	(1.25% total)	(1.75% total)
COST OF EXCESS EXPENSE				
Additional Annual Savings Needed	$4,800	$10,700	$6,000	$13,200
Delay Retirement by:	4 Years	7 Years	4 Years	7 Years
Reduce Annual Retirement Income by	$16,000	$28,900	$19,100	$34,500
Increased Risk of Outliving Resources	60%	114%	59%	119%
Reduction to Age 65 Portfolio Values:				
Likely More than:	$176,241	$146,054	$200,777	$170,827
Likely Less than:	$1,419,624	$1,419,624	$1,622,791	$2,961,948

Allocation: **45% Stock/55% Bonds**				
Base Comfortable "In Balance" Case:				
Maximum Fair Total Expense	0.75%		0.75%	
Retirement Income @ Age 65	$67,900		$84,400	
Age 65 Range of Portfolio Values	$1,008,548 to $5,918,179		$1,275,778 to $6,850,442	
EXCESS EXPENSE:	**0.50%**	**1.00%**	**0.50%**	**1.00%**
	(1.25% total)	(1.75% total)	(1.25% total)	(1.75% total)
COST OF EXCESS EXPENSE				
Additional Annual Savings Needed	$4,600	$10,100	$5,500	$12,100
Delay Retirement by:	4 Years	8 Years	4 Years	7 Years
Reduce Annual Retirement Income by	$13,300	$23,900	$15,400	$28,400
Increased Risk of Outliving Resources	67%	143%	64%	144%
Reduction to Age 65 Portfolio Values:				
Likely More than:	$157,507	$123,370	$179,442	$152,669
Likely Less than:	$919,550	$919,550	$1,030,471	$1,884,456

Total annual savings is COMBINED annual employee AND employer contribution

AGE 30 WITH CURRENT 401(K) BALANCE OF $25,000

Total Annual Savings	$2,500		$5,000	
Allocation: **80% Stock/20% Bonds**				
Base Comfortable "In Balance" Case:				
Maximum Fair Total Expense	0.75%		0.75%	
Retirement Income @ Age 65	$13,300		$21,400	
Age 65 Range of Portfolio Values	$160,661 to $1,384,456		$273,252 to $2,113,527	
EXCESS EXPENSE:	**0.50%**	**1.00%**	**0.50%**	**1.00%**
	(1.25% total)	(1.75% total)	(1.25% total)	(1.75% total)
COST OF EXCESS EXPENSE				
Additional Annual Savings Needed	$800	$1,600	$1,100	$2,400
Delay Retirement by:	3 Years	6 Years	3 Years	5 Years
Reduce Annual Retirement Income by	$2,300	$4,100	$3,200	$6,000
Increased Risk of Outliving Resources	39%	91%	38%	92%
Reduction to Age 65 Portfolio Values:				
Likely More than:	$19,886	$16,563	$30,505	$25,885
Likely Less than:	$183,101	$183,101	$247,554	$475,984

Allocation: **60% Stock/40% Bonds**				
Base Comfortable "In Balance" Case:				
Maximum Fair Total Expense	0.75%		0.75%	
Retirement Income @ Age 65	$11,200		$18,500	
Age 65 Range of Portfolio Values	$157,646 to $896,444		$269,266 to $1,387,361	
EXCESS EXPENSE:	**0.50%**	**1.00%**	**0.50%**	**1.00%**
	(1.25% total)	(1.75% total)	(1.25% total)	(1.75% total)
COST OF EXCESS EXPENSE				
Additional Annual Savings Needed	$700	$1,600	$1,200	$2,500
Delay Retirement by:	3 Years	6 Years	3 Years	6 Years
Reduce Annual Retirement Income by	$1,800	$3,300	$2,900	$5,300
Increased Risk of Outliving Resources	60%	120%	57%	118%
Reduction to Age 65 Portfolio Values:				
Likely More than:	$18,917	$16,395	$31,155	$26,483
Likely Less than:	$114,046	$114,046	$165,908	$309,354

Allocation: **45% Stock/55% Bonds**				
Base Comfortable "In Balance" Case:				
Maximum Fair Total Expense	0.75%		0.75%	
Retirement Income @ Age 65	$9,500		$15,900	
Age 65 Range of Portfolio Values	$150,316 to $653,618		$258,564 to $1,025,987	
EXCESS EXPENSE:	**0.50%**	**1.00%**	**0.50%**	**1.00%**
	(1.25% total)	(1.75% total)	(1.25% total)	(1.75% total)
COST OF EXCESS EXPENSE				
Additional Annual Savings Needed	$800	$1,600	$1,200	$2,500
Delay Retirement by:	3 Years	6 Years	3 Years	6 Years
Reduce Annual Retirement Income by	$1,600	$2,900	$2,500	$4,700
Increased Risk of Outliving Resources	72%	154%	72%	151%
Reduction to Age 65 Portfolio Values:				
Likely More than:	$17,526	$15,417	$28,302	$24,202
Likely Less than:	$83,188	$83,188	$120,998	$228,658

Total annual savings is COMBINED annual employee AND employer contribution

AGE 30 WITH CURRENT 401(K) BALANCE OF $25,000

Total Annual Savings	$10,000		$15,000	
Allocation: **80% Stock/20% Bonds**				
Base Comfortable "In Balance" Case:				
Maximum Fair Total Expense	0.75%		0.75%	
Retirement Income @ Age 65	$38,600		$54,800	
Age 65 Range of Portfolio Values	$498,867 to $3,541,208		$729,957 to $4,924,284	
EXCESS EXPENSE:	**0.50%**	**1.00%**	**0.50%**	**1.00%**
	(1.25% total)	(1.75% total)	(1.25% total)	(1.75% total)
COST OF EXCESS EXPENSE				
Additional Annual Savings Needed	$2,100	$4,400	$2,800	$5,900
Delay Retirement by:	3 Years	5 Years	2 Years	5 Years
Reduce Annual Retirement Income by	$6,100	$10,800	$7,900	$14,800
Increased Risk of Outliving Resources	37%	92%	33%	88%
Reduction to Age 65 Portfolio Values:				
Likely More than:	$52,177	$45,743	$74,974	$68,737
Likely Less than:	$426,752	$426,752	$569,085	$1,069,087

Allocation: **60% Stock/40% Bonds**				
Base Comfortable "In Balance" Case:				
Maximum Fair Total Expense	0.75%		0.75%	
Retirement Income @ Age 65	$33,100		$47,300	
Age 65 Range of Portfolio Values	$486,473 to $2,407,034		$710,602 to $3,395,754	
EXCESS EXPENSE:	**0.50%**	**1.00%**	**0.50%**	**1.00%**
	(1.25% total)	(1.75% total)	(1.25% total)	(1.75% total)
COST OF EXCESS EXPENSE				
Additional Annual Savings Needed	$2,000	$4,300	$2,800	$6,000
Delay Retirement by:	3 Years	5 Years	3 Years	5 Years
Reduce Annual Retirement Income by	$5,000	$9,200	$6,900	$12,800
Increased Risk of Outliving Resources	52%	118%	50%	117%
Reduction to Age 65 Portfolio Values:				
Likely More than:	$50,597	$45,184	$73,282	$62,450
Likely Less than:	$278,421	$278,421	$385,440	$712,196

Allocation: **45% Stock/55% Bonds**				
Base Comfortable "In Balance" Case:				
Maximum Fair Total Expense	0.75%		0.75%	
Retirement Income @ Age 65	$28,300		$41,100	
Age 65 Range of Portfolio Values	$471,934 to $1,770,271		$682,500 to $2,513,084	
EXCESS EXPENSE:	**0.50%**	**1.00%**	**0.50%**	**1.00%**
	(1.25% total)	(1.75% total)	(1.25% total)	(1.75% total)
COST OF EXCESS EXPENSE				
Additional Annual Savings Needed	$2,000	$4,200	$2,900	$6,100
Delay Retirement by:	3 Years	6 Years	3 Years	6 Years
Reduce Annual Retirement Income by	$4,200	$7,800	$6,300	$11,300
Increased Risk of Outliving Resources	66%	152%	64%	147%
Reduction to Age 65 Portfolio Values:				
Likely More than:	$49,352	$44,113	$68,422	$62,867
Likely Less than:	$199,800	$199,800	$278,498	$532,604

Total annual savings is COMBINED annual employee AND employer contribution

AGE 30 WITH CURRENT 401(K) BALANCE OF $75,000

Total Annual Savings	$2,500		$5,000	
Allocation: **80% Stock/20% Bonds**				
Base Comfortable "In Balance" Case:				
Maximum Fair Total Expense	0.75%		0.75%	
Retirement Income @ Age 65	$23,100		$31,700	
Age 65 Range of Portfolio Values	$260,848 to $2,752,331		$373,077 to $3,454,180	
EXCESS EXPENSE:	**0.50%**	**1.00%**	**0.50%**	**1.00%**
	(1.25% total)	(1.75% total)	(1.25% total)	(1.75% total)
COST OF EXCESS EXPENSE				
Additional Annual Savings Needed	$1,400	$3,000	$1,900	$4,100
Delay Retirement by:	4 Years	7 Years	3 Years	6 Years
Reduce Annual Retirement Income by	$4,100	$7,500	$5,500	$10,100
Increased Risk of Outliving Resources	49%	96%	47%	95%
Reduction to Age 65 Portfolio Values:				
Likely More than:	$37,489	$32,232	$48,085	$39,277
Likely Less than:	$387,247	$387,247	$458,735	$855,777

Allocation: **60% Stock/40% Bonds**				
Base Comfortable "In Balance" Case:				
Maximum Fair Total Expense	0.75%		0.75%	
Retirement Income @ Age 65	$18,800		$26,500	
Age 65 Range of Portfolio Values	$245,613 to $1,689,162		$361,492 to $2,200,207	
EXCESS EXPENSE:	**0.50%**	**1.00%**	**0.50%**	**1.00%**
	(1.25% total)	(1.75% total)	(1.25% total)	(1.75% total)
COST OF EXCESS EXPENSE				
Additional Annual Savings Needed	$1,300	$2,800	$1,800	$3,800
Delay Retirement by:	3 Years	7 Years	3 Years	7 Years
Reduce Annual Retirement Income by	$3,200	$6,000	$4,500	$8,200
Increased Risk of Outliving Resources	62%	121%	64%	123%
Reduction to Age 65 Portfolio Values:				
Likely More than:	$34,025	$28,205	$48,108	$37,728
Likely Less than:	$237,817	$237,817	$287,814	$539,275

Allocation: **45% Stock/55% Bonds**				
Base Comfortable "In Balance" Case:				
Maximum Fair Total Expense	0.75%		0.75%	
Retirement Income @ Age 65	$15,700		$22,200	
Age 65 Range of Portfolio Values	$235,547 to $1,201,429		$345,310 to $1,582,025	
EXCESS EXPENSE:	**0.50%**	**1.00%**	**0.50%**	**1.00%**
	(1.25% total)	(1.75% total)	(1.25% total)	(1.75% total)
COST OF EXCESS EXPENSE				
Additional Annual Savings Needed	$1,300	$2,700	$1,800	$3,800
Delay Retirement by:	4 Years	7 Years	4 Years	7 Years
Reduce Annual Retirement Income by	$2,900	$5,200	$3,800	$6,900
Increased Risk of Outliving Resources	73%	156%	77%	160%
Reduction to Age 65 Portfolio Values:				
Likely More than:	$31,627	$27,363	$43,428	$37,665
Likely Less than:	$167,763	$167,763	$206,511	$385,633

Total annual savings is COMBINED annual employee AND employer contribution

AGE 30 WITH CURRENT 401(K) BALANCE OF $75,000

Total Annual Savings	$10,000		$15,000	
Allocation: **80% Stock/20% Bonds**				
Base Comfortable "In Balance" Case:				
Maximum Fair Total Expense	0.75%		0.75%	
Retirement Income @ Age 65	$47,900		$64,400	
Age 65 Range of Portfolio Values	$591,738 to $4,850,275		$819,514 to $6,340,339	
EXCESS EXPENSE:	**0.50%**	**1.00%**	**0.50%**	**1.00%**
	(1.25% total)	(1.75% total)	(1.25% total)	(1.75% total)
COST OF EXCESS EXPENSE				
Additional Annual Savings Needed	$2,700	$5,700	$3,400	$7,300
Delay Retirement by:	3 Years	5 Years	3 Years	5 Years
Reduce Annual Retirement Income by	$7,500	$13,900	$9,600	$18,100
Increased Risk of Outliving Resources	38%	90%	37%	92%
Reduction to Age 65 Portfolio Values:				
Likely More than:	$67,379	$58,952	$91,517	$77,655
Likely Less than:	$593,782	$593,782	$742,664	$1,427,952

Allocation: **60% Stock/40% Bonds**				
Base Comfortable "In Balance" Case:				
Maximum Fair Total Expense	0.75%		0.75%	
Retirement Income @ Age 65	$41,100		$55,600	
Age 65 Range of Portfolio Values	$587,279 to $3,192,618		$807,677 to $4,161,960	
EXCESS EXPENSE:	**0.50%**	**1.00%**	**0.50%**	**1.00%**
	(1.25% total)	(1.75% total)	(1.25% total)	(1.75% total)
COST OF EXCESS EXPENSE				
Additional Annual Savings Needed	$2,700	$5,600	$3,400	$7,500
Delay Retirement by:	3 Years	6 Years	3 Years	6 Years
Reduce Annual Retirement Income by	$6,500	$12,200	$8,600	$16,000
Increased Risk of Outliving Resources	63%	120%	57%	117%
Reduction to Age 65 Portfolio Values:				
Likely More than:	$68,801	$61,284	$93,465	$79,450
Likely Less than:	$400,036	$400,036	$497,721	$928,061

Allocation: **45% Stock/55% Bonds**				
Base Comfortable "In Balance" Case:				
Maximum Fair Total Expense	0.75%		0.75%	
Retirement Income @ Age 65	$34,900		$47,800	
Age 65 Range of Portfolio Values	$560,759 to $2,334,584		$775,572 to $3,077,839	
EXCESS EXPENSE:	**0.50%**	**1.00%**	**0.50%**	**1.00%**
	(1.25% total)	(1.75% total)	(1.25% total)	(1.75% total)
COST OF EXCESS EXPENSE				
Additional Annual Savings Needed	$2,600	$5,500	$3,500	$7,600
Delay Retirement by:	3 Years	6 Years	3 Years	6 Years
Reduce Annual Retirement Income by	$5,600	$10,400	$7,500	$14,000
Increased Risk of Outliving Resources	71%	154%	72%	151%
Reduction to Age 65 Portfolio Values:				
Likely More than:	$63,355	$55,504	$84,906	$72,606
Likely Less than:	$289,652	$289,652	$362,992	$685,973

Total annual savings is COMBINED annual employee AND employer contribution

AGE 30 WITH CURRENT 401(K) BALANCE OF $150,000

Total Annual Savings	$2,500		$5,000	
Allocation: **80% Stock/20% Bonds**				
Base Comfortable "In Balance" Case:				
Maximum Fair Total Expense	0.75%		0.75%	
Retirement Income @ Age 65	$36,700		$46,200	
Age 65 Range of Portfolio Values	$410,117 to $4,828,576		$521,696 to $5,504,662	
EXCESS EXPENSE:	**0.50%**	**1.00%**	**0.50%**	**1.00%**
	(1.25% total)	(1.75% total)	(1.25% total)	(1.75% total)
COST OF EXCESS EXPENSE				
Additional Annual Savings Needed	$2,000	$4,700	$2,800	$6,000
Delay Retirement by:	4 Years	7 Years	4 Years	7 Years
Reduce Annual Retirement Income by	$6,800	$12,200	$8,200	$14,900
Increased Risk of Outliving Resources	41%	96%	49%	96%
Reduction to Age 65 Portfolio Values:				
Likely More than:	$62,964	$56,393	$74,977	$64,464
Likely Less than:	$698,678	$698,678	$774,494	$1,441,010

Allocation: **60% Stock/40% Bonds**				
Base Comfortable "In Balance" Case:				
Maximum Fair Total Expense	0.75%		0.75%	
Retirement Income @ Age 65	$30,200		$37,700	
Age 65 Range of Portfolio Values	$385,243 to $2,909,969		$491,105 to $3,378,203	
EXCESS EXPENSE:	**0.50%**	**1.00%**	**0.50%**	**1.00%**
	(1.25% total)	(1.75% total)	(1.25% total)	(1.75% total)
COST OF EXCESS EXPENSE				
Additional Annual Savings Needed	$2,200	$4,500	$2,500	$5,500
Delay Retirement by:	4 Years	8 Years	4 Years	7 Years
Reduce Annual Retirement Income by	$5,700	$10,400	$6,400	$12,100
Increased Risk of Outliving Resources	57%	120%	60%	120%
Reduction to Age 65 Portfolio Values:				
Likely More than:	$56,104	$50,734	$68,050	$56,410
Likely Less than:	$425,323	$425,323	$475,634	$882,268

Allocation: **45% Stock/55% Bonds**				
Base Comfortable "In Balance" Case:				
Maximum Fair Total Expense	0.75%		0.75%	
Retirement Income @ Age 65	$24,900		$31,400	
Age 65 Range of Portfolio Values	$361,014 to $2,061,452		$471,094 to $2,402,857	
EXCESS EXPENSE:	**0.50%**	**1.00%**	**0.50%**	**1.00%**
	(1.25% total)	(1.75% total)	(1.25% total)	(1.75% total)
COST OF EXCESS EXPENSE				
Additional Annual Savings Needed	$2,100	$4,400	$2,500	$5,400
Delay Retirement by:	4 Years	8 Years	4 Years	7 Years
Reduce Annual Retirement Income by	$4,600	$8,500	$5,700	$10,300
Increased Risk of Outliving Resources	75%	156%	73%	156%
Reduction to Age 65 Portfolio Values:				
Likely More than:	$52,753	$44,770	$63,253	$54,728
Likely Less than:	$301,849	$301,849	$335,525	$624,114

Total annual savings is COMBINED annual employee AND employer contribution

AGE 30 WITH CURRENT 401(K) BALANCE OF $150,000

Total Annual Savings	$10,000		$15,000	
Allocation: **80% Stock/20% Bonds**				
Base Comfortable "In Balance" Case:				
Maximum Fair Total Expense	0.75%		0.75%	
Retirement Income @ Age 65	$63,400		$80,000	
Age 65 Range of Portfolio Values	$746,154 to $6,908,359		$963,723 to $8,306,496	
EXCESS EXPENSE:	**0.50%**	**1.00%**	**0.50%**	**1.00%**
	(1.25% total)	(1.75% total)	(1.25% total)	(1.75% total)
COST OF EXCESS EXPENSE				
Additional Annual Savings Needed	$3,800	$8,100	$4,700	$9,700
Delay Retirement by:	3 Years	6 Years	3 Years	6 Years
Reduce Annual Retirement Income by	$11,000	$20,100	$13,500	$24,300
Increased Risk of Outliving Resources	47%	95%	40%	92%
Reduction to Age 65 Portfolio Values:				
Likely More than:	$96,171	$78,553	$119,316	$99,377
Likely Less than:	$917,468	$917,468	$1,098,608	$2,049,457
Allocation: **60% Stock/40% Bonds**				
Base Comfortable "In Balance" Case:				
Maximum Fair Total Expense	0.75%		0.75%	
Retirement Income @ Age 65	$53,100		$67,400	
Age 65 Range of Portfolio Values	$722,862 to $4,400,293		$945,636 to $5,378,419	
EXCESS EXPENSE:	**0.50%**	**1.00%**	**0.50%**	**1.00%**
	(1.25% total)	(1.75% total)	(1.25% total)	(1.75% total)
COST OF EXCESS EXPENSE				
Additional Annual Savings Needed	$3,500	$7,600	$4,300	$9,200
Delay Retirement by:	3 Years	7 Years	3 Years	6 Years
Reduce Annual Retirement Income by	$9,100	$16,500	$10,900	$19,900
Increased Risk of Outliving Resources	64%	123%	59%	119%
Reduction to Age 65 Portfolio Values:				
Likely More than:	$96,215	$75,457	$113,507	$98,370
Likely Less than:	$575,628	$575,628	$684,271	$1,277,954
Allocation: **45% Stock/55% Bonds**				
Base Comfortable "In Balance" Case:				
Maximum Fair Total Expense	0.75%		0.75%	
Retirement Income @ Age 65	$44,500		$57,100	
Age 65 Range of Portfolio Values	$690,498 to $3,163,928		$901,777 to $3,921,586	
EXCESS EXPENSE:	**0.50%**	**1.00%**	**0.50%**	**1.00%**
	(1.25% total)	(1.75% total)	(1.25% total)	(1.75% total)
COST OF EXCESS EXPENSE				
Additional Annual Savings Needed	$3,600	$7,500	$4,300	$9,200
Delay Retirement by:	4 Years	7 Years	3 Years	6 Years
Reduce Annual Retirement Income by	$7,600	$13,900	$9,500	$17,300
Increased Risk of Outliving Resources	77%	160%	72%	153%
Reduction to Age 65 Portfolio Values:				
Likely More than:	$86,855	$75,331	$105,161	$92,498
Likely Less than:	$413,021	$413,021	$499,127	$924,725

Total annual savings is COMBINED annual employee AND employer contribution

AGE 30 WITH CURRENT 401(K) BALANCE OF $250,000

	Total Annual Savings		$2,500		$5,000	
Allocation: **80% Stock/20% Bonds**						
Base Comfortable "In Balance" Case:						
Maximum Fair Total Expense			0.75%		0.75%	
Retirement Income @ Age 65			$54,800		$64,400	
Age 65 Range of Portfolio Values			$606,654 to $7,595,338		$717,876 to $8,271,991	
EXCESS EXPENSE:		**0.50%**	**1.00%**	**0.50%**	**1.00%**	
		(1.25% total)	(1.75% total)	(1.25% total)	(1.75% total)	
COST OF EXCESS EXPENSE						
Additional Annual Savings Needed		$3,100	$6,700	$3,600	$8,200	
Delay Retirement by:		4 Years	7 Years	3 Years	7 Years	
Reduce Annual Retirement Income by		$10,500	$18,900	$11,700	$21,500	
Increased Risk of Outliving Resources		40%	92%	41%	97%	
Reduction to Age 65 Portfolio Values:						
Likely More than:		$99,482	$84,690	$106,430	$95,105	
Likely Less than:		$1,112,313	$1,112,313	$1,189,480	$2,219,101	

Allocation: **60% Stock/40% Bonds**						
Base Comfortable "In Balance" Case:						
Maximum Fair Total Expense			0.75%		0.75%	
Retirement Income @ Age 65			$45,000		$53,000	
Age 65 Range of Portfolio Values			$564,738 to $4,528,970		$680,688 to $5,005,689	
EXCESS EXPENSE:		**0.50%**	**1.00%**	**0.50%**	**1.00%**	
		(1.25% total)	(1.75% total)	(1.25% total)	(1.75% total)	
COST OF EXCESS EXPENSE						
Additional Annual Savings Needed		$3,200	$6,800	$3,600	$7,700	
Delay Retirement by:		4 Years	8 Years	4 Years	7 Years	
Reduce Annual Retirement Income by		$8,700	$15,800	$9,900	$17,800	
Increased Risk of Outliving Resources		53%	117%	60%	121%	
Reduction to Age 65 Portfolio Values:						
Likely More than:		$90,563	$76,945	$102,414	$87,426	
Likely Less than:		$676,019	$676,019	$726,416	$1,348,903	

Allocation: **45% Stock/55% Bonds**						
Base Comfortable "In Balance" Case:						
Maximum Fair Total Expense			0.75%		0.75%	
Retirement Income @ Age 65			$37,100		$43,800	
Age 65 Range of Portfolio Values			$527,191 to $3,211,588		$641,518 to $3,544,082	
EXCESS EXPENSE:		**0.50%**	**1.00%**	**0.50%**	**1.00%**	
		(1.25% total)	(1.75% total)	(1.25% total)	(1.75% total)	
COST OF EXCESS EXPENSE						
Additional Annual Savings Needed		$3,200	$6,900	$3,700	$7,700	
Delay Retirement by:		4 Years	8 Years	4 Years	8 Years	
Reduce Annual Retirement Income by		$7,200	$13,000	$8,400	$14,900	
Increased Risk of Outliving Resources		74%	154%	77%	160%	
Reduction to Age 65 Portfolio Values:						
Likely More than:		$83,347	$68,800	$96,219	$80,088	
Likely Less than:		$476,095	$476,095	$508,916	$948,168	

Total annual savings is COMBINED annual employee AND employer contribution

AGE 30 WITH CURRENT 401(K) BALANCE OF $250,000

Total Annual Savings	$10,000		$15,000	
Allocation: **80% Stock/20% Bonds**				
Base Comfortable "In Balance" Case:				
Maximum Fair Total Expense	0.75%		0.75%	
Retirement Income @ Age 65	$82,000		$100,300	
Age 65 Range of Portfolio Values	$940,685 to $9,627,239		$1,171,121 to $11,009,958	
EXCESS EXPENSE:	**0.50%** (1.25% total)	**1.00%** (1.75% total)	**0.50%** (1.25% total)	**1.00%** (1.75% total)
COST OF EXCESS EXPENSE				
Additional Annual Savings Needed	$4,800	$10,500	$6,200	$12,900
Delay Retirement by:	3 Years	7 Years	3 Years	7 Years
Reduce Annual Retirement Income by	$13,700	$25,600	$17,900	$31,600
Increased Risk of Outliving Resources	49%	93%	50%	97%
Reduction to Age 65 Portfolio Values:				
Likely More than:	$132,744	$112,198	$151,827	$134,377
Likely Less than:	$1,341,829	$1,341,829	$1,473,517	$2,747,820
Allocation: **60% Stock/40% Bonds**				
Base Comfortable "In Balance" Case:				
Maximum Fair Total Expense	0.75%		0.75%	
Retirement Income @ Age 65	$68,600		$83,500	
Age 65 Range of Portfolio Values	$894,447 to $5,964,031		$1,131,526 to $6,987,202	
EXCESS EXPENSE:	**0.50%** (1.25% total)	**1.00%** (1.75% total)	**0.50%** (1.25% total)	**1.00%** (1.75% total)
COST OF EXCESS EXPENSE				
Additional Annual Savings Needed	$4,600	$10,100	$5,600	$11,900
Delay Retirement by:	4 Years	7 Years	3 Years	7 Years
Reduce Annual Retirement Income by	$11,900	$22,200	$13,900	$25,900
Increased Risk of Outliving Resources	64%	122%	64%	122%
Reduction to Age 65 Portfolio Values:				
Likely More than:	$117,063	$99,857	$145,374	$132,603
Likely Less than:	$828,445	$828,445	$929,407	$1,720,362
Allocation: **45% Stock/55% Bonds**				
Base Comfortable "In Balance" Case:				
Maximum Fair Total Expense	0.75%		0.75%	
Retirement Income @ Age 65	$56,700		$70,000	
Age 65 Range of Portfolio Values	$860,803 to $4,260,710		$1,078,998 to $5,028,313	
EXCESS EXPENSE:	**0.50%** (1.25% total)	**1.00%** (1.75% total)	**0.50%** (1.25% total)	**1.00%** (1.75% total)
COST OF EXCESS EXPENSE				
Additional Annual Savings Needed	$4,400	$9,700	$5,600	$11,900
Delay Retirement by:	4 Years	7 Years	4 Years	7 Years
Reduce Annual Retirement Income by	$10,000	$18,300	$12,000	$22,100
Increased Risk of Outliving Resources	73%	156%	76%	159%
Reduction to Age 65 Portfolio Values:				
Likely More than:	$114,591	$98,714	$137,786	$118,214
Likely Less than:	$587,299	$587,299	$671,569	$1,239,421

Total annual savings is COMBINED annual employee AND employer contribution

AGE 35 WITH CURRENT 401(K) BALANCE OF $25,000

Total Annual Savings	$2,500		$5,000	
Allocation: **80% Stock/20% Bonds**				
Base Comfortable "In Balance" Case:				
Maximum Fair Total Expense	0.75%		0.75%	
Retirement Income @ Age 65	$10,200		$16,600	
Age 65 Range of Portfolio Values	$131,176 to $988,433		$218,961 to $1,454,462	
EXCESS EXPENSE:	**0.50%**	**1.00%**	**0.50%**	**1.00%**
	(1.25% total)	(1.75% total)	(1.25% total)	(1.75% total)
COST OF EXCESS EXPENSE				
Additional Annual Savings Needed	$700	$1,500	$1,000	$2,200
Delay Retirement by:	3 Years	5 Years	3 Years	4 Years
Reduce Annual Retirement Income by	$1,500	$2,800	$2,300	$4,300
Increased Risk of Outliving Resources	31%	85%	34%	87%
Reduction to Age 65 Portfolio Values:				
Likely More than:	$14,392	$11,489	$19,826	$18,197
Likely Less than:	$107,943	$107,943	$148,059	$279,878

Allocation: **60% Stock/40% Bonds**				
Base Comfortable "In Balance" Case:				
Maximum Fair Total Expense	0.75%		0.75%	
Retirement Income @ Age 65	$8,800		$14,400	
Age 65 Range of Portfolio Values	$129,494 to $659,543		$217,091 to $1,004,552	
EXCESS EXPENSE:	**0.50%**	**1.00%**	**0.50%**	**1.00%**
	(1.25% total)	(1.75% total)	(1.25% total)	(1.75% total)
COST OF EXCESS EXPENSE				
Additional Annual Savings Needed	$700	$1,500	$1,100	$2,200
Delay Retirement by:	3 Years	5 Years	3 Years	5 Years
Reduce Annual Retirement Income by	$1,400	$2,500	$2,100	$3,900
Increased Risk of Outliving Resources	54%	118%	48%	111%
Reduction to Age 65 Portfolio Values:				
Likely More than:	$12,710	$11,891	$20,987	$17,141
Likely Less than:	$70,880	$70,880	$104,399	$195,664

Allocation: **45% Stock/55% Bonds**				
Base Comfortable "In Balance" Case:				
Maximum Fair Total Expense	0.75%		0.75%	
Retirement Income @ Age 65	$7,600		$12,700	
Age 65 Range of Portfolio Values	$125,436 to $496,354		$212,438 to $752,955	
EXCESS EXPENSE:	**0.50%**	**1.00%**	**0.50%**	**1.00%**
	(1.25% total)	(1.75% total)	(1.25% total)	(1.75% total)
COST OF EXCESS EXPENSE				
Additional Annual Savings Needed	$600	$1,400	$1,100	$2,300
Delay Retirement by:	3 Years	6 Years	3 Years	5 Years
Reduce Annual Retirement Income by	$1,100	$2,100	$1,900	$3,400
Increased Risk of Outliving Resources	69%	152%	69%	157%
Reduction to Age 65 Portfolio Values:				
Likely More than:	$12,595	$11,427	$19,723	$17,019
Likely Less than:	$53,719	$53,719	$72,960	$138,312

Total annual savings is COMBINED annual employee AND employer contribution

AGE 35 WITH CURRENT 401(K) BALANCE OF $25,000

Total Annual Savings	$10,000		$15,000	
Allocation: **80% Stock/20% Bonds**				
Base Comfortable "In Balance" Case:				
Maximum Fair Total Expense	0.75%		0.75%	
Retirement Income @ Age 65	$29,400		$42,300	
Age 65 Range of Portfolio Values	$398,139 to $2,467,936		$572,106 to $3,441,296	
EXCESS EXPENSE:	**0.50%**	**1.00%**	**0.50%**	**1.00%**
	(1.25% total)	(1.75% total)	(1.25% total)	(1.75% total)
COST OF EXCESS EXPENSE				
Additional Annual Savings Needed	$1,700	$3,700	$2,400	$5,100
Delay Retirement by:	2 Years	4 Years	2 Years	4 Years
Reduce Annual Retirement Income by	$3,900	$7,300	$5,500	$10,300
Increased Risk of Outliving Resources	32%	83%	34%	86%
Reduction to Age 65 Portfolio Values:				
Likely More than:	$34,668	$35,426	$52,615	$49,944
Likely Less than:	$250,602	$250,602	$337,971	$639,494

Allocation: **60% Stock/40% Bonds**				
Base Comfortable "In Balance" Case:				
Maximum Fair Total Expense	0.75%		0.75%	
Retirement Income @ Age 65	$25,700		$37,100	
Age 65 Range of Portfolio Values	$397,786 to $1,704,860		$577,420 to $2,436,363	
EXCESS EXPENSE:	**0.50%**	**1.00%**	**0.50%**	**1.00%**
	(1.25% total)	(1.75% total)	(1.25% total)	(1.75% total)
COST OF EXCESS EXPENSE				
Additional Annual Savings Needed	$1,800	$3,800	$2,500	$5,400
Delay Retirement by:	3 Years	5 Years	3 Years	5 Years
Reduce Annual Retirement Income by	$3,600	$6,600	$5,000	$9,300
Increased Risk of Outliving Resources	48%	114%	51%	118%
Reduction to Age 65 Portfolio Values:				
Likely More than:	$34,280	$30,361	$50,618	$44,181
Likely Less than:	$158,762	$158,762	$222,040	$432,778

Allocation: **45% Stock/55% Bonds**				
Base Comfortable "In Balance" Case:				
Maximum Fair Total Expense	0.75%		0.75%	
Retirement Income @ Age 65	$22,600		$32,600	
Age 65 Range of Portfolio Values	$385,566 to $1,299,881		$562,993 to $1,844,123	
EXCESS EXPENSE:	**0.50%**	**1.00%**	**0.50%**	**1.00%**
	(1.25% total)	(1.75% total)	(1.25% total)	(1.75% total)
COST OF EXCESS EXPENSE				
Additional Annual Savings Needed	$1,800	$4,000	$2,700	$5,800
Delay Retirement by:	3 Years	5 Years	3 Years	5 Years
Reduce Annual Retirement Income by	$3,100	$5,900	$4,600	$8,500
Increased Risk of Outliving Resources	63%	156%	63%	155%
Reduction to Age 65 Portfolio Values:				
Likely More than:	$32,476	$30,419	$49,283	$44,371
Likely Less than:	$122,489	$122,489	$168,877	$334,100

Total annual savings is COMBINED annual employee AND employer contribution

AGE 35 WITH CURRENT 401(K) BALANCE OF $75,000

Total Annual Savings	$2,500		$5,000	
Allocation: **80% Stock/20% Bonds**				
Base Comfortable "In Balance" Case:				
Maximum Fair Total Expense	0.75%		0.75%	
Retirement Income @ Age 65	$17,700		$24,100	
Age 65 Range of Portfolio Values	$204,977 to $2,048,600		$304,942 to $2,499,392	
EXCESS EXPENSE:	**0.50%**	**1.00%**	**0.50%**	**1.00%**
	(1.25% total)	(1.75% total)	(1.25% total)	(1.75% total)
COST OF EXCESS EXPENSE				
Additional Annual Savings Needed	$1,300	$2,700	$1,600	$3,300
Delay Retirement by:	3 Years	6 Years	3 Years	5 Years
Reduce Annual Retirement Income by	$2,800	$5,200	$3,700	$6,800
Increased Risk of Outliving Resources	39%	88%	33%	86%
Reduction to Age 65 Portfolio Values:				
Likely More than:	$23,951	$21,064	$33,739	$28,218
Likely Less than:	$242,255	$242,255	$287,432	$543,865

Allocation: **60% Stock/40% Bonds**				
Base Comfortable "In Balance" Case:				
Maximum Fair Total Expense	0.75%		0.75%	
Retirement Income @ Age 65	$14,900		$20,800	
Age 65 Range of Portfolio Values	$210,607 to $1,288,681		$301,501 to $1,632,534	
EXCESS EXPENSE:	**0.50%**	**1.00%**	**0.50%**	**1.00%**
	(1.25% total)	(1.75% total)	(1.25% total)	(1.75% total)
COST OF EXCESS EXPENSE				
Additional Annual Savings Needed	$1,200	$2,500	$1,600	$3,600
Delay Retirement by:	3 Years	6 Years	3 Years	6 Years
Reduce Annual Retirement Income by	$2,500	$4,500	$3,300	$6,000
Increased Risk of Outliving Resources	51%	114%	57%	119%
Reduction to Age 65 Portfolio Values:				
Likely More than:	$24,850	$21,827	$32,511	$28,404
Likely Less than:	$157,846	$157,846	$188,079	$353,471

Allocation: **45% Stock/55% Bonds**				
Base Comfortable "In Balance" Case:				
Maximum Fair Total Expense	0.75%		0.75%	
Retirement Income @ Age 65	$12,500		$17,700	
Age 65 Range of Portfolio Values	$203,253 to $931,839		$290,389 to $1,225,516	
EXCESS EXPENSE:	**0.50%**	**1.00%**	**0.50%**	**1.00%**
	(1.25% total)	(1.75% total)	(1.25% total)	(1.75% total)
COST OF EXCESS EXPENSE				
Additional Annual Savings Needed	$1,200	$2,400	$1,500	$3,200
Delay Retirement by:	3 Years	6 Years	3 Years	6 Years
Reduce Annual Retirement Income by	$2,000	$3,700	$2,700	$5,000
Increased Risk of Outliving Resources	58%	139%	66%	146%
Reduction to Age 65 Portfolio Values:				
Likely More than:	$24,075	$20,795	$31,547	$27,522
Likely Less than:	$113,092	$113,092	$138,466	$260,732

Total annual savings is COMBINED annual employee AND employer contribution

AGE 35 WITH CURRENT 401(K) BALANCE OF $75,000

Total Annual Savings	$10,000		$15,000	
Allocation: **80% Stock/20% Bonds**				
Base Comfortable "In Balance" Case:				
Maximum Fair Total Expense	0.75%		0.75%	
Retirement Income @ Age 65	$37,200		$49,900	
Age 65 Range of Portfolio Values	$481,484 to $3,411,221		$656,760 to $4,363,265	
EXCESS EXPENSE:	**0.50%**	**1.00%**	**0.50%**	**1.00%**
	(1.25% total)	(1.75% total)	(1.25% total)	(1.75% total)
COST OF EXCESS EXPENSE				
Additional Annual Savings Needed	$2,400	$5,100	$3,100	$6,500
Delay Retirement by:	3 Years	5 Years	3 Years	5 Years
Reduce Annual Retirement Income by	$5,300	$10,000	$7,000	$13,000
Increased Risk of Outliving Resources	32%	85%	32%	84%
Reduction to Age 65 Portfolio Values:				
Likely More than:	$46,563	$45,459	$59,475	$54,593
Likely Less than:	$364,109	$364,109	$444,176	$839,634

Allocation: **60% Stock/40% Bonds**				
Base Comfortable "In Balance" Case:				
Maximum Fair Total Expense	0.75%		0.75%	
Retirement Income @ Age 65	$32,100		$43,200	
Age 65 Range of Portfolio Values	$477,733 to $2,331,808		$651,273 to $3,013,655	
EXCESS EXPENSE:	**0.50%**	**1.00%**	**0.50%**	**1.00%**
	(1.25% total)	(1.75% total)	(1.25% total)	(1.75% total)
COST OF EXCESS EXPENSE				
Additional Annual Savings Needed	$2,500	$5,200	$3,100	$6,600
Delay Retirement by:	3 Years	5 Years	3 Years	5 Years
Reduce Annual Retirement Income by	$4,900	$8,900	$6,100	$11,500
Increased Risk of Outliving Resources	51%	114%	48%	111%
Reduction to Age 65 Portfolio Values:				
Likely More than:	$47,181	$43,791	$62,962	$51,421
Likely Less than:	$261,930	$261,930	$313,196	$586,991

Allocation: **45% Stock/55% Bonds**				
Base Comfortable "In Balance" Case:				
Maximum Fair Total Expense	0.75%		0.75%	
Retirement Income @ Age 65	$28,000		$38,100	
Age 65 Range of Portfolio Values	$463,039 to $1,754,237		$637,313 to $2,258,866	
EXCESS EXPENSE:	**0.50%**	**1.00%**	**0.50%**	**1.00%**
	(1.25% total)	(1.75% total)	(1.25% total)	(1.75% total)
COST OF EXCESS EXPENSE				
Additional Annual Savings Needed	$2,300	$5,100	$3,100	$6,700
Delay Retirement by:	3 Years	6 Years	3 Years	5 Years
Reduce Annual Retirement Income by	$3,900	$7,500	$5,600	$10,200
Increased Risk of Outliving Resources	71%	157%	69%	157%
Reduction to Age 65 Portfolio Values:				
Likely More than:	$44,947	$38,682	$59,167	$51,058
Likely Less than:	$185,598	$185,598	$218,882	$414,937

Total annual savings is COMBINED annual employee AND employer contribution

AGE 35 WITH CURRENT 401(K) BALANCE OF $150,000

Total Annual Savings	$2,500		$5,000	
Allocation: **80% Stock/20% Bonds**				
Base Comfortable "In Balance" Case:				
Maximum Fair Total Expense	0.75%		0.75%	
Retirement Income @ Age 65	$28,800		$35,500	
Age 65 Range of Portfolio Values	$320,869 to $3,589,868		$409,833 to $4,097,079	
EXCESS EXPENSE:	**0.50%**	**1.00%**	**0.50%**	**1.00%**
	(1.25% total)	(1.75% total)	(1.25% total)	(1.75% total)
COST OF EXCESS EXPENSE				
Additional Annual Savings Needed	$2,100	$4,600	$2,600	$5,400
Delay Retirement by:	4 Years	7 Years	3 Years	6 Years
Reduce Annual Retirement Income by	$4,700	$8,800	$5,700	$10,500
Increased Risk of Outliving Resources	38%	86%	38%	87%
Reduction to Age 65 Portfolio Values:				
Likely More than:	$43,105	$37,443	$47,903	$42,127
Likely Less than:	$446,201	$446,201	$484,511	$921,050

Allocation: **60% Stock/40% Bonds**				
Base Comfortable "In Balance" Case:				
Maximum Fair Total Expense	0.75%		0.75%	
Retirement Income @ Age 65	$24,000		$29,800	
Age 65 Range of Portfolio Values	$323,839 to $2,228,147		$421,215 to $2,577,361	
EXCESS EXPENSE:	**0.50%**	**1.00%**	**0.50%**	**1.00%**
	(1.25% total)	(1.75% total)	(1.25% total)	(1.75% total)
COST OF EXCESS EXPENSE				
Additional Annual Savings Needed	$2,000	$4,200	$2,400	$5,000
Delay Retirement by:	4 Years	7 Years	3 Years	6 Years
Reduce Annual Retirement Income by	$4,000	$7,400	$4,900	$9,000
Increased Risk of Outliving Resources	52%	109%	51%	114%
Reduction to Age 65 Portfolio Values:				
Likely More than:	$42,228	$36,848	$49,702	$43,652
Likely Less than:	$279,897	$279,897	$315,692	$593,079

Allocation: **45% Stock/55% Bonds**				
Base Comfortable "In Balance" Case:				
Maximum Fair Total Expense	0.75%		0.75%	
Retirement Income @ Age 65	$20,200		$25,100	
Age 65 Range of Portfolio Values	$319,553 to $1,587,014		$406,384 to $1,863,557	
EXCESS EXPENSE:	**0.50%**	**1.00%**	**0.50%**	**1.00%**
	(1.25% total)	(1.75% total)	(1.25% total)	(1.75% total)
COST OF EXCESS EXPENSE				
Additional Annual Savings Needed	$2,000	$4,200	$2,300	$4,700
Delay Retirement by:	4 Years	7 Years	3 Years	6 Years
Reduce Annual Retirement Income by	$3,500	$6,300	$4,100	$7,500
Increased Risk of Outliving Resources	63%	146%	60%	141%
Reduction to Age 65 Portfolio Values:				
Likely More than:	$41,584	$36,221	$48,150	$41,589
Likely Less than:	$199,305	$199,305	$226,185	$423,243

Total annual savings is COMBINED annual employee AND employer contribution

AGE 35 WITH CURRENT 401(K) BALANCE OF $150,000

Total Annual Savings	$10,000		$15,000	
Allocation: **80% Stock/20% Bonds**				
Base Comfortable "In Balance" Case:				
Maximum Fair Total Expense	0.75%		0.75%	
Retirement Income @ Age 65	$48,200		$61,300	
Age 65 Range of Portfolio Values	$609,884 to $4,998,784		$786,932 to $5,930,478	
EXCESS EXPENSE:	**0.50%**	**1.00%**	**0.50%**	**1.00%**
	(1.25% total)	(1.75% total)	(1.25% total)	(1.75% total)
COST OF EXCESS EXPENSE				
Additional Annual Savings Needed	$3,200	$6,600	$3,900	$8,600
Delay Retirement by:	3 Years	5 Years	3 Years	5 Years
Reduce Annual Retirement Income by	$7,300	$13,600	$9,100	$16,700
Increased Risk of Outliving Resources	33%	86%	31%	86%
Reduction to Age 65 Portfolio Values:				
Likely More than:	$67,479	$56,435	$86,351	$68,931
Likely Less than:	$574,865	$574,865	$647,659	$1,244,369
Allocation: **60% Stock/40% Bonds**				
Base Comfortable "In Balance" Case:				
Maximum Fair Total Expense	0.75%		0.75%	
Retirement Income @ Age 65	$41,600		$53,200	
Age 65 Range of Portfolio Values	$603,001 to $3,265,069		$776,477 to $3,956,775	
EXCESS EXPENSE:	**0.50%**	**1.00%**	**0.50%**	**1.00%**
	(1.25% total)	(1.75% total)	(1.25% total)	(1.75% total)
COST OF EXCESS EXPENSE				
Additional Annual Savings Needed	$3,200	$7,100	$4,300	$8,800
Delay Retirement by:	3 Years	6 Years	3 Years	5 Years
Reduce Annual Retirement Income by	$6,500	$11,900	$8,300	$15,200
Increased Risk of Outliving Resources	57%	119%	54%	118%
Reduction to Age 65 Portfolio Values:				
Likely More than:	$65,020	$56,809	$76,259	$71,343
Likely Less than:	$376,158	$376,158	$425,284	$802,994
Allocation: **45% Stock/55% Bonds**				
Base Comfortable "In Balance" Case:				
Maximum Fair Total Expense	0.75%		0.75%	
Retirement Income @ Age 65	$35,500		$45,800	
Age 65 Range of Portfolio Values	$580,657 to $2,450,910		$752,374 to $2,977,880	
EXCESS EXPENSE:	**0.50%**	**1.00%**	**0.50%**	**1.00%**
	(1.25% total)	(1.75% total)	(1.25% total)	(1.75% total)
COST OF EXCESS EXPENSE				
Additional Annual Savings Needed	$3,000	$6,300	$3,700	$8,200
Delay Retirement by:	3 Years	6 Years	3 Years	6 Years
Reduce Annual Retirement Income by	$5,500	$10,000	$6,600	$12,300
Increased Risk of Outliving Resources	67%	147%	69%	150%
Reduction to Age 65 Portfolio Values:				
Likely More than:	$63,095	$55,043	$75,570	$68,560
Likely Less than:	$276,932	$276,932	$322,313	$607,923

Total annual savings is COMBINED annual employee AND employer contribution

AGE 35 WITH CURRENT 401(K) BALANCE OF $250,000

Total Annual Savings	$2,500		$5,000	
Allocation: **80% Stock/20% Bonds**				
Base Comfortable "In Balance" Case:				
Maximum Fair Total Expense		0.75%		0.75%
Retirement Income @ Age 65		$43,000		$50,200
Age 65 Range of Portfolio Values	$481,768 to $5,631,026		$563,199 to $6,156,829	
EXCESS EXPENSE:	**0.50%**	**1.00%**	**0.50%**	**1.00%**
	(1.25% total)	(1.75% total)	(1.25% total)	(1.75% total)
COST OF EXCESS EXPENSE				
Additional Annual Savings Needed	$2,800	$6,600	$3,600	$8,000
Delay Retirement by:	4 Years	7 Years	3 Years	7 Years
Reduce Annual Retirement Income by	$7,200	$13,300	$8,000	$15,300
Increased Risk of Outliving Resources	38%	86%	39%	88%
Reduction to Age 65 Portfolio Values:				
Likely More than:	$66,001	$59,976	$74,030	$65,137
Likely Less than:	$710,928	$710,928	$758,508	$1,425,093

Allocation: **60% Stock/40% Bonds**				
Base Comfortable "In Balance" Case:				
Maximum Fair Total Expense		0.75%		0.75%
Retirement Income @ Age 65		$36,500		$41,900
Age 65 Range of Portfolio Values	$479,033 to $3,465,980		$571,221 to $3,827,406	
EXCESS EXPENSE:	**0.50%**	**1.00%**	**0.50%**	**1.00%**
	(1.25% total)	(1.75% total)	(1.25% total)	(1.75% total)
COST OF EXCESS EXPENSE				
Additional Annual Savings Needed	$3,300	$6,900	$3,500	$7,300
Delay Retirement by:	4 Years	7 Years	4 Years	7 Years
Reduce Annual Retirement Income by	$6,400	$11,900	$7,000	$12,800
Increased Risk of Outliving Resources	55%	113%	51%	111%
Reduction to Age 65 Portfolio Values:				
Likely More than:	$65,403	$57,716	$72,097	$64,314
Likely Less than:	$448,344	$448,344	$474,631	$891,220

Allocation: **45% Stock/55% Bonds**				
Base Comfortable "In Balance" Case:				
Maximum Fair Total Expense		0.75%		0.75%
Retirement Income @ Age 65		$30,100		$35,200
Age 65 Range of Portfolio Values	$473,156 to $2,462,291		$562,859 to $2,741,644	
EXCESS EXPENSE:	**0.50%**	**1.00%**	**0.50%**	**1.00%**
	(1.25% total)	(1.75% total)	(1.25% total)	(1.75% total)
COST OF EXCESS EXPENSE				
Additional Annual Savings Needed	$2,900	$6,200	$3,300	$7,100
Delay Retirement by:	4 Years	7 Years	4 Years	7 Years
Reduce Annual Retirement Income by	$5,300	$9,600	$5,800	$10,700
Increased Risk of Outliving Resources	61%	137%	62%	143%
Reduction to Age 65 Portfolio Values:				
Likely More than:	$64,414	$56,057	$71,901	$63,243
Likely Less than:	$315,025	$315,025	$340,032	$638,296

Total annual savings is COMBINED annual employee AND employer contribution

AGE 35 WITH CURRENT 401(K) BALANCE OF $250,000

Total Annual Savings		$10,000		$15,000	
Allocation: **80% Stock/20% Bonds**					
Base Comfortable "In Balance" Case:					
Maximum Fair Total Expense		0.75%		0.75%	
Retirement Income @ Age 65		$63,600		$75,800	
Age 65 Range of Portfolio Values		$751,544 to $7,153,645		$954,870 to $8,020,945	
EXCESS EXPENSE:		**0.50%**	**1.00%**	**0.50%**	**1.00%**
		(1.25% total)	(1.75% total)	(1.25% total)	(1.75% total)
COST OF EXCESS EXPENSE					
Additional Annual Savings Needed		$4,700	$9,300	$4,900	$10,500
Delay Retirement by:		3 Years	6 Years	3 Years	5 Years
Reduce Annual Retirement Income by		$10,100	$18,700	$11,400	$21,600
Increased Risk of Outliving Resources		36%	89%	31%	85%
Reduction to Age 65 Portfolio Values:					
Likely More than:		$89,491	$74,951	$105,111	$97,796
Likely Less than:		$859,076	$859,076	$918,971	$1,747,165

Allocation: **60% Stock/40% Bonds**					
Base Comfortable "In Balance" Case:					
Maximum Fair Total Expense		0.75%		0.75%	
Retirement Income @ Age 65		$53,500		$65,100	
Age 65 Range of Portfolio Values		$765,989 to $4,507,266		$951,963 to $5,220,966	
EXCESS EXPENSE:		**0.50%**	**1.00%**	**0.50%**	**1.00%**
		(1.25% total)	(1.75% total)	(1.25% total)	(1.75% total)
COST OF EXCESS EXPENSE					
Additional Annual Savings Needed		$4,200	$8,900	$4,800	$11,000
Delay Retirement by:		3 Years	6 Years	3 Years	6 Years
Reduce Annual Retirement Income by		$8,900	$15,800	$10,000	$18,600
Increased Risk of Outliving Resources		51%	114%	53%	118%
Reduction to Age 65 Portfolio Values:					
Likely More than:		$86,740	$78,973	$108,042	$95,174
Likely Less than:		$533,688	$533,688	$609,129	$1,143,046

Allocation: **45% Stock/55% Bonds**					
Base Comfortable "In Balance" Case:					
Maximum Fair Total Expense		0.75%		0.75%	
Retirement Income @ Age 65		$45,300		$55,600	
Age 65 Range of Portfolio Values		$737,722 to $3,293,407		$916,110 to $3,887,146	
EXCESS EXPENSE:		**0.50%**	**1.00%**	**0.50%**	**1.00%**
		(1.25% total)	(1.75% total)	(1.25% total)	(1.75% total)
COST OF EXCESS EXPENSE					
Additional Annual Savings Needed		$3,900	$8,300	$4,600	$9,800
Delay Retirement by:		3 Years	6 Years	3 Years	6 Years
Reduce Annual Retirement Income by		$7,500	$13,300	$8,500	$15,800
Increased Risk of Outliving Resources		59%	142%	63%	143%
Reduction to Age 65 Portfolio Values:					
Likely More than:		$86,745	$74,366	$104,108	$88,528
Likely Less than:		$387,513	$387,513	$438,231	$825,658

Total annual savings is COMBINED annual employee AND employer contribution

AGE 40 WITH CURRENT 401(K) BALANCE OF $25,000

Total Annual Savings		$2,500		$5,000	
Allocation: **80% Stock/20% Bonds**					
Base Comfortable "In Balance" Case:					
Maximum Fair Total Expense		0.75%		0.75%	
Retirement Income @ Age 65		$7,500		$12,100	
Age 65 Range of Portfolio Values		$101,132 to $650,685		$165,936 to $949,110	
EXCESS EXPENSE:		**0.50%**	**1.00%**	**0.50%**	**1.00%**
		(1.25% total)	(1.75% total)	(1.25% total)	(1.75% total)
COST OF EXCESS EXPENSE					
Additional Annual Savings Needed		$600	$1,400	$1,000	$2,000
Delay Retirement by:		3 Years	5 Years	2 Years	4 Years
Reduce Annual Retirement Income by		$1,000	$1,900	$1,600	$2,900
Increased Risk of Outliving Resources		39%	82%	37%	80%
Reduction to Age 65 Portfolio Values:					
Likely More than:		$8,650	$8,144	$13,084	$11,095
Likely Less than:		$61,313	$61,313	$82,139	$157,963

Allocation: **60% Stock/40% Bonds**					
Base Comfortable "In Balance" Case:					
Maximum Fair Total Expense		0.75%		0.75%	
Retirement Income @ Age 65		$6,500		$10,700	
Age 65 Range of Portfolio Values		$100,394 to $455,780		$169,184 to $682,395	
EXCESS EXPENSE:		**0.50%**	**1.00%**	**0.50%**	**1.00%**
		(1.25% total)	(1.75% total)	(1.25% total)	(1.75% total)
COST OF EXCESS EXPENSE					
Additional Annual Savings Needed		$600	$1,200	$900	$2,000
Delay Retirement by:		2 Years	5 Years	2 Years	4 Years
Reduce Annual Retirement Income by		$800	$1,600	$1,400	$2,600
Increased Risk of Outliving Resources		42%	106%	38%	105%
Reduction to Age 65 Portfolio Values:					
Likely More than:		$8,923	$7,954	$13,150	$12,196
Likely Less than:		$41,521	$41,521	$59,536	$113,645

Allocation: **45% Stock/55% Bonds**					
Base Comfortable "In Balance" Case:					
Maximum Fair Total Expense		0.75%		0.75%	
Retirement Income @ Age 65		$5,700		$9,400	
Age 65 Range of Portfolio Values		$102,050 to $344,786		$170,546 to $530,781	
EXCESS EXPENSE:		**0.50%**	**1.00%**	**0.50%**	**1.00%**
		(1.25% total)	(1.75% total)	(1.25% total)	(1.75% total)
COST OF EXCESS EXPENSE					
Additional Annual Savings Needed		$600	$1,300	$1,000	$2,000
Delay Retirement by:		3 Years	5 Years	2 Years	5 Years
Reduce Annual Retirement Income by		$800	$1,500	$1,200	$2,300
Increased Risk of Outliving Resources		47%	118%	46%	117%
Reduction to Age 65 Portfolio Values:					
Likely More than:		$8,948	$8,064	$14,118	$12,079
Likely Less than:		$32,265	$32,265	$44,955	$84,449

Total annual savings is COMBINED annual employee AND employer contribution

AGE 40 WITH CURRENT 401(K) BALANCE OF $25,000

Total Annual Savings	$10,000		$15,000	
Allocation: **80% Stock/20% Bonds**				
Base Comfortable "In Balance" Case:				
Maximum Fair Total Expense	0.75%		0.75%	
Retirement Income @ Age 65	$21,100		$30,300	
Age 65 Range of Portfolio Values	$297,302 to $1,555,037		$430,621 to $2,192,923	
EXCESS EXPENSE:	**0.50%**	**1.00%**	**0.50%**	**1.00%**
	(1.25% total)	(1.75% total)	(1.25% total)	(1.75% total)
COST OF EXCESS EXPENSE				
Additional Annual Savings Needed	$1,600	$3,300	$2,200	$4,700
Delay Retirement by:	2 Years	4 Years	2 Years	4 Years
Reduce Annual Retirement Income by	$2,500	$4,800	$3,700	$6,900
Increased Risk of Outliving Resources	33%	68%	34%	69%
Reduction to Age 65 Portfolio Values:				
Likely More than:	$20,059	$19,669	$30,266	$27,831
Likely Less than:	$127,165	$127,165	$171,106	$328,416
Allocation: **60% Stock/40% Bonds**				
Base Comfortable "In Balance" Case:				
Maximum Fair Total Expense	0.75%		0.75%	
Retirement Income @ Age 65	$18,900		$27,200	
Age 65 Range of Portfolio Values	$307,414 to $1,128,064		$442,541 to $1,579,146	
EXCESS EXPENSE:	**0.50%**	**1.00%**	**0.50%**	**1.00%**
	(1.25% total)	(1.75% total)	(1.25% total)	(1.75% total)
COST OF EXCESS EXPENSE				
Additional Annual Savings Needed	$1,600	$3,400	$2,200	$4,900
Delay Retirement by:	2 Years	4 Years	2 Years	4 Years
Reduce Annual Retirement Income by	$2,300	$4,300	$3,300	$6,200
Increased Risk of Outliving Resources	35%	99%	39%	96%
Reduction to Age 65 Portfolio Values:				
Likely More than:	$23,179	$19,905	$29,169	$28,232
Likely Less than:	$92,018	$92,018	$122,030	$232,023
Allocation: **45% Stock/55% Bonds**				
Base Comfortable "In Balance" Case:				
Maximum Fair Total Expense	0.75%		0.75%	
Retirement Income @ Age 65	$16,700		$24,000	
Age 65 Range of Portfolio Values	$306,389 to $901,296		$442,520 to $1,269,782	
EXCESS EXPENSE:	**0.50%**	**1.00%**	**0.50%**	**1.00%**
	(1.25% total)	(1.75% total)	(1.25% total)	(1.75% total)
COST OF EXCESS EXPENSE				
Additional Annual Savings Needed	$1,600	$3,400	$2,200	$4,900
Delay Retirement by:	2 Years	4 Years	2 Years	4 Years
Reduce Annual Retirement Income by	$2,100	$3,900	$2,900	$5,500
Increased Risk of Outliving Resources	43%	112%	46%	113%
Reduction to Age 65 Portfolio Values:				
Likely More than:	$22,603	$20,699	$32,299	$28,494
Likely Less than:	$69,089	$69,089	$95,711	$183,489

Total annual savings is COMBINED annual employee AND employer contribution

AGE 40 WITH CURRENT 401(K) BALANCE OF $75,000

Total Annual Savings	$2,500		$5,000	
Allocation: **80% Stock/20% Bonds**				
Base Comfortable "In Balance" Case:				
Maximum Fair Total Expense	0.75%		0.75%	
Retirement Income @ Age 65	$13,100		$17,800	
Age 65 Range of Portfolio Values	$165,446 to $1,322,446		$232,781 to $1,634,043	
EXCESS EXPENSE:	**0.50%**	**1.00%**	**0.50%**	**1.00%**
	(1.25% total)	(1.75% total)	(1.25% total)	(1.75% total)
COST OF EXCESS EXPENSE				
Additional Annual Savings Needed	$1,100	$2,400	$1,400	$3,100
Delay Retirement by:	3 Years	5 Years	3 Years	5 Years
Reduce Annual Retirement Income by	$1,900	$3,500	$2,400	$4,500
Increased Risk of Outliving Resources	36%	80%	36%	81%
Reduction to Age 65 Portfolio Values:				
Likely More than:	$17,453	$16,577	$21,316	$19,236
Likely Less than:	$136,407	$136,407	$162,856	$303,168
Allocation: **60% Stock/40% Bonds**				
Base Comfortable "In Balance" Case:				
Maximum Fair Total Expense	0.75%		0.75%	
Retirement Income @ Age 65	$11,600		$15,700	
Age 65 Range of Portfolio Values	$166,956 to $894,724		$235,218 to $1,125,381	
EXCESS EXPENSE:	**0.50%**	**1.00%**	**0.50%**	**1.00%**
	(1.25% total)	(1.75% total)	(1.25% total)	(1.75% total)
COST OF EXCESS EXPENSE				
Additional Annual Savings Needed	$1,200	$2,500	$1,600	$3,200
Delay Retirement by:	3 Years	6 Years	3 Years	5 Years
Reduce Annual Retirement Income by	$1,700	$3,300	$2,200	$4,100
Increased Risk of Outliving Resources	51%	104%	47%	103%
Reduction to Age 65 Portfolio Values:				
Likely More than:	$17,340	$15,696	$21,665	$20,052
Likely Less than:	$92,036	$92,036	$106,627	$202,916
Allocation: **45% Stock/55% Bonds**				
Base Comfortable "In Balance" Case:				
Maximum Fair Total Expense	0.75%		0.75%	
Retirement Income @ Age 65	$9,900		$13,700	
Age 65 Range of Portfolio Values	$165,045 to $668,951		$235,597 to $846,206	
EXCESS EXPENSE:	**0.50%**	**1.00%**	**0.50%**	**1.00%**
	(1.25% total)	(1.75% total)	(1.25% total)	(1.75% total)
COST OF EXCESS EXPENSE				
Additional Annual Savings Needed	$1,100	$2,400	$1,600	$3,300
Delay Retirement by:	3 Years	6 Years	3 Years	6 Years
Reduce Annual Retirement Income by	$1,500	$2,700	$2,000	$3,700
Increased Risk of Outliving Resources	53%	117%	52%	118%
Reduction to Age 65 Portfolio Values:				
Likely More than:	$16,342	$14,786	$21,171	$18,989
Likely Less than:	$67,868	$67,868	$81,847	$154,451

Total annual savings is COMBINED annual employee AND employer contribution

AGE 40 WITH CURRENT 401(K) BALANCE OF $75,000

Total Annual Savings	$10,000		$15,000	
Allocation: **80% Stock/20% Bonds**				
Base Comfortable "In Balance" Case:				
Maximum Fair Total Expense	0.75%		0.75%	
Retirement Income @ Age 65	$27,300		$36,300	
Age 65 Range of Portfolio Values	$371,871 to $2,248,148		$497,809 to $2,847,331	
EXCESS EXPENSE:	**0.50%**	**1.00%**	**0.50%**	**1.00%**
	(1.25% total)	(1.75% total)	(1.25% total)	(1.75% total)
COST OF EXCESS EXPENSE				
Additional Annual Savings Needed	$2,300	$4,800	$3,000	$6,000
Delay Retirement by:	2 Years	5 Years	2 Years	4 Years
Reduce Annual Retirement Income by	$3,700	$6,800	$4,800	$8,700
Increased Risk of Outliving Resources	39%	83%	37%	80%
Reduction to Age 65 Portfolio Values:				
Likely More than:	$31,958	$28,855	$39,253	$33,285
Likely Less than:	$208,136	$208,136	$246,418	$473,890
Allocation: **60% Stock/40% Bonds**				
Base Comfortable "In Balance" Case:				
Maximum Fair Total Expense	0.75%		0.75%	
Retirement Income @ Age 65	$24,000		$32,200	
Age 65 Range of Portfolio Values	$370,135 to $1,593,409		$507,432 to $2,047,065	
EXCESS EXPENSE:	**0.50%**	**1.00%**	**0.50%**	**1.00%**
	(1.25% total)	(1.75% total)	(1.25% total)	(1.75% total)
COST OF EXCESS EXPENSE				
Additional Annual Savings Needed	$2,200	$4,600	$2,800	$5,900
Delay Retirement by:	3 Years	5 Years	2 Years	4 Years
Reduce Annual Retirement Income by	$3,200	$5,900	$4,100	$7,700
Increased Risk of Outliving Resources	40%	103%	37%	103%
Reduction to Age 65 Portfolio Values:				
Likely More than:	$29,299	$28,313	$39,451	$36,590
Likely Less than:	$142,555	$142,555	$178,609	$340,935
Allocation: **45% Stock/55% Bonds**				
Base Comfortable "In Balance" Case:				
Maximum Fair Total Expense	0.75%		0.75%	
Retirement Income @ Age 65	$20,900		$28,200	
Age 65 Range of Portfolio Values	$373,810 to $1,217,411		$511,639 to $1,592,342	
EXCESS EXPENSE:	**0.50%**	**1.00%**	**0.50%**	**1.00%**
	(1.25% total)	(1.75% total)	(1.25% total)	(1.75% total)
COST OF EXCESS EXPENSE				
Additional Annual Savings Needed	$2,200	$4,500	$2,800	$5,900
Delay Retirement by:	3 Years	5 Years	2 Years	5 Years
Reduce Annual Retirement Income by	$2,800	$5,300	$3,600	$6,900
Increased Risk of Outliving Resources	45%	114%	46%	117%
Reduction to Age 65 Portfolio Values:				
Likely More than:	$29,069	$28,837	$42,355	$36,238
Likely Less than:	$106,781	$106,781	$134,864	$253,346

Total annual savings is COMBINED annual employee AND employer contribution

AGE 40 WITH CURRENT 401(K) BALANCE OF $150,000

Total Annual Savings	$2,500		$5,000	
Allocation: **80% Stock/20% Bonds**				
Base Comfortable "In Balance" Case:				
Maximum Fair Total Expense	0.75%		0.75%	
Retirement Income @ Age 65	$21,400		$26,200	
Age 65 Range of Portfolio Values	$257,976 to $2,350,616		$330,892 to $2,644,892	
EXCESS EXPENSE:	**0.50%**	**1.00%**	**0.50%**	**1.00%**
	(1.25% total)	(1.75% total)	(1.25% total)	(1.75% total)
COST OF EXCESS EXPENSE				
Additional Annual Savings Needed	$1,900	$4,000	$2,200	$4,700
Delay Retirement by:	3 Years	6 Years	3 Years	5 Years
Reduce Annual Retirement Income by	$3,300	$6,000	$3,800	$7,000
Increased Risk of Outliving Resources	35%	82%	36%	80%
Reduction to Age 65 Portfolio Values:				
Likely More than:	$28,055	$24,932	$34,905	$33,156
Likely Less than:	$249,447	$249,447	$272,815	$517,990
Allocation: **60% Stock/40% Bonds**				
Base Comfortable "In Balance" Case:				
Maximum Fair Total Expense	0.75%		0.75%	
Retirement Income @ Age 65	$18,900		$23,300	
Age 65 Range of Portfolio Values	$260,416 to $1,574,001		$333,791 to $1,789,327	
EXCESS EXPENSE:	**0.50%**	**1.00%**	**0.50%**	**1.00%**
	(1.25% total)	(1.75% total)	(1.25% total)	(1.75% total)
COST OF EXCESS EXPENSE				
Additional Annual Savings Needed	$1,900	$4,200	$2,500	$5,100
Delay Retirement by:	3 Years	6 Years	3 Years	6 Years
Reduce Annual Retirement Income by	$2,800	$5,300	$3,500	$6,600
Increased Risk of Outliving Resources	49%	101%	53%	105%
Reduction to Age 65 Portfolio Values:				
Likely More than:	$29,271	$26,298	$34,680	$31,392
Likely Less than:	$169,235	$169,235	$184,073	$349,446
Allocation: **45% Stock/55% Bonds**				
Base Comfortable "In Balance" Case:				
Maximum Fair Total Expense	0.75%		0.75%	
Retirement Income @ Age 65	$16,100		$19,800	
Age 65 Range of Portfolio Values	$259,757 to $1,168,506		$330,090 to $1,337,903	
EXCESS EXPENSE:	**0.50%**	**1.00%**	**0.50%**	**1.00%**
	(1.25% total)	(1.75% total)	(1.25% total)	(1.75% total)
COST OF EXCESS EXPENSE				
Additional Annual Savings Needed	$1,800	$3,900	$2,100	$4,700
Delay Retirement by:	3 Years	6 Years	3 Years	6 Years
Reduce Annual Retirement Income by	$2,500	$4,700	$2,900	$5,400
Increased Risk of Outliving Resources	53%	120%	53%	117%
Reduction to Age 65 Portfolio Values:				
Likely More than:	$28,433	$25,753	$32,683	$29,573
Likely Less than:	$126,256	$126,256	$135,737	$257,672

Total annual savings is COMBINED annual employee AND employer contribution

AGE 40 WITH CURRENT 401(K) BALANCE OF $150,000

Total Annual Savings	$10,000		$15,000	
Allocation: **80% Stock/20% Bonds**				
Base Comfortable "In Balance" Case:				
Maximum Fair Total Expense	0.75%		0.75%	
Retirement Income @ Age 65	$35,700		$45,300	
Age 65 Range of Portfolio Values	$465,440 to $3,267,966		$606,430 to $3,903,744	
EXCESS EXPENSE:	**0.50%**	**1.00%**	**0.50%**	**1.00%**
	(1.25% total)	(1.75% total)	(1.25% total)	(1.75% total)
COST OF EXCESS EXPENSE				
Additional Annual Savings Needed	$2,800	$6,300	$3,700	$8,100
Delay Retirement by:	3 Years	5 Years	3 Years	5 Years
Reduce Annual Retirement Income by	$4,900	$9,100	$6,100	$11,200
Increased Risk of Outliving Resources	35%	80%	40%	83%
Reduction to Age 65 Portfolio Values:				
Likely More than:	$42,632	$38,472	$51,901	$48,867
Likely Less than:	$325,713	$325,713	$367,877	$700,609

Allocation: **60% Stock/40% Bonds**				
Base Comfortable "In Balance" Case:				
Maximum Fair Total Expense	0.75%		0.75%	
Retirement Income @ Age 65	$31,500		$39,500	
Age 65 Range of Portfolio Values	$470,314 to $2,250,640		$601,757 to $2,734,070	
EXCESS EXPENSE:	**0.50%**	**1.00%**	**0.50%**	**1.00%**
	(1.25% total)	(1.75% total)	(1.25% total)	(1.75% total)
COST OF EXCESS EXPENSE				
Additional Annual Savings Needed	$3,200	$6,300	$3,500	$7,500
Delay Retirement by:	3 Years	5 Years	3 Years	5 Years
Reduce Annual Retirement Income by	$4,500	$8,300	$5,200	$9,800
Increased Risk of Outliving Resources	48%	104%	40%	102%
Reduction to Age 65 Portfolio Values:				
Likely More than:	$43,329	$40,104	$53,540	$47,722
Likely Less than:	$213,254	$213,254	$249,123	$478,723

Allocation: **45% Stock/55% Bonds**				
Base Comfortable "In Balance" Case:				
Maximum Fair Total Expense	0.75%		0.75%	
Retirement Income @ Age 65	$27,400		$34,400	
Age 65 Range of Portfolio Values	$471,193 to $1,692,411		$612,058 to $2,068,474	
EXCESS EXPENSE:	**0.50%**	**1.00%**	**0.50%**	**1.00%**
	(1.25% total)	(1.75% total)	(1.25% total)	(1.75% total)
COST OF EXCESS EXPENSE				
Additional Annual Savings Needed	$3,100	$6,500	$3,500	$7,700
Delay Retirement by:	3 Years	6 Years	3 Years	5 Years
Reduce Annual Retirement Income by	$3,900	$7,300	$4,800	$8,700
Increased Risk of Outliving Resources	52%	118%	46%	113%
Reduction to Age 65 Portfolio Values:				
Likely More than:	$42,340	$37,979	$53,691	$48,384
Likely Less than:	$163,694	$163,694	$193,591	$358,946

Total annual savings is COMBINED annual employee AND employer contribution

AGE 40 WITH CURRENT 401(K) BALANCE OF $250,000

Total Annual Savings	$2,500		$5,000	
Allocation: **80% Stock/20% Bonds**				
Base Comfortable "In Balance" Case:				
Maximum Fair Total Expense	0.75%		0.75%	
Retirement Income @ Age 65	$32,600		$37,400	
Age 65 Range of Portfolio Values	$378,895 to $3,700,618		$461,064 to $4,017,171	
EXCESS EXPENSE:	**0.50%** (1.25% total)	**1.00%** (1.75% total)	**0.50%** (1.25% total)	**1.00%** (1.75% total)
COST OF EXCESS EXPENSE				
Additional Annual Savings Needed	$3,000	$6,200	$3,300	$7,100
Delay Retirement by:	3 Years	6 Years	3 Years	6 Years
Reduce Annual Retirement Income by	$5,000	$9,500	$5,700	$10,400
Increased Risk of Outliving Resources	34%	82%	34%	79%
Reduction to Age 65 Portfolio Values:				
Likely More than:	$44,504	$39,515	$51,311	$46,418
Likely Less than:	$399,042	$399,042	$426,759	$809,583

Allocation: **60% Stock/40% Bonds**				
Base Comfortable "In Balance" Case:				
Maximum Fair Total Expense	0.75%		0.75%	
Retirement Income @ Age 65	$28,600		$33,100	
Age 65 Range of Portfolio Values	$387,662 to $2,476,925		$456,201 to $2,687,330	
EXCESS EXPENSE:	**0.50%** (1.25% total)	**1.00%** (1.75% total)	**0.50%** (1.25% total)	**1.00%** (1.75% total)
COST OF EXCESS EXPENSE				
Additional Annual Savings Needed	$2,700	$6,400	$3,400	$7,200
Delay Retirement by:	3 Years	7 Years	3 Years	6 Years
Reduce Annual Retirement Income by	$4,500	$8,300	$4,900	$9,200
Increased Risk of Outliving Resources	47%	100%	51%	102%
Reduction to Age 65 Portfolio Values:				
Likely More than:	$46,146	$41,039	$49,323	$44,231
Likely Less than:	$268,179	$268,179	$284,001	$538,654

Allocation: **45% Stock/55% Bonds**				
Base Comfortable "In Balance" Case:				
Maximum Fair Total Expense	0.75%		0.75%	
Retirement Income @ Age 65	$24,300		$28,000	
Age 65 Range of Portfolio Values	$388,752 to $1,839,842		$455,938 to $1,996,235	
EXCESS EXPENSE:	**0.50%** (1.25% total)	**1.00%** (1.75% total)	**0.50%** (1.25% total)	**1.00%** (1.75% total)
COST OF EXCESS EXPENSE				
Additional Annual Savings Needed	$3,000	$6,100	$3,100	$6,800
Delay Retirement by:	4 Years	7 Years	3 Years	6 Years
Reduce Annual Retirement Income by	$3,900	$7,100	$4,300	$8,000
Increased Risk of Outliving Resources	54%	118%	54%	119%
Reduction to Age 65 Portfolio Values:				
Likely More than:	$45,407	$40,396	$48,280	$43,449
Likely Less than:	$201,308	$201,308	$214,013	$405,608

Total annual savings is COMBINED annual employee AND employer contribution

AGE 40 WITH CURRENT 401(K) BALANCE OF $250,000

Total Annual Savings	$10,000		$15,000	
Allocation: **80% Stock/20% Bonds**				
Base Comfortable "In Balance" Case:				
Maximum Fair Total Expense	0.75%		0.75%	
Retirement Income @ Age 65	$46,800		$56,300	
Age 65 Range of Portfolio Values	$592,312 to $4,596,160		$735,309 to $5,242,840	
EXCESS EXPENSE:	**0.50%**	**1.00%**	**0.50%**	**1.00%**
	(1.25% total)	(1.75% total)	(1.25% total)	(1.75% total)
COST OF EXCESS EXPENSE				
Additional Annual Savings Needed	$4,000	$8,100	$4,500	$9,600
Delay Retirement by:	3 Years	5 Years	3 Years	5 Years
Reduce Annual Retirement Income by	$6,400	$12,400	$7,700	$14,400
Increased Risk of Outliving Resources	36%	78%	36%	80%
Reduction to Age 65 Portfolio Values:				
Likely More than:	$62,106	$53,973	$74,374	$61,426
Likely Less than:	$472,514	$472,514	$507,289	$980,067

	$10,000		$15,000	
Allocation: **60% Stock/40% Bonds**				
Base Comfortable "In Balance" Case:				
Maximum Fair Total Expense	0.75%		0.75%	
Retirement Income @ Age 65	$41,400		$49,500	
Age 65 Range of Portfolio Values	$601,459 to $3,134,658		$736,601 to $3,588,075	
EXCESS EXPENSE:	**0.50%**	**1.00%**	**0.50%**	**1.00%**
	(1.25% total)	(1.75% total)	(1.25% total)	(1.75% total)
COST OF EXCESS EXPENSE				
Additional Annual Savings Needed	$4,100	$8,800	$4,700	$9,900
Delay Retirement by:	3 Years	6 Years	3 Years	5 Years
Reduce Annual Retirement Income by	$6,300	$11,300	$6,700	$12,900
Increased Risk of Outliving Resources	48%	101%	47%	102%
Reduction to Age 65 Portfolio Values:				
Likely More than:	$61,016	$55,021	$67,716	$62,050
Likely Less than:	$315,136	$315,136	$344,178	$654,719

	$10,000		$15,000	
Allocation: **45% Stock/55% Bonds**				
Base Comfortable "In Balance" Case:				
Maximum Fair Total Expense	0.75%		0.75%	
Retirement Income @ Age 65	$35,600		$43,100	
Age 65 Range of Portfolio Values	$598,544 to $2,353,831		$738,291 to $2,693,751	
EXCESS EXPENSE:	**0.50%**	**1.00%**	**0.50%**	**1.00%**
	(1.25% total)	(1.75% total)	(1.25% total)	(1.75% total)
COST OF EXCESS EXPENSE				
Additional Annual Savings Needed	$4,000	$8,400	$4,600	$10,300
Delay Retirement by:	3 Years	6 Years	3 Years	6 Years
Reduce Annual Retirement Income by	$5,200	$9,600	$6,200	$11,400
Increased Risk of Outliving Resources	51%	117%	51%	117%
Reduction to Age 65 Portfolio Values:				
Likely More than:	$58,602	$52,534	$66,761	$62,023
Likely Less than:	$239,259	$239,259	$256,158	$490,845

Total annual savings is COMBINED annual employee AND employer contribution

AGE 45 WITH CURRENT 401(K) BALANCE OF $25,000

Total Annual Savings	$2,500		$5,000	
Allocation: **80% Stock/20% Bonds**				
Base Comfortable "In Balance" Case:				
Maximum Fair Total Expense	0.75%		0.75%	
Retirement Income @ Age 65	$5,500		$8,700	
Age 65 Range of Portfolio Values	$76,870 to $414,961		$127,045 to $599,041	
EXCESS EXPENSE:	**0.50%**	**1.00%**	**0.50%**	**1.00%**
	(1.25% total)	(1.75% total)	(1.25% total)	(1.75% total)
COST OF EXCESS EXPENSE				
Additional Annual Savings Needed	$600	$1,200	$800	$1,700
Delay Retirement by:	2 Years	4 Years	2 Years	3 Years
Reduce Annual Retirement Income by	$700	$1,300	$1,000	$1,800
Increased Risk of Outliving Resources	35%	73%	31%	76%
Reduction to Age 65 Portfolio Values:				
Likely More than:	$5,494	$5,086	$8,109	$6,795
Likely Less than:	$31,502	$31,502	$43,216	$81,207

Allocation: **60% Stock/40% Bonds**				
Base Comfortable "In Balance" Case:				
Maximum Fair Total Expense	0.75%		0.75%	
Retirement Income @ Age 65	$4,900		$7,900	
Age 65 Range of Portfolio Values	$79,614 to $299,971		$131,075 to $438,447	
EXCESS EXPENSE:	**0.50%**	**1.00%**	**0.50%**	**1.00%**
	(1.25% total)	(1.75% total)	(1.25% total)	(1.75% total)
COST OF EXCESS EXPENSE				
Additional Annual Savings Needed	$600	$1,200	$800	$1,800
Delay Retirement by:	2 Years	4 Years	2 Years	4 Years
Reduce Annual Retirement Income by	$600	$1,100	$900	$1,700
Increased Risk of Outliving Resources	40%	93%	43%	93%
Reduction to Age 65 Portfolio Values:				
Likely More than:	$5,593	$5,547	$8,210	$8,148
Likely Less than:	$23,182	$23,182	$29,942	$59,655

Allocation: **45% Stock/55% Bonds**				
Base Comfortable "In Balance" Case:				
Maximum Fair Total Expense	0.75%		0.75%	
Retirement Income @ Age 65	$4,400		$7,000	
Age 65 Range of Portfolio Values	$80,197 to $242,827		$131,008 to $363,704	
EXCESS EXPENSE:	**0.50%**	**1.00%**	**0.50%**	**1.00%**
	(1.25% total)	(1.75% total)	(1.25% total)	(1.75% total)
COST OF EXCESS EXPENSE				
Additional Annual Savings Needed	$600	$1,200	$800	$1,800
Delay Retirement by:	2 Years	4 Years	2 Years	4 Years
Reduce Annual Retirement Income by	$600	$1,100	$800	$1,500
Increased Risk of Outliving Resources	41%	112%	46%	112%
Reduction to Age 65 Portfolio Values:				
Likely More than:	$5,629	$5,650	$8,200	$7,288
Likely Less than:	$18,590	$18,590	$24,914	$47,950

Total annual savings is COMBINED annual employee AND employer contribution

AGE 45 WITH CURRENT 401(K) BALANCE OF $25,000

Total Annual Savings	$10,000		$15,000	
Allocation: **80% Stock/20% Bonds**				
Base Comfortable "In Balance" Case:				
Maximum Fair Total Expense	0.75%		0.75%	
Retirement Income @ Age 65	$15,400		$21,800	
Age 65 Range of Portfolio Values	$226,258 to $978,841		$323,311 to $1,356,334	
EXCESS EXPENSE:	**0.50%**	**1.00%**	**0.50%**	**1.00%**
	(1.25% total)	(1.75% total)	(1.25% total)	(1.75% total)
COST OF EXCESS EXPENSE				
Additional Annual Savings Needed	$1,500	$3,100	$2,000	$4,200
Delay Retirement by:	2 Years	4 Years	2 Years	3 Years
Reduce Annual Retirement Income by	$1,700	$3,300	$2,400	$4,400
Increased Risk of Outliving Resources	40%	81%	38%	79%
Reduction to Age 65 Portfolio Values:				
Likely More than:	$13,812	$12,865	$18,895	$17,724
Likely Less than:	$63,588	$63,588	$90,334	$172,079

Allocation: **60% Stock/40% Bonds**				
Base Comfortable "In Balance" Case:				
Maximum Fair Total Expense	0.75%		0.75%	
Retirement Income @ Age 65	$13,800		$19,800	
Age 65 Range of Portfolio Values	$233,164 to $719,358		$332,132 to $1,020,595	
EXCESS EXPENSE:	**0.50%**	**1.00%**	**0.50%**	**1.00%**
	(1.25% total)	(1.75% total)	(1.25% total)	(1.75% total)
COST OF EXCESS EXPENSE				
Additional Annual Savings Needed	$1,400	$3,100	$2,100	$4,400
Delay Retirement by:	2 Years	4 Years	2 Years	4 Years
Reduce Annual Retirement Income by	$1,500	$2,900	$2,200	$4,200
Increased Risk of Outliving Resources	49%	96%	50%	96%
Reduction to Age 65 Portfolio Values:				
Likely More than:	$14,180	$12,501	$18,856	$16,613
Likely Less than:	$45,004	$45,004	$63,897	$127,241

Allocation: **45% Stock/55% Bonds**				
Base Comfortable "In Balance" Case:				
Maximum Fair Total Expense	0.75%		0.75%	
Retirement Income @ Age 65	$12,400		$17,800	
Age 65 Range of Portfolio Values	$234,154 to $609,085		$335,598 to $854,822	
EXCESS EXPENSE:	**0.50%**	**1.00%**	**0.50%**	**1.00%**
	(1.25% total)	(1.75% total)	(1.25% total)	(1.75% total)
COST OF EXCESS EXPENSE				
Additional Annual Savings Needed	$1,400	$3,000	$2,000	$4,300
Delay Retirement by:	2 Years	4 Years	2 Years	3 Years
Reduce Annual Retirement Income by	$1,400	$2,600	$1,900	$3,700
Increased Risk of Outliving Resources	47%	109%	50%	114%
Reduction to Age 65 Portfolio Values:				
Likely More than:	$14,292	$12,717	$20,192	$16,950
Likely Less than:	$38,237	$38,237	$55,294	$105,518

Total annual savings is COMBINED annual employee AND employer contribution

AGE 45 WITH CURRENT 401(K) BALANCE OF $75,000

Total Annual Savings	$2,500		$5,000	
Allocation: **80% Stock/20% Bonds**				
Base Comfortable "In Balance" Case:				
Maximum Fair Total Expense	0.75%		0.75%	
Retirement Income @ Age 65	$9,800		$13,200	
Age 65 Range of Portfolio Values	$131,506 to $861,817		$178,157 to $1,052,522	
EXCESS EXPENSE:	**0.50%**	**1.00%**	**0.50%**	**1.00%**
	(1.25% total)	(1.75% total)	(1.25% total)	(1.75% total)
COST OF EXCESS EXPENSE				
Additional Annual Savings Needed	$1,000	$2,200	$1,400	$3,000
Delay Retirement by:	2 Years	5 Years	2 Years	4 Years
Reduce Annual Retirement Income by	$1,300	$2,400	$1,600	$3,100
Increased Risk of Outliving Resources	37%	70%	37%	72%
Reduction to Age 65 Portfolio Values:				
Likely More than:	$11,209	$10,731	$13,935	$11,770
Likely Less than:	$70,731	$70,731	$81,272	$156,022
Allocation: **60% Stock/40% Bonds**				
Base Comfortable "In Balance" Case:				
Maximum Fair Total Expense	0.75%		0.75%	
Retirement Income @ Age 65	$8,800		$11,700	
Age 65 Range of Portfolio Values	$133,789 to $617,086		$187,635 to $768,545	
EXCESS EXPENSE:	**0.50%**	**1.00%**	**0.50%**	**1.00%**
	(1.25% total)	(1.75% total)	(1.25% total)	(1.75% total)
COST OF EXCESS EXPENSE				
Additional Annual Savings Needed	$1,100	$2,300	$1,300	$2,700
Delay Retirement by:	3 Years	5 Years	2 Years	4 Years
Reduce Annual Retirement Income by	$1,200	$2,200	$1,400	$2,700
Increased Risk of Outliving Resources	39%	86%	40%	90%
Reduction to Age 65 Portfolio Values:				
Likely More than:	$10,559	$10,271	$13,761	$12,781
Likely Less than:	$50,398	$50,398	$60,682	$116,540
Allocation: **45% Stock/55% Bonds**				
Base Comfortable "In Balance" Case:				
Maximum Fair Total Expense	0.75%		0.75%	
Retirement Income @ Age 65	$7,900		$10,500	
Age 65 Range of Portfolio Values	$135,415 to $486,273		$187,629 to $605,528	
EXCESS EXPENSE:	**0.50%**	**1.00%**	**0.50%**	**1.00%**
	(1.25% total)	(1.75% total)	(1.25% total)	(1.75% total)
COST OF EXCESS EXPENSE				
Additional Annual Savings Needed	$1,100	$2,300	$1,300	$2,900
Delay Retirement by:	3 Years	5 Years	2 Years	4 Years
Reduce Annual Retirement Income by	$1,100	$2,000	$1,400	$2,400
Increased Risk of Outliving Resources	49%	116%	42%	113%
Reduction to Age 65 Portfolio Values:				
Likely More than:	$11,283	$10,490	$13,421	$12,888
Likely Less than:	$40,679	$40,679	$46,920	$90,131

Total annual savings is COMBINED annual employee AND employer contribution

AGE 45 WITH CURRENT 401(K) BALANCE OF $75,000

Total Annual Savings	$10,000		$15,000	
Allocation: **80% Stock/20% Bonds**				
Base Comfortable "In Balance" Case:				
Maximum Fair Total Expense	0.75%		0.75%	
Retirement Income @ Age 65	$19,600		$26,100	
Age 65 Range of Portfolio Values	$280,137 to $1,427,136		$381,136 to $1,797,124	
EXCESS EXPENSE:	**0.50%**	**1.00%**	**0.50%**	**1.00%**
	(1.25% total)	(1.75% total)	(1.25% total)	(1.75% total)
COST OF EXCESS EXPENSE				
Additional Annual Savings Needed	$1,900	$3,900	$2,400	$5,000
Delay Retirement by:	2 Years	4 Years	2 Years	3 Years
Reduce Annual Retirement Income by	$2,300	$4,300	$2,900	$5,400
Increased Risk of Outliving Resources	33%	74%	31%	76%
Reduction to Age 65 Portfolio Values:				
Likely More than:	$19,476	$17,724	$24,327	$20,386
Likely Less than:	$101,428	$101,428	$129,650	$243,622

Allocation: **60% Stock/40% Bonds**				
Base Comfortable "In Balance" Case:				
Maximum Fair Total Expense	0.75%		0.75%	
Retirement Income @ Age 65	$17,800		$23,900	
Age 65 Range of Portfolio Values	$289,391 to $1,039,095		$392,982 to $1,315,099	
EXCESS EXPENSE:	**0.50%**	**1.00%**	**0.50%**	**1.00%**
	(1.25% total)	(1.75% total)	(1.25% total)	(1.75% total)
COST OF EXCESS EXPENSE				
Additional Annual Savings Needed	$1,800	$4,000	$2,600	$5,400
Delay Retirement by:	2 Years	4 Years	2 Years	4 Years
Reduce Annual Retirement Income by	$2,100	$4,000	$2,800	$5,200
Increased Risk of Outliving Resources	39%	90%	45%	97%
Reduction to Age 65 Portfolio Values:				
Likely More than:	$19,169	$17,734	$24,631	$24,443
Likely Less than:	$75,990	$75,990	$89,827	$178,967

Allocation: **45% Stock/55% Bonds**				
Base Comfortable "In Balance" Case:				
Maximum Fair Total Expense	0.75%		0.75%	
Retirement Income @ Age 65	$15,900		$21,100	
Age 65 Range of Portfolio Values	$290,667 to $845,017		$392,902 to $1,090,991	
EXCESS EXPENSE:	**0.50%**	**1.00%**	**0.50%**	**1.00%**
	(1.25% total)	(1.75% total)	(1.25% total)	(1.75% total)
COST OF EXCESS EXPENSE				
Additional Annual Savings Needed	$2,000	$4,200	$2,400	$5,400
Delay Retirement by:	2 Years	4 Years	2 Years	4 Years
Reduce Annual Retirement Income by	$1,900	$3,700	$2,400	$4,500
Increased Risk of Outliving Resources	42%	111%	45%	110%
Reduction to Age 65 Portfolio Values:				
Likely More than:	$19,651	$19,214	$24,599	$21,866
Likely Less than:	$59,695	$59,695	$74,741	$143,851

Total annual savings is COMBINED annual employee AND employer contribution

AGE 45 WITH CURRENT 401(K) BALANCE OF $150,000

Total Annual Savings	$2,500		$5,000	
Allocation: **80% Stock/20% Bonds**				
Base Comfortable "In Balance" Case:				
Maximum Fair Total Expense	0.75%		0.75%	
Retirement Income @ Age 65	$16,400		$19,700	
Age 65 Range of Portfolio Values	$211,548 to $1,555,325		$262,891 to $1,723,512	
EXCESS EXPENSE:	**0.50%** (1.25% total)	**1.00%** (1.75% total)	**0.50%** (1.25% total)	**1.00%** (1.75% total)
COST OF EXCESS EXPENSE				
Additional Annual Savings Needed	$1,900	$3,900	$2,100	$4,500
Delay Retirement by:	3 Years	5 Years	2 Years	5 Years
Reduce Annual Retirement Income by	$2,100	$4,100	$2,600	$4,800
Increased Risk of Outliving Resources	36%	74%	35%	67%
Reduction to Age 65 Portfolio Values:				
Likely More than:	$19,897	$18,136	$22,419	$21,461
Likely Less than:	$135,235	$135,235	$141,462	$271,482

Allocation: **60% Stock/40% Bonds**	$2,500		$5,000	
Base Comfortable "In Balance" Case:				
Maximum Fair Total Expense	0.75%		0.75%	
Retirement Income @ Age 65	$14,700		$17,700	
Age 65 Range of Portfolio Values	$213,276 to $1,089,509		$267,457 to $1,234,050	
EXCESS EXPENSE:	**0.50%** (1.25% total)	**1.00%** (1.75% total)	**0.50%** (1.25% total)	**1.00%** (1.75% total)
COST OF EXCESS EXPENSE				
Additional Annual Savings Needed	$1,900	$4,000	$2,300	$4,600
Delay Retirement by:	3 Years	5 Years	3 Years	5 Years
Reduce Annual Retirement Income by	$2,000	$3,800	$2,400	$4,500
Increased Risk of Outliving Resources	40%	90%	40%	89%
Reduction to Age 65 Portfolio Values:				
Likely More than:	$20,077	$18,291	$21,118	$20,542
Likely Less than:	$95,631	$95,631	$100,795	$193,597

Allocation: **45% Stock/55% Bonds**	$2,500		$5,000	
Base Comfortable "In Balance" Case:				
Maximum Fair Total Expense	0.75%		0.75%	
Retirement Income @ Age 65	$13,200		$15,900	
Age 65 Range of Portfolio Values	$219,078 to $847,761		$270,709 to $972,425	
EXCESS EXPENSE:	**0.50%** (1.25% total)	**1.00%** (1.75% total)	**0.50%** (1.25% total)	**1.00%** (1.75% total)
COST OF EXCESS EXPENSE				
Additional Annual Savings Needed	$1,900	$4,100	$2,400	$4,600
Delay Retirement by:	3 Years	6 Years	3 Years	5 Years
Reduce Annual Retirement Income by	$1,800	$3,500	$2,200	$4,100
Increased Risk of Outliving Resources	50%	119%	49%	117%
Reduction to Age 65 Portfolio Values:				
Likely More than:	$19,470	$18,028	$22,567	$20,979
Likely Less than:	$74,096	$74,096	$81,359	$157,186

Total annual savings is COMBINED annual employee AND employer contribution

AGE 45 WITH CURRENT 401(K) BALANCE OF $150,000

Total Annual Savings	$10,000		$15,000	
Allocation: **80% Stock/20% Bonds**				
Base Comfortable "In Balance" Case:				
Maximum Fair Total Expense	0.75%		0.75%	
Retirement Income @ Age 65	$26,400		$33,000	
Age 65 Range of Portfolio Values	$356,313 to $2,105,044		$461,219 to $2,489,768	
EXCESS EXPENSE:	**0.50%**	**1.00%**	**0.50%**	**1.00%**
	(1.25% total)	(1.75% total)	(1.25% total)	(1.75% total)
COST OF EXCESS EXPENSE				
Additional Annual Savings Needed	$2,700	$5,900	$3,400	$7,100
Delay Retirement by:	2 Years	4 Years	2 Years	4 Years
Reduce Annual Retirement Income by	$3,200	$6,200	$3,900	$7,600
Increased Risk of Outliving Resources	37%	72%	35%	73%
Reduction to Age 65 Portfolio Values:				
Likely More than:	$27,869	$23,540	$32,965	$30,514
Likely Less than:	$162,544	$162,544	$189,012	$363,597

Allocation: **60% Stock/40% Bonds**				
Base Comfortable "In Balance" Case:				
Maximum Fair Total Expense	0.75%		0.75%	
Retirement Income @ Age 65	$23,500		$29,500	
Age 65 Range of Portfolio Values	$375,148 to $1,536,969		$477,564 to $1,799,705	
EXCESS EXPENSE:	**0.50%**	**1.00%**	**0.50%**	**1.00%**
	(1.25% total)	(1.75% total)	(1.25% total)	(1.75% total)
COST OF EXCESS EXPENSE				
Additional Annual Savings Needed	$2,600	$5,500	$3,200	$6,800
Delay Retirement by:	2 Years	4 Years	2 Years	4 Years
Reduce Annual Retirement Income by	$2,900	$5,400	$3,400	$6,500
Increased Risk of Outliving Resources	36%	86%	41%	92%
Reduction to Age 65 Portfolio Values:				
Likely More than:	$27,522	$25,562	$33,559	$33,280
Likely Less than:	$121,364	$121,364	$139,090	$267,282

Allocation: **45% Stock/55% Bonds**				
Base Comfortable "In Balance" Case:				
Maximum Fair Total Expense	0.75%		0.75%	
Retirement Income @ Age 65	$21,000		$26,400	
Age 65 Range of Portfolio Values	$375,257 to $1,211,057		$481,181 to $1,456,962	
EXCESS EXPENSE:	**0.50%**	**1.00%**	**0.50%**	**1.00%**
	(1.25% total)	(1.75% total)	(1.25% total)	(1.75% total)
COST OF EXCESS EXPENSE				
Additional Annual Savings Needed	$2,600	$5,700	$3,200	$7,100
Delay Retirement by:	2 Years	4 Years	2 Years	4 Years
Reduce Annual Retirement Income by	$2,700	$4,800	$3,200	$6,100
Increased Risk of Outliving Resources	42%	113%	41%	112%
Reduction to Age 65 Portfolio Values:				
Likely More than:	$26,841	$25,777	$33,775	$33,901
Likely Less than:	$93,842	$93,842	$111,543	$213,492

Total annual savings is COMBINED annual employee AND employer contribution

AGE 45 WITH CURRENT 401(K) BALANCE OF $250,000

Total Annual Savings	$2,500		$5,000	
Allocation: **80% Stock/20% Bonds**				
Base Comfortable "In Balance" Case:				
Maximum Fair Total Expense	0.75%		0.75%	
Retirement Income @ Age 65	$25,300		$28,500	
Age 65 Range of Portfolio Values	$320,274 to $2,500,480		$369,218 to $2,635,693	
EXCESS EXPENSE:	**0.50%**	**1.00%**	**0.50%**	**1.00%**
	(1.25% total)	(1.75% total)	(1.25% total)	(1.75% total)
COST OF EXCESS EXPENSE				
Additional Annual Savings Needed	$3,000	$6,200	$3,100	$6,600
Delay Retirement by:	3 Years	5 Years	3 Years	5 Years
Reduce Annual Retirement Income by	$3,400	$6,500	$3,800	$7,100
Increased Risk of Outliving Resources	35%	73%	34%	69%
Reduction to Age 65 Portfolio Values:				
Likely More than:	$31,707	$28,858	$33,848	$30,885
Likely Less than:	$216,845	$216,845	$228,151	$437,395

Allocation: **60% Stock/40% Bonds**				
Base Comfortable "In Balance" Case:				
Maximum Fair Total Expense	0.75%		0.75%	
Retirement Income @ Age 65	$22,600		$25,600	
Age 65 Range of Portfolio Values	$326,125 to $1,733,569		$372,067 to $1,857,535	
EXCESS EXPENSE:	**0.50%**	**1.00%**	**0.50%**	**1.00%**
	(1.25% total)	(1.75% total)	(1.25% total)	(1.75% total)
COST OF EXCESS EXPENSE				
Additional Annual Savings Needed	$2,900	$6,400	$3,300	$6,900
Delay Retirement by:	3 Years	6 Years	3 Years	5 Years
Reduce Annual Retirement Income by	$3,200	$6,000	$3,500	$6,600
Increased Risk of Outliving Resources	42%	89%	40%	90%
Reduction to Age 65 Portfolio Values:				
Likely More than:	$32,042	$28,562	$32,322	$29,536
Likely Less than:	$152,048	$152,048	$156,626	$300,716

Allocation: **45% Stock/55% Bonds**				
Base Comfortable "In Balance" Case:				
Maximum Fair Total Expense	0.75%		0.75%	
Retirement Income @ Age 65	$20,100		$23,000	
Age 65 Range of Portfolio Values	$331,578 to $1,331,759		$383,084 to $1,455,409	
EXCESS EXPENSE:	**0.50%**	**1.00%**	**0.50%**	**1.00%**
	(1.25% total)	(1.75% total)	(1.25% total)	(1.75% total)
COST OF EXCESS EXPENSE				
Additional Annual Savings Needed	$2,800	$6,200	$3,400	$7,000
Delay Retirement by:	3 Years	6 Years	3 Years	6 Years
Reduce Annual Retirement Income by	$2,900	$5,400	$3,200	$6,000
Increased Risk of Outliving Resources	53%	119%	51%	123%
Reduction to Age 65 Portfolio Values:				
Likely More than:	$31,522	$28,701	$34,823	$31,759
Likely Less than:	$119,660	$119,660	$125,935	$241,271

Total annual savings is COMBINED annual employee AND employer contribution

AGE 45 WITH CURRENT 401(K) BALANCE OF $250,000

Total Annual Savings	$10,000		$15,000	
Allocation: **80% Stock/20% Bonds**				
Base Comfortable "In Balance" Case:				
Maximum Fair Total Expense	0.75%		0.75%	
Retirement Income @ Age 65	$34,900		$42,000	
Age 65 Range of Portfolio Values	$469,451 to $3,007,179		$559,410 to $3,388,079	
EXCESS EXPENSE:	**0.50%**	**1.00%**	**0.50%**	**1.00%**
	(1.25% total)	(1.75% total)	(1.25% total)	(1.75% total)
COST OF EXCESS EXPENSE				
Additional Annual Savings Needed	$3,400	$7,800	$4,500	$9,400
Delay Retirement by:	2 Years	4 Years	2 Years	4 Years
Reduce Annual Retirement Income by	$4,200	$8,200	$5,300	$10,100
Increased Risk of Outliving Resources	36%	70%	36%	72%
Reduction to Age 65 Portfolio Values:				
Likely More than:	$41,420	$37,853	$41,920	$40,878
Likely Less than:	$243,449	$243,449	$271,763	$519,979
Allocation: **60% Stock/40% Bonds**				
Base Comfortable "In Balance" Case:				
Maximum Fair Total Expense	0.75%		0.75%	
Retirement Income @ Age 65	$31,500		$37,100	
Age 65 Range of Portfolio Values	$484,636 to $2,151,400		$586,381 to $2,459,887	
EXCESS EXPENSE:	**0.50%**	**1.00%**	**0.50%**	**1.00%**
	(1.25% total)	(1.75% total)	(1.25% total)	(1.75% total)
COST OF EXCESS EXPENSE				
Additional Annual Savings Needed	$4,000	$8,000	$4,000	$8,700
Delay Retirement by:	3 Years	5 Years	2 Years	4 Years
Reduce Annual Retirement Income by	$4,300	$7,900	$4,600	$8,500
Increased Risk of Outliving Resources	40%	87%	38%	87%
Reduction to Age 65 Portfolio Values:				
Likely More than:	$40,134	$38,543	$42,309	$39,003
Likely Less than:	$179,413	$179,413	$189,466	$365,490
Allocation: **45% Stock/55% Bonds**				
Base Comfortable "In Balance" Case:				
Maximum Fair Total Expense	0.75%		0.75%	
Retirement Income @ Age 65	$28,200		$33,500	
Age 65 Range of Portfolio Values	$485,239 to $1,701,411		$587,354 to $1,940,187	
EXCESS EXPENSE:	**0.50%**	**1.00%**	**0.50%**	**1.00%**
	(1.25% total)	(1.75% total)	(1.25% total)	(1.75% total)
COST OF EXCESS EXPENSE				
Additional Annual Savings Needed	$3,800	$8,000	$4,300	$9,400
Delay Retirement by:	3 Years	5 Years	3 Years	5 Years
Reduce Annual Retirement Income by	$3,800	$7,100	$4,300	$8,000
Increased Risk of Outliving Resources	48%	117%	46%	115%
Reduction to Age 65 Portfolio Values:				
Likely More than:	$39,609	$36,285	$42,334	$39,506
Likely Less than:	$141,701	$141,701	$153,236	$296,991

Total annual savings is COMBINED annual employee AND employer contribution

AGE 50 WITH CURRENT 401(K) BALANCE OF $25,000

Total Annual Savings	$2,500		$5,000	
Allocation: **80% Stock/20% Bonds**				
Base Comfortable "In Balance" Case:				
Maximum Fair Total Expense	0.75%		0.75%	
Retirement Income @ Age 65	$4,100		$6,300	
Age 65 Range of Portfolio Values	$59,148 to $264,454		$92,518 to $374,859	
EXCESS EXPENSE:	**0.50%**	**1.00%**	**0.50%**	**1.00%**
	(1.25% total)	(1.75% total)	(1.25% total)	(1.75% total)
COST OF EXCESS EXPENSE				
Additional Annual Savings Needed	$600	$1,200	$800	$1,700
Delay Retirement by:	2 Years	3 Years	2 Years	3 Years
Reduce Annual Retirement Income by	$500	$900	$700	$1,200
Increased Risk of Outliving Resources	40%	83%	41%	84%
Reduction to Age 65 Portfolio Values:				
Likely More than:	$3,263	$3,063	$4,402	$4,165
Likely Less than:	$15,238	$15,238	$19,997	$38,885

Allocation: **60% Stock/40% Bonds**				
Base Comfortable "In Balance" Case:				
Maximum Fair Total Expense	0.75%		0.75%	
Retirement Income @ Age 65	$3,700		$5,700	
Age 65 Range of Portfolio Values	$62,753 to $199,591		$98,780 to $292,950	
EXCESS EXPENSE:	**0.50%**	**1.00%**	**0.50%**	**1.00%**
	(1.25% total)	(1.75% total)	(1.25% total)	(1.75% total)
COST OF EXCESS EXPENSE				
Additional Annual Savings Needed	$600	$1,100	$800	$1,600
Delay Retirement by:	2 Years	3 Years	2 Years	3 Years
Reduce Annual Retirement Income by	$400	$800	$600	$1,100
Increased Risk of Outliving Resources	36%	92%	39%	94%
Reduction to Age 65 Portfolio Values:				
Likely More than:	$3,570	$3,356	$5,067	$4,527
Likely Less than:	$11,950	$11,950	$14,883	$28,963

Allocation: **45% Stock/55% Bonds**				
Base Comfortable "In Balance" Case:				
Maximum Fair Total Expense	0.75%		0.75%	
Retirement Income @ Age 65	$3,300		$5,200	
Age 65 Range of Portfolio Values	$63,958 to $165,948		$100,971 to $243,553	
EXCESS EXPENSE:	**0.50%**	**1.00%**	**0.50%**	**1.00%**
	(1.25% total)	(1.75% total)	(1.25% total)	(1.75% total)
COST OF EXCESS EXPENSE				
Additional Annual Savings Needed	$500	$1,000	$700	$1,600
Delay Retirement by:	2 Years	3 Years	2 Years	3 Years
Reduce Annual Retirement Income by	$300	$700	$500	$1,000
Increased Risk of Outliving Resources	43%	112%	41%	115%
Reduction to Age 65 Portfolio Values:				
Likely More than:	$3,498	$3,457	$5,123	$4,914
Likely Less than:	$9,355	$9,355	$12,395	$24,116

Total annual savings is COMBINED annual employee AND employer contribution

AGE 50 WITH CURRENT 401(K) BALANCE OF $25,000

Total Annual Savings	$10,000		$15,000	
Allocation: **80% Stock/20% Bonds**				
Base Comfortable "In Balance" Case:				
Maximum Fair Total Expense	0.75%		0.75%	
Retirement Income @ Age 65	$10,600		$15,000	
Age 65 Range of Portfolio Values	$162,645 to $603,191		$230,620 to $824,449	
EXCESS EXPENSE:	**0.50%**	**1.00%**	**0.50%**	**1.00%**
	(1.25% total)	(1.75% total)	(1.25% total)	(1.75% total)
COST OF EXCESS EXPENSE				
Additional Annual Savings Needed	$1,300	$2,800	$1,900	$4,000
Delay Retirement by:	2 Years	3 Years	2 Years	3 Years
Reduce Annual Retirement Income by	$1,000	$2,000	$1,500	$2,900
Increased Risk of Outliving Resources	39%	78%	39%	80%
Reduction to Age 65 Portfolio Values:				
Likely More than:	$7,562	$7,160	$10,476	$9,070
Likely Less than:	$28,105	$28,105	$37,504	$73,031

Allocation: **60% Stock/40% Bonds**				
Base Comfortable "In Balance" Case:				
Maximum Fair Total Expense	0.75%		0.75%	
Retirement Income @ Age 65	$9,800		$13,900	
Age 65 Range of Portfolio Values	$169,122 to $472,915		$238,973 to $647,011	
EXCESS EXPENSE:	**0.50%**	**1.00%**	**0.50%**	**1.00%**
	(1.25% total)	(1.75% total)	(1.25% total)	(1.75% total)
COST OF EXCESS EXPENSE				
Additional Annual Savings Needed	$1,200	$2,900	$1,900	$4,000
Delay Retirement by:	2 Years	3 Years	2 Years	3 Years
Reduce Annual Retirement Income by	$900	$1,900	$1,400	$2,700
Increased Risk of Outliving Resources	47%	101%	51%	103%
Reduction to Age 65 Portfolio Values:				
Likely More than:	$8,021	$7,557	$10,415	$9,950
Likely Less than:	$23,677	$23,677	$29,573	$57,697

Allocation: **45% Stock/55% Bonds**				
Base Comfortable "In Balance" Case:				
Maximum Fair Total Expense	0.75%		0.75%	
Retirement Income @ Age 65	$8,900		$12,700	
Age 65 Range of Portfolio Values	$172,762 to $396,438		$244,769 to $558,068	
EXCESS EXPENSE:	**0.50%**	**1.00%**	**0.50%**	**1.00%**
	(1.25% total)	(1.75% total)	(1.25% total)	(1.75% total)
COST OF EXCESS EXPENSE				
Additional Annual Savings Needed	$1,200	$2,700	$1,800	$3,800
Delay Retirement by:	1 Years	3 Years	2 Years	3 Years
Reduce Annual Retirement Income by	$900	$1,700	$1,300	$2,400
Increased Risk of Outliving Resources	45%	118%	51%	121%
Reduction to Age 65 Portfolio Values:				
Likely More than:	$7,405	$6,969	$10,656	$10,041
Likely Less than:	$17,407	$17,407	$24,429	$49,138

Total annual savings is COMBINED annual employee AND employer contribution

AGE 50 WITH CURRENT 401(K) BALANCE OF $75,000

Total Annual Savings		$2,500		$5,000	
Allocation: ***80% Stock/20% Bonds***					
Base Comfortable "In Balance" Case:					
Maximum Fair Total Expense		0.75%		0.75%	
Retirement Income @ Age 65		$7,800		$10,100	
Age 65 Range of Portfolio Values		$106,109 to $576,952		$142,300 to $689,562	
EXCESS EXPENSE:		**0.50%**	**1.00%**	**0.50%**	**1.00%**
		(1.25% total)	(1.75% total)	(1.25% total)	(1.75% total)
COST OF EXCESS EXPENSE					
Additional Annual Savings Needed		$1,100	$2,200	$1,300	$2,800
Delay Retirement by:		2 Years	4 Years	2 Years	4 Years
Reduce Annual Retirement Income by		$900	$1,700	$1,100	$2,100
Increased Risk of Outliving Resources		36%	80%	35%	79%
Reduction to Age 65 Portfolio Values:					
Likely More than:		$7,257	$6,690	$8,311	$8,448
Likely Less than:		$36,817	$36,817	$41,341	$80,236
Allocation: ***60% Stock/40% Bonds***					
Base Comfortable "In Balance" Case:					
Maximum Fair Total Expense		0.75%		0.75%	
Retirement Income @ Age 65		$7,100		$9,100	
Age 65 Range of Portfolio Values		$113,403 to $429,270		$151,736 to $509,258	
EXCESS EXPENSE:		**0.50%**	**1.00%**	**0.50%**	**1.00%**
		(1.25% total)	(1.75% total)	(1.25% total)	(1.75% total)
COST OF EXCESS EXPENSE					
Additional Annual Savings Needed		$1,100	$2,400	$1,400	$2,900
Delay Retirement by:		2 Years	4 Years	2 Years	4 Years
Reduce Annual Retirement Income by		$900	$1,600	$1,100	$2,000
Increased Risk of Outliving Resources		40%	95%	36%	94%
Reduction to Age 65 Portfolio Values:					
Likely More than:		$7,676	$7,148	$9,302	$8,845
Likely Less than:		$27,838	$27,838	$31,021	$60,179
Allocation: ***45% Stock/55% Bonds***					
Base Comfortable "In Balance" Case:					
Maximum Fair Total Expense		0.75%		0.75%	
Retirement Income @ Age 65		$6,300		$8,200	
Age 65 Range of Portfolio Values		$115,013 to $343,304		$153,507 to $416,874	
EXCESS EXPENSE:		**0.50%**	**1.00%**	**0.50%**	**1.00%**
		(1.25% total)	(1.75% total)	(1.25% total)	(1.75% total)
COST OF EXCESS EXPENSE					
Additional Annual Savings Needed		$1,000	$2,200	$1,300	$2,800
Delay Retirement by:		2 Years	4 Years	2 Years	4 Years
Reduce Annual Retirement Income by		$700	$1,400	$900	$1,700
Increased Risk of Outliving Resources		43%	108%	41%	108%
Reduction to Age 65 Portfolio Values:					
Likely More than:		$7,525	$7,035	$9,199	$8,308
Likely Less than:		$21,865	$21,865	$24,759	$48,034

Total annual savings is COMBINED annual employee AND employer contribution

AGE 50 WITH CURRENT 401(K) BALANCE OF $75,000

Total Annual Savings		$10,000		$15,000	
Allocation: *80% Stock/20% Bonds*					
Base Comfortable "In Balance" Case:					
Maximum Fair Total Expense		0.75%		0.75%	
Retirement Income @ Age 65		$14,500		$18,900	
Age 65 Range of Portfolio Values		$211,032 to $893,304		$277,553 to $1,124,577	
EXCESS EXPENSE:		**0.50%**	**1.00%**	**0.50%**	**1.00%**
		(1.25% total)	(1.75% total)	(1.25% total)	(1.75% total)
COST OF EXCESS EXPENSE					
Additional Annual Savings Needed		$1,800	$3,900	$2,300	$5,100
Delay Retirement by:		2 Years	3 Years	2 Years	3 Years
Reduce Annual Retirement Income by		$1,400	$2,900	$1,900	$3,600
Increased Risk of Outliving Resources		40%	84%	41%	84%
Reduction to Age 65 Portfolio Values:					
Likely More than:		$11,060	$11,522	$13,204	$12,496
Likely Less than:		$50,904	$50,904	$59,991	$116,656
Allocation: *60% Stock/40% Bonds*					
Base Comfortable "In Balance" Case:					
Maximum Fair Total Expense		0.75%		0.75%	
Retirement Income @ Age 65		$13,100		$17,200	
Age 65 Range of Portfolio Values		$225,202 to $697,768		$296,217 to $878,730	
EXCESS EXPENSE:		**0.50%**	**1.00%**	**0.50%**	**1.00%**
		(1.25% total)	(1.75% total)	(1.25% total)	(1.75% total)
COST OF EXCESS EXPENSE					
Additional Annual Savings Needed		$1,800	$3,800	$2,300	$4,800
Delay Retirement by:		2 Years	3 Years	2 Years	3 Years
Reduce Annual Retirement Income by		$1,300	$2,600	$1,700	$3,300
Increased Risk of Outliving Resources		35%	90%	39%	96%
Reduction to Age 65 Portfolio Values:					
Likely More than:		$12,016	$12,104	$15,199	$13,580
Likely Less than:		$37,593	$37,593	$44,651	$86,890
Allocation: *45% Stock/55% Bonds*					
Base Comfortable "In Balance" Case:					
Maximum Fair Total Expense		0.75%		0.75%	
Retirement Income @ Age 65		$12,000		$15,800	
Age 65 Range of Portfolio Values		$229,195 to $574,580		$302,671 to $730,415	
EXCESS EXPENSE:		**0.50%**	**1.00%**	**0.50%**	**1.00%**
		(1.25% total)	(1.75% total)	(1.25% total)	(1.75% total)
COST OF EXCESS EXPENSE					
Additional Annual Savings Needed		$1,900	$3,900	$2,400	$5,200
Delay Retirement by:		2 Years	3 Years	2 Years	3 Years
Reduce Annual Retirement Income by		$1,300	$2,400	$1,600	$3,200
Increased Risk of Outliving Resources		42%	114%	44%	117%
Reduction to Age 65 Portfolio Values:					
Likely More than:		$12,161	$11,451	$15,369	$14,743
Likely Less than:		$32,058	$32,058	$37,183	$72,348

Total annual savings is COMBINED annual employee AND employer contribution

AGE 50 WITH CURRENT 401(K) BALANCE OF $150,000

Total Annual Savings	$2,500		$5,000	
Allocation: *80% Stock/20% Bonds*				
Base Comfortable "In Balance" Case:				
Maximum Fair Total Expense	0.75%		0.75%	
Retirement Income @ Age 65	$13,400		$15,700	
Age 65 Range of Portfolio Values	$178,764 to $1,041,173		$212,097 to $1,153,783	
EXCESS EXPENSE:	**0.50%**	**1.00%**	**0.50%**	**1.00%**
	(1.25% total)	(1.75% total)	(1.25% total)	(1.75% total)
COST OF EXCESS EXPENSE				
Additional Annual Savings Needed	$1,800	$3,900	$2,200	$4,500
Delay Retirement by:	2 Years	4 Years	2 Years	4 Years
Reduce Annual Retirement Income by	$1,500	$3,000	$1,800	$3,400
Increased Risk of Outliving Resources	36%	73%	36%	79%
Reduction to Age 65 Portfolio Values:				
Likely More than:	$13,252	$12,345	$14,514	$13,380
Likely Less than:	$68,452	$68,452	$73,634	$143,475

Allocation: *60% Stock/40% Bonds*				
Base Comfortable "In Balance" Case:				
Maximum Fair Total Expense	0.75%		0.75%	
Retirement Income @ Age 65	$12,100		$14,200	
Age 65 Range of Portfolio Values	$190,302 to $769,101		$226,806 to $858,540	
EXCESS EXPENSE:	**0.50%**	**1.00%**	**0.50%**	**1.00%**
	(1.25% total)	(1.75% total)	(1.25% total)	(1.75% total)
COST OF EXCESS EXPENSE				
Additional Annual Savings Needed	$1,800	$4,000	$2,200	$4,800
Delay Retirement by:	2 Years	5 Years	2 Years	4 Years
Reduce Annual Retirement Income by	$1,400	$2,700	$1,700	$3,100
Increased Risk of Outliving Resources	43%	101%	40%	95%
Reduction to Age 65 Portfolio Values:				
Likely More than:	$13,685	$12,922	$15,352	$14,296
Likely Less than:	$51,890	$51,890	$55,676	$107,880

Allocation: *45% Stock/55% Bonds*				
Base Comfortable "In Balance" Case:				
Maximum Fair Total Expense	0.75%		0.75%	
Retirement Income @ Age 65	$10,800		$12,700	
Age 65 Range of Portfolio Values	$191,653 to $608,998		$229,906 to $686,487	
EXCESS EXPENSE:	**0.50%**	**1.00%**	**0.50%**	**1.00%**
	(1.25% total)	(1.75% total)	(1.25% total)	(1.75% total)
COST OF EXCESS EXPENSE				
Additional Annual Savings Needed	$1,800	$4,000	$2,100	$4,600
Delay Retirement by:	3 Years	5 Years	2 Years	4 Years
Reduce Annual Retirement Income by	$1,300	$2,500	$1,500	$2,800
Increased Risk of Outliving Resources	46%	106%	44%	108%
Reduction to Age 65 Portfolio Values:				
Likely More than:	$13,743	$12,769	$15,050	$14,072
Likely Less than:	$41,061	$41,061	$43,730	$85,814

Total annual savings is COMBINED annual employee AND employer contribution

AGE 50 WITH CURRENT 401(K) BALANCE OF $150,000

Total Annual Savings	$10,000		$15,000	
Allocation: **80% Stock/20% Bonds**				
Base Comfortable "In Balance" Case:				
Maximum Fair Total Expense	0.75%		0.75%	
Retirement Income @ Age 65	$20,200		$24,800	
Age 65 Range of Portfolio Values	$284,600 to $1,379,124		$354,644 to $1,586,482	
EXCESS EXPENSE:	**0.50%**	**1.00%**	**0.50%**	**1.00%**
	(1.25% total)	(1.75% total)	(1.25% total)	(1.75% total)
COST OF EXCESS EXPENSE				
Additional Annual Savings Needed	$2,600	$5,500	$3,300	$7,000
Delay Retirement by:	2 Years	4 Years	2 Years	3 Years
Reduce Annual Retirement Income by	$2,200	$4,100	$2,700	$5,100
Increased Risk of Outliving Resources	35%	79%	39%	85%
Reduction to Age 65 Portfolio Values:				
Likely More than:	$16,621	$16,897	$19,577	$18,380
Likely Less than:	$82,683	$82,683	$91,431	$179,920
Allocation: **60% Stock/40% Bonds**				
Base Comfortable "In Balance" Case:				
Maximum Fair Total Expense	0.75%		0.75%	
Retirement Income @ Age 65	$18,200		$22,200	
Age 65 Range of Portfolio Values	$303,471 to $1,018,516		$376,521 to $1,197,543	
EXCESS EXPENSE:	**0.50%**	**1.00%**	**0.50%**	**1.00%**
	(1.25% total)	(1.75% total)	(1.25% total)	(1.75% total)
COST OF EXCESS EXPENSE				
Additional Annual Savings Needed	$2,800	$5,700	$3,100	$6,500
Delay Retirement by:	2 Years	4 Years	2 Years	3 Years
Reduce Annual Retirement Income by	$2,100	$3,900	$2,400	$4,500
Increased Risk of Outliving Resources	36%	94%	36%	92%
Reduction to Age 65 Portfolio Values:				
Likely More than:	$18,602	$17,692	$21,421	$20,138
Likely Less than:	$62,043	$62,043	$71,694	$137,754
Allocation: **45% Stock/55% Bonds**				
Base Comfortable "In Balance" Case:				
Maximum Fair Total Expense	0.75%		0.75%	
Retirement Income @ Age 65	$16,500		$20,200	
Age 65 Range of Portfolio Values	$306,893 to $833,626		$383,260 to $995,203	
EXCESS EXPENSE:	**0.50%**	**1.00%**	**0.50%**	**1.00%**
	(1.25% total)	(1.75% total)	(1.25% total)	(1.75% total)
COST OF EXCESS EXPENSE				
Additional Annual Savings Needed	$2,700	$5,700	$3,100	$6,600
Delay Retirement by:	2 Years	4 Years	2 Years	4 Years
Reduce Annual Retirement Income by	$1,900	$3,500	$2,200	$4,200
Increased Risk of Outliving Resources	42%	109%	40%	112%
Reduction to Age 65 Portfolio Values:				
Likely More than:	$18,398	$16,617	$20,986	$20,740
Likely Less than:	$49,518	$49,518	$56,133	$109,004

Total annual savings is COMBINED annual employee AND employer contribution

AGE 50 WITH CURRENT 401(K) BALANCE OF $250,000

Total Annual Savings	$2,500		$5,000	
Allocation: **80% Stock/20% Bonds**				
Base Comfortable "In Balance" Case:				
Maximum Fair Total Expense	0.75%		0.75%	
Retirement Income @ Age 65	$21,000		$23,300	
Age 65 Range of Portfolio Values	$274,560 to $1,673,387		$308,809 to $1,772,583	
EXCESS EXPENSE:	**0.50%**	**1.00%**	**0.50%**	**1.00%**
	(1.25% total)	(1.75% total)	(1.25% total)	(1.75% total)
COST OF EXCESS EXPENSE				
Additional Annual Savings Needed	$3,000	$6,400	$3,200	$6,900
Delay Retirement by:	3 Years	5 Years	2 Years	4 Years
Reduce Annual Retirement Income by	$2,500	$4,800	$2,800	$5,100
Increased Risk of Outliving Resources	37%	74%	36%	76%
Reduction to Age 65 Portfolio Values:				
Likely More than:	$21,165	$19,702	$22,507	$20,977
Likely Less than:	$112,413	$112,413	$115,668	$224,161

Allocation: **60% Stock/40% Bonds**				
Base Comfortable "In Balance" Case:				
Maximum Fair Total Expense	0.75%		0.75%	
Retirement Income @ Age 65	$18,900		$20,900	
Age 65 Range of Portfolio Values	$290,798 to $1,223,682		$329,192 to $1,308,061	
EXCESS EXPENSE:	**0.50%**	**1.00%**	**0.50%**	**1.00%**
	(1.25% total)	(1.75% total)	(1.25% total)	(1.75% total)
COST OF EXCESS EXPENSE				
Additional Annual Savings Needed	$3,100	$6,300	$3,200	$6,900
Delay Retirement by:	3 Years	5 Years	2 Years	5 Years
Reduce Annual Retirement Income by	$2,300	$4,400	$2,400	$4,700
Increased Risk of Outliving Resources	44%	99%	41%	98%
Reduction to Age 65 Portfolio Values:				
Likely More than:	$22,047	$20,530	$23,558	$21,970
Likely Less than:	$82,741	$82,741	$86,612	$167,770

Allocation: **45% Stock/55% Bonds**				
Base Comfortable "In Balance" Case:				
Maximum Fair Total Expense	0.75%		0.75%	
Retirement Income @ Age 65	$16,800		$18,800	
Age 65 Range of Portfolio Values	$295,013 to $965,391		$332,050 to $1,039,663	
EXCESS EXPENSE:	**0.50%**	**1.00%**	**0.50%**	**1.00%**
	(1.25% total)	(1.75% total)	(1.25% total)	(1.75% total)
COST OF EXCESS EXPENSE				
Additional Annual Savings Needed	$2,900	$6,200	$3,400	$7,100
Delay Retirement by:	3 Years	5 Years	3 Years	5 Years
Reduce Annual Retirement Income by	$2,100	$4,000	$2,400	$4,400
Increased Risk of Outliving Resources	47%	108%	46%	109%
Reduction to Age 65 Portfolio Values:				
Likely More than:	$22,061	$20,548	$23,113	$21,998
Likely Less than:	$66,364	$66,364	$68,845	$133,329

Total annual savings is COMBINED annual employee AND employer contribution

AGE 50 WITH CURRENT 401(K) BALANCE OF $250,000

Total Annual Savings	$10,000		$15,000	
Allocation: ***80% Stock/20% Bonds***				
Base Comfortable "In Balance" Case:				
Maximum Fair Total Expense	0.75%		0.75%	
Retirement Income @ Age 65	$27,700		$32,100	
Age 65 Range of Portfolio Values	$376,891 to $1,990,497		$449,396 to $2,222,463	
EXCESS EXPENSE:	**0.50%**	**1.00%**	**0.50%**	**1.00%**
	(1.25% total)	(1.75% total)	(1.25% total)	(1.75% total)
COST OF EXCESS EXPENSE				
Additional Annual Savings Needed	$3,700	$7,800	$4,000	$8,800
Delay Retirement by:	2 Years	4 Years	2 Years	4 Years
Reduce Annual Retirement Income by	$3,100	$5,900	$3,400	$6,600
Increased Risk of Outliving Resources	31%	78%	34%	79%
Reduction to Age 65 Portfolio Values:				
Likely More than:	$25,332	$23,678	$28,285	$24,946
Likely Less than:	$126,958	$126,958	$133,598	$260,223

Allocation: ***60% Stock/40% Bonds***				
Base Comfortable "In Balance" Case:				
Maximum Fair Total Expense	0.75%		0.75%	
Retirement Income @ Age 65	$24,900		$29,000	
Age 65 Range of Portfolio Values	$403,084 to $1,480,367		$479,923 to $1,640,647	
EXCESS EXPENSE:	**0.50%**	**1.00%**	**0.50%**	**1.00%**
	(1.25% total)	(1.75% total)	(1.25% total)	(1.75% total)
COST OF EXCESS EXPENSE				
Additional Annual Savings Needed	$3,700	$8,000	$4,500	$9,200
Delay Retirement by:	2 Years	4 Years	2 Years	4 Years
Reduce Annual Retirement Income by	$2,800	$5,300	$3,200	$6,200
Increased Risk of Outliving Resources	41%	98%	36%	95%
Reduction to Age 65 Portfolio Values:				
Likely More than:	$25,553	$22,616	$28,441	$26,638
Likely Less than:	$94,827	$94,827	$100,950	$195,720

Allocation: ***45% Stock/55% Bonds***				
Base Comfortable "In Balance" Case:				
Maximum Fair Total Expense	0.75%		0.75%	
Retirement Income @ Age 65	$22,500		$26,200	
Age 65 Range of Portfolio Values	$409,740 to $1,193,225		$485,757 to $1,335,598	
EXCESS EXPENSE:	**0.50%**	**1.00%**	**0.50%**	**1.00%**
	(1.25% total)	(1.75% total)	(1.25% total)	(1.75% total)
COST OF EXCESS EXPENSE				
Additional Annual Savings Needed	$3,800	$8,000	$4,400	$9,000
Delay Retirement by:	2 Years	4 Years	2 Years	4 Years
Reduce Annual Retirement Income by	$2,600	$5,000	$3,000	$5,600
Increased Risk of Outliving Resources	40%	107%	40%	106%
Reduction to Age 65 Portfolio Values:				
Likely More than:	$26,805	$25,060	$29,632	$27,218
Likely Less than:	$76,207	$76,207	$80,324	$155,801

Total annual savings is COMBINED annual employee AND employer contribution

AGE 55 WITH CURRENT 401(K) BALANCE OF $25,000

Total Annual Savings	$2,500		$5,000	
Allocation: **80% Stock/20% Bonds**				
Base Comfortable "In Balance" Case:				
Maximum Fair Total Expense	0.75%		0.75%	
Retirement Income @ Age 65	$2,800		$4,200	
Age 65 Range of Portfolio Values	$44,649 to $150,039		$67,706 to $204,743	
EXCESS EXPENSE:	**0.50%**	**1.00%**	**0.50%**	**1.00%**
	(1.25% total)	(1.75% total)	(1.25% total)	(1.75% total)
COST OF EXCESS EXPENSE				
Additional Annual Savings Needed	$400	$1,000	$700	$1,600
Delay Retirement by:	1 Year	2 Years	1 Year	2 Years
Reduce Annual Retirement Income by	$200	$500	$400	$800
Increased Risk of Outliving Resources	32%	74%	38%	80%
Reduction to Age 65 Portfolio Values:				
Likely More than:	$1,813	$1,737	$2,396	$2,503
Likely Less than:	$5,991	$5,991	$7,794	$15,260

Allocation: **60% Stock/40% Bonds**				
Base Comfortable "In Balance" Case:				
Maximum Fair Total Expense	0.75%		0.75%	
Retirement Income @ Age 65	$2,600		$3,800	
Age 65 Range of Portfolio Values	$46,684 to $123,897		$70,477 to $172,367	
EXCESS EXPENSE:	**0.50%**	**1.00%**	**0.50%**	**1.00%**
	(1.25% total)	(1.75% total)	(1.25% total)	(1.75% total)
COST OF EXCESS EXPENSE				
Additional Annual Savings Needed	$500	$1,100	$600	$1,500
Delay Retirement by:	1 Year	3 Years	1 Year	2 Years
Reduce Annual Retirement Income by	$200	$500	$300	$600
Increased Risk of Outliving Resources	41%	93%	44%	99%
Reduction to Age 65 Portfolio Values:				
Likely More than:	$1,850	$1,849	$2,413	$2,403
Likely Less than:	$5,035	$5,035	$6,074	$12,018

Allocation: **45% Stock/55% Bonds**				
Base Comfortable "In Balance" Case:				
Maximum Fair Total Expense	0.75%		0.75%	
Retirement Income @ Age 65	$2,400		$3,500	
Age 65 Range of Portfolio Values	$47,517 to $109,721		$72,154 to $153,344	
EXCESS EXPENSE:	**0.50%**	**1.00%**	**0.50%**	**1.00%**
	(1.25% total)	(1.75% total)	(1.25% total)	(1.75% total)
COST OF EXCESS EXPENSE				
Additional Annual Savings Needed	$500	$1,100	$600	$1,400
Delay Retirement by:	1 Year	3 Years	1 Year	2 Years
Reduce Annual Retirement Income by	$200	$500	$300	$600
Increased Risk of Outliving Resources	57%	114%	49%	114%
Reduction to Age 65 Portfolio Values:				
Likely More than:	$1,806	$1,797	$2,548	$2,534
Likely Less than:	$4,416	$4,416	$5,621	$11,029

Total annual savings is COMBINED annual employee AND employer contribution

AGE 55 WITH CURRENT 401(K) BALANCE OF $25,000

Total Annual Savings	$10,000		$15,000	
Allocation: **80% Stock/20% Bonds**				
Base Comfortable "In Balance" Case:				
Maximum Fair Total Expense	0.75%		0.75%	
Retirement Income @ Age 65	$6,800		$9,400	
Age 65 Range of Portfolio Values	$114,062 to $313,730		$159,352 to $424,927	
EXCESS EXPENSE:	**0.50%**	**1.00%**	**0.50%**	**1.00%**
	(1.25% total)	(1.75% total)	(1.25% total)	(1.75% total)
COST OF EXCESS EXPENSE				
Additional Annual Savings Needed	$1,100	$2,500	$1,500	$3,300
Delay Retirement by:	1 Year	2 Years	1 Year	2 Years
Reduce Annual Retirement Income by	$600	$1,100	$800	$1,500
Increased Risk of Outliving Resources	32%	73%	31%	74%
Reduction to Age 65 Portfolio Values:				
Likely More than:	$3,561	$3,552	$4,545	$4,605
Likely Less than:	$10,250	$10,250	$13,205	$25,977

Allocation: **60% Stock/40% Bonds**	$10,000		$15,000	
Base Comfortable "In Balance" Case:				
Maximum Fair Total Expense	0.75%		0.75%	
Retirement Income @ Age 65	$6,300		$8,800	
Age 65 Range of Portfolio Values	$118,405 to $268,197		$165,860 to $365,888	
EXCESS EXPENSE:	**0.50%**	**1.00%**	**0.50%**	**1.00%**
	(1.25% total)	(1.75% total)	(1.25% total)	(1.75% total)
COST OF EXCESS EXPENSE				
Additional Annual Savings Needed	$1,100	$2,400	$1,700	$3,500
Delay Retirement by:	1 Year	2 Years	1 Year	2 Years
Reduce Annual Retirement Income by	$500	$1,100	$800	$1,500
Increased Risk of Outliving Resources	45%	96%	44%	92%
Reduction to Age 65 Portfolio Values:				
Likely More than:	$3,580	$3,455	$5,154	$4,625
Likely Less than:	$8,279	$8,279	$11,166	$21,967

Allocation: **45% Stock/55% Bonds**	$10,000		$15,000	
Base Comfortable "In Balance" Case:				
Maximum Fair Total Expense	0.75%		0.75%	
Retirement Income @ Age 65	$5,900		$8,200	
Age 65 Range of Portfolio Values	$120,936 to $240,466		$170,158 to $327,803	
EXCESS EXPENSE:	**0.50%**	**1.00%**	**0.50%**	**1.00%**
	(1.25% total)	(1.75% total)	(1.25% total)	(1.75% total)
COST OF EXCESS EXPENSE				
Additional Annual Savings Needed	$1,300	$2,500	$1,600	$3,500
Delay Retirement by:	1 Year	2 Years	1 Year	2 Years
Reduce Annual Retirement Income by	$600	$1,100	$700	$1,400
Increased Risk of Outliving Resources	54%	116%	51%	111%
Reduction to Age 65 Portfolio Values:				
Likely More than:	$3,721	$3,607	$5,041	$4,974
Likely Less than:	$7,421	$7,421	$10,421	$20,492

Total annual savings is COMBINED annual employee AND employer contribution

AGE 55 WITH CURRENT 401(K) BALANCE OF $75,000

Total Annual Savings	$2,500		$5,000	
Allocation: **80% Stock/20% Bonds**				
Base Comfortable "In Balance" Case:				
Maximum Fair Total Expense	0.75%		0.75%	
Retirement Income @ Age 65	$5,800		$7,200	
Age 65 Range of Portfolio Values	$87,593 to $339,088		$111,390 to $394,481	
EXCESS EXPENSE:	**0.50%**	**1.00%**	**0.50%**	**1.00%**
	(1.25% total)	(1.75% total)	(1.25% total)	(1.75% total)
COST OF EXCESS EXPENSE				
Additional Annual Savings Needed	$1,100	$2,300	$1,300	$2,700
Delay Retirement by:	2 Years	3 Years	2 Years	3 Years
Reduce Annual Retirement Income by	$600	$1,100	$700	$1,300
Increased Risk of Outliving Resources	28%	66%	32%	67%
Reduction to Age 65 Portfolio Values:				
Likely More than:	$4,277	$4,081	$4,799	$4,840
Likely Less than:	$15,188	$15,188	$16,671	$32,610

Allocation: **60% Stock/40% Bonds**				
Base Comfortable "In Balance" Case:				
Maximum Fair Total Expense	0.75%		0.75%	
Retirement Income @ Age 65	$5,300		$6,600	
Age 65 Range of Portfolio Values	$90,461 to $275,898		$115,132 to $325,871	
EXCESS EXPENSE:	**0.50%**	**1.00%**	**0.50%**	**1.00%**
	(1.25% total)	(1.75% total)	(1.25% total)	(1.75% total)
COST OF EXCESS EXPENSE				
Additional Annual Savings Needed	$1,000	$2,200	$1,300	$2,700
Delay Retirement by:	2 Years	3 Years	2 Years	3 Years
Reduce Annual Retirement Income by	$500	$1,000	$600	$1,200
Increased Risk of Outliving Resources	34%	93%	36%	90%
Reduction to Age 65 Portfolio Values:				
Likely More than:	$4,369	$4,135	$5,052	$4,833
Likely Less than:	$12,597	$12,597	$13,451	$26,357

Allocation: **45% Stock/55% Bonds**				
Base Comfortable "In Balance" Case:				
Maximum Fair Total Expense	0.75%		0.75%	
Retirement Income @ Age 65	$4,900		$6,100	
Age 65 Range of Portfolio Values	$94,017 to $238,911		$117,826 to $283,565	
EXCESS EXPENSE:	**0.50%**	**1.00%**	**0.50%**	**1.00%**
	(1.25% total)	(1.75% total)	(1.25% total)	(1.75% total)
COST OF EXCESS EXPENSE				
Additional Annual Savings Needed	$1,000	$2,200	$1,200	$2,800
Delay Retirement by:	2 Years	4 Years	2 Years	3 Years
Reduce Annual Retirement Income by	$500	$900	$600	$1,100
Increased Risk of Outliving Resources	56%	113%	54%	110%
Reduction to Age 65 Portfolio Values:				
Likely More than:	$4,429	$4,378	$5,039	$4,887
Likely Less than:	$10,715	$10,715	$11,893	$23,301

Total annual savings is COMBINED annual employee AND employer contribution

AGE 55 WITH CURRENT 401(K) BALANCE OF $75,000

Total Annual Savings		$10,000		$15,000	
Allocation: **80% Stock/20% Bonds**					
Base Comfortable "In Balance" Case:					
Maximum Fair Total Expense		0.75%		0.75%	
Retirement Income @ Age 65		$10,000		$12,600	
Age 65 Range of Portfolio Values		$156,762 to $505,267		$203,118 to $614,230	
EXCESS EXPENSE:		**0.50%**	**1.00%**	**0.50%**	**1.00%**
		(1.25% total)	(1.75% total)	(1.25% total)	(1.75% total)
COST OF EXCESS EXPENSE					
Additional Annual Savings Needed		$1,800	$3,900	$2,100	$4,800
Delay Retirement by:		1 Year	3 Years	1 Year	2 Years
Reduce Annual Retirement Income by		$1,000	$1,800	$1,100	$2,200
Increased Risk of Outliving Resources		35%	75%	38%	80%
Reduction to Age 65 Portfolio Values:					
Likely More than:		$6,023	$5,777	$7,188	$7,508
Likely Less than:		$19,635	$19,635	$23,382	$45,780

Allocation: **60% Stock/40% Bonds**					
Base Comfortable "In Balance" Case:					
Maximum Fair Total Expense		0.75%		0.75%	
Retirement Income @ Age 65		$9,200		$11,600	
Age 65 Range of Portfolio Values		$163,315 to $416,749		$211,187 to $516,858	
EXCESS EXPENSE:		**0.50%**	**1.00%**	**0.50%**	**1.00%**
		(1.25% total)	(1.75% total)	(1.25% total)	(1.75% total)
COST OF EXCESS EXPENSE					
Additional Annual Savings Needed		$1,800	$4,100	$2,200	$4,800
Delay Retirement by:		2 Years	3 Years	1 Year	2 Years
Reduce Annual Retirement Income by		$900	$1,700	$1,100	$2,000
Increased Risk of Outliving Resources		43%	93%	40%	89%
Reduction to Age 65 Portfolio Values:					
Likely More than:		$6,472	$5,978	$7,238	$7,209
Likely Less than:		$15,487	$15,487	$18,223	$36,053

Allocation: **45% Stock/55% Bonds**					
Base Comfortable "In Balance" Case:					
Maximum Fair Total Expense		0.75%		0.75%	
Retirement Income @ Age 65		$8,400		$10,700	
Age 65 Range of Portfolio Values		$167,449 to $372,987		$216,220 to $459,789	
EXCESS EXPENSE:		**0.50%**	**1.00%**	**0.50%**	**1.00%**
		(1.25% total)	(1.75% total)	(1.25% total)	(1.75% total)
COST OF EXCESS EXPENSE					
Additional Annual Savings Needed		$1,700	$3,800	$2,100	$4,700
Delay Retirement by:		1 Years	3 Years	1 Year	3 Years
Reduce Annual Retirement Income by		$700	$1,500	$1,000	$1,900
Increased Risk of Outliving Resources		52%	109%	51%	108%
Reduction to Age 65 Portfolio Values:					
Likely More than:		$6,642	$6,228	$7,644	$7,604
Likely Less than:		$14,240	$14,240	$16,861	$33,088

Total annual savings is COMBINED annual employee AND employer contribution

AGE 55 WITH CURRENT 401(K) BALANCE OF $150,000

Total Annual Savings	$2,500		$5,000	
Allocation: **80% Stock/20% Bonds**				
Base Comfortable "In Balance" Case:				
Maximum Fair Total Expense	0.75%		0.75%	
Retirement Income @ Age 65	$10,300		$11,600	
Age 65 Range of Portfolio Values	$150,656 to $623,482		$175,185 to $678,175	
EXCESS EXPENSE:	**0.50%**	**1.00%**	**0.50%**	**1.00%**
	(1.25% total)	(1.75% total)	(1.25% total)	(1.75% total)
COST OF EXCESS EXPENSE				
Additional Annual Savings Needed	$2,100	$4,200	$2,200	$4,500
Delay Retirement by:	2 Years	4 Years	2 Years	3 Years
Reduce Annual Retirement Income by	$1,100	$2,000	$1,100	$2,200
Increased Risk of Outliving Resources	28%	65%	28%	66%
Reduction to Age 65 Portfolio Values:				
Likely More than:	$7,831	$7,465	$8,552	$8,162
Likely Less than:	$28,549	$28,549	$30,376	$59,488

Allocation: **60% Stock/40% Bonds**				
Base Comfortable "In Balance" Case:				
Maximum Fair Total Expense	0.75%		0.75%	
Retirement Income @ Age 65	$9,500		$10,700	
Age 65 Range of Portfolio Values	$157,110 to $505,456		$180,800 to $551,675	
EXCESS EXPENSE:	**0.50%**	**1.00%**	**0.50%**	**1.00%**
	(1.25% total)	(1.75% total)	(1.25% total)	(1.75% total)
COST OF EXCESS EXPENSE				
Additional Annual Savings Needed	$2,100	$4,400	$2,200	$4,600
Delay Retirement by:	2 Years	4 Years	2 Years	3 Years
Reduce Annual Retirement Income by	$1,000	$1,900	$1,100	$2,100
Increased Risk of Outliving Resources	35%	86%	33%	90%
Reduction to Age 65 Portfolio Values:				
Likely More than:	$8,003	$7,741	$8,737	$8,271
Likely Less than:	$23,467	$23,467	$25,195	$48,923

Allocation: **45% Stock/55% Bonds**				
Base Comfortable "In Balance" Case:				
Maximum Fair Total Expense	0.75%		0.75%	
Retirement Income @ Age 65	$8,700		$9,900	
Age 65 Range of Portfolio Values	$162,101 to $435,212		$187,913 to $477,700	
EXCESS EXPENSE:	**0.50%**	**1.00%**	**0.50%**	**1.00%**
	(1.25% total)	(1.75% total)	(1.25% total)	(1.75% total)
COST OF EXCESS EXPENSE				
Additional Annual Savings Needed	$2,000	$4,200	$2,200	$4,600
Delay Retirement by:	2 Years	4 Years	2 Years	4 Years
Reduce Annual Retirement Income by	$900	$1,700	$1,000	$1,900
Increased Risk of Outliving Resources	53%	111%	51%	105%
Reduction to Age 65 Portfolio Values:				
Likely More than:	$8,309	$7,924	$8,858	$8,756
Likely Less than:	$20,488	$20,488	$21,430	$41,966

Total annual savings is COMBINED annual employee AND employer contribution

AGE 55 WITH CURRENT 401(K) BALANCE OF $150,000

Total Annual Savings	$10,000		$15,000	
Allocation: **80% Stock/20% Bonds**				
Base Comfortable "In Balance" Case:				
Maximum Fair Total Expense	0.75%		0.75%	
Retirement Income @ Age 65	$14,400		$17,200	
Age 65 Range of Portfolio Values	$222,781 to $788,962		$267,411 to $899,748	
EXCESS EXPENSE:	**0.50%**	**1.00%**	**0.50%**	**1.00%**
	(1.25% total)	(1.75% total)	(1.25% total)	(1.75% total)
COST OF EXCESS EXPENSE				
Additional Annual Savings Needed	$2,600	$5,400	$3,100	$6,500
Delay Retirement by:	2 Years	3 Years	1 Year	3 Years
Reduce Annual Retirement Income by	$1,400	$2,600	$1,600	$3,000
Increased Risk of Outliving Resources	32%	67%	33%	73%
Reduction to Age 65 Portfolio Values:				
Likely More than:	$9,599	$9,680	$10,881	$10,424
Likely Less than:	$33,341	$33,341	$35,948	$70,413
Allocation: **60% Stock/40% Bonds**				
Base Comfortable "In Balance" Case:				
Maximum Fair Total Expense	0.75%		0.75%	
Retirement Income @ Age 65	$13,200		$15,800	
Age 65 Range of Portfolio Values	$230,263 to $651,743		$279,860 to $743,141	
EXCESS EXPENSE:	**0.50%**	**1.00%**	**0.50%**	**1.00%**
	(1.25% total)	(1.75% total)	(1.25% total)	(1.75% total)
COST OF EXCESS EXPENSE				
Additional Annual Savings Needed	$2,500	$5,400	$3,000	$6,600
Delay Retirement by:	2 Years	3 Years	2 Years	3 Years
Reduce Annual Retirement Income by	$1,200	$2,400	$1,400	$2,800
Increased Risk of Outliving Resources	36%	90%	39%	90%
Reduction to Age 65 Portfolio Values:				
Likely More than:	$10,104	$9,666	$11,100	$11,094
Likely Less than:	$26,903	$26,903	$30,210	$59,221
Allocation: **45% Stock/55% Bonds**				
Base Comfortable "In Balance" Case:				
Maximum Fair Total Expense	0.75%		0.75%	
Retirement Income @ Age 65	$12,300		$14,600	
Age 65 Range of Portfolio Values	$235,531 to $567,010		$284,858 to $658,085	
EXCESS EXPENSE:	**0.50%**	**1.00%**	**0.50%**	**1.00%**
	(1.25% total)	(1.75% total)	(1.25% total)	(1.75% total)
COST OF EXCESS EXPENSE				
Additional Annual Savings Needed	$2,700	$5,900	$3,100	$6,700
Delay Retirement by:	2 Years	3 Years	2 Years	3 Years
Reduce Annual Retirement Income by	$1,200	$2,300	$1,400	$2,700
Increased Risk of Outliving Resources	53%	110%	55%	110%
Reduction to Age 65 Portfolio Values:				
Likely More than:	$10,079	$9,773	$10,837	$10,779
Likely Less than:	$23,787	$23,787	$26,496	$52,140

Total annual savings is COMBINED annual employee AND employer contribution

AGE 55 WITH CURRENT 401(K) BALANCE OF $250,000

Total Annual Savings	$2,500		$5,000	
Allocation: **80% Stock/20% Bonds**				
Base Comfortable "In Balance" Case:				
Maximum Fair Total Expense	0.75%		0.75%	
Retirement Income @ Age 65	$16,200		$17,600	
Age 65 Range of Portfolio Values	$233,971 to $1,009,023		$259,605 to $1,056,272	
EXCESS EXPENSE:	**0.50%**	**1.00%**	**0.50%**	**1.00%**
	(1.25% total)	(1.75% total)	(1.25% total)	(1.75% total)
COST OF EXCESS EXPENSE				
Additional Annual Savings Needed	$3,100	$6,700	$3,500	$7,100
Delay Retirement by:	2 Years	4 Years	2 Years	4 Years
Reduce Annual Retirement Income by	$1,600	$3,200	$1,800	$3,400
Increased Risk of Outliving Resources	26%	62%	28%	66%
Reduction to Age 65 Portfolio Values:				
Likely More than:	$12,641	$12,043	$13,145	$12,539
Likely Less than:	$46,760	$46,760	$48,650	$95,249

Allocation: **60% Stock/40% Bonds**				
Base Comfortable "In Balance" Case:				
Maximum Fair Total Expense	0.75%		0.75%	
Retirement Income @ Age 65	$15,100		$16,200	
Age 65 Range of Portfolio Values	$243,219 to $813,860		$269,450 to $856,709	
EXCESS EXPENSE:	**0.50%**	**1.00%**	**0.50%**	**1.00%**
	(1.25% total)	(1.75% total)	(1.25% total)	(1.75% total)
COST OF EXCESS EXPENSE				
Additional Annual Savings Needed	$3,600	$7,100	$3,500	$7,200
Delay Retirement by:	3 Years	5 Years	2 Years	4 Years
Reduce Annual Retirement Income by	$1,700	$3,100	$1,600	$3,200
Increased Risk of Outliving Resources	36%	89%	33%	85%
Reduction to Age 65 Portfolio Values:				
Likely More than:	$12,794	$12,194	$14,015	$13,363
Likely Less than:	$38,343	$38,343	$39,496	$77,323

Allocation: **45% Stock/55% Bonds**				
Base Comfortable "In Balance" Case:				
Maximum Fair Total Expense	0.75%		0.75%	
Retirement Income @ Age 65	$13,800		$15,000	
Age 65 Range of Portfolio Values	$252,278 to $698,105		$278,358 to $738,057	
EXCESS EXPENSE:	**0.50%**	**1.00%**	**0.50%**	**1.00%**
	(1.25% total)	(1.75% total)	(1.25% total)	(1.75% total)
COST OF EXCESS EXPENSE				
Additional Annual Savings Needed	$3,400	$7,000	$3,600	$7,400
Delay Retirement by:	3 Years	5 Years	2 Years	4 Years
Reduce Annual Retirement Income by	$1,500	$2,800	$1,600	$3,000
Increased Risk of Outliving Resources	48%	108%	51%	108%
Reduction to Age 65 Portfolio Values:				
Likely More than:	$13,292	$12,668	$13,924	$13,282
Likely Less than:	$33,219	$33,219	$34,496	$67,515

Total annual savings is COMBINED annual employee AND employer contribution

AGE 55 WITH CURRENT 401(K) BALANCE OF $250,000

Total Annual Savings	$10,000		$15,000	
Allocation: **80% Stock/20% Bonds**				
Base Comfortable "In Balance" Case:				
Maximum Fair Total Expense	0.75%		0.75%	
Retirement Income @ Age 65	$20,300		$23,000	
Age 65 Range of Portfolio Values	$307,306 to $1,164,933		$353,769 to $1,279,049	
EXCESS EXPENSE:	**0.50%**	**1.00%**	**0.50%**	**1.00%**
	(1.25% total)	(1.75% total)	(1.25% total)	(1.75% total)
COST OF EXCESS EXPENSE				
Additional Annual Savings Needed	$3,800	$7,800	$4,100	$8,500
Delay Retirement by:	2 Years	3 Years	2 Years	3 Years
Reduce Annual Retirement Income by	$2,000	$3,800	$2,100	$4,100
Increased Risk of Outliving Resources	29%	66%	32%	68%
Reduction to Age 65 Portfolio Values:				
Likely More than:	$14,642	$13,981	$14,952	$14,840
Likely Less than:	$50,685	$50,685	$53,322	$105,203
Allocation: **60% Stock/40% Bonds**				
Base Comfortable "In Balance" Case:				
Maximum Fair Total Expense	0.75%		0.75%	
Retirement Income @ Age 65	$18,800		$21,200	
Age 65 Range of Portfolio Values	$317,987 to $951,145		$368,111 to $1,054,077	
EXCESS EXPENSE:	**0.50%**	**1.00%**	**0.50%**	**1.00%**
	(1.25% total)	(1.75% total)	(1.25% total)	(1.75% total)
COST OF EXCESS EXPENSE				
Additional Annual Savings Needed	$4,000	$8,300	$4,000	$8,700
Delay Retirement by:	2 Years	3 Years	2 Years	3 Years
Reduce Annual Retirement Income by	$1,900	$3,600	$2,000	$3,800
Increased Risk of Outliving Resources	34%	92%	37%	94%
Reduction to Age 65 Portfolio Values:				
Likely More than:	$14,795	$14,136	$16,533	$15,715
Likely Less than:	$41,510	$41,510	$45,484	$87,830
Allocation: **45% Stock/55% Bonds**				
Base Comfortable "In Balance" Case:				
Maximum Fair Total Expense	0.75%		0.75%	
Retirement Income @ Age 65	$17,400		$19,800	
Age 65 Range of Portfolio Values	$327,705 to $826,090		$376,305 to $915,228	
EXCESS EXPENSE:	**0.50%**	**1.00%**	**0.50%**	**1.00%**
	(1.25% total)	(1.75% total)	(1.25% total)	(1.75% total)
COST OF EXCESS EXPENSE				
Additional Annual Savings Needed	$3,900	$8,400	$4,500	$9,600
Delay Retirement by:	2 Years	4 Years	2 Years	3 Years
Reduce Annual Retirement Income by	$1,800	$3,400	$2,000	$3,700
Increased Risk of Outliving Resources	53%	109%	52%	111%
Reduction to Age 65 Portfolio Values:				
Likely More than:	$15,755	$14,661	$16,597	$15,878
Likely Less than:	$36,379	$36,379	$39,025	$76,586

Total annual savings is COMBINED annual employee AND employer contribution

AGE 60 WITH CURRENT 401(K) BALANCE OF $25,000

Total Annual Savings	$2,500		$5,000	
Allocation: **80% Stock/20% Bonds**				
Base Comfortable "In Balance" Case:				
Maximum Fair Total Expense	0.75%		0.75%	
Retirement Income @ Age 65	$1,800		$2,400	
Age 65 Range of Portfolio Values	$30,994 to $81,028		$43,621 to $102,461	
EXCESS EXPENSE:	**0.50%**	**1.00%**	**0.50%**	**1.00%**
	(1.25% total)	(1.75% total)	(1.25% total)	(1.75% total)
COST OF EXCESS EXPENSE				
Additional Annual Savings Needed	$600	$1,200	$500	$1,400
Delay Retirement by:	1 Year	2 Years	1 Year	2 Years
Reduce Annual Retirement Income by	$200	$300	$200	$300
Increased Risk of Outliving Resources	28%	64%	28%	60%
Reduction to Age 65 Portfolio Values:				
Likely More than:	$756	$740	$903	$933
Likely Less than:	$1,796	$1,796	$2,174	$4,307

Allocation: **60% Stock/40% Bonds**				
Base Comfortable "In Balance" Case:				
Maximum Fair Total Expense	0.75%		0.75%	
Retirement Income @ Age 65	$1,700		$2,300	
Age 65 Range of Portfolio Values	$32,470 to $71,438		$45,590 to $91,243	
EXCESS EXPENSE:	**0.50%**	**1.00%**	**0.50%**	**1.00%**
	(1.25% total)	(1.75% total)	(1.25% total)	(1.75% total)
COST OF EXCESS EXPENSE				
Additional Annual Savings Needed	$500	$1,200	$700	$1,600
Delay Retirement by:	1 Year	2 Years	1 Year	2 Years
Reduce Annual Retirement Income by	$200	$300	$200	$400
Increased Risk of Outliving Resources	36%	71%	32%	71%
Reduction to Age 65 Portfolio Values:				
Likely More than:	$780	$764	$952	$918
Likely Less than:	$1,620	$1,620	$1,871	$3,706

Allocation: **45% Stock/55% Bonds**				
Base Comfortable "In Balance" Case:				
Maximum Fair Total Expense	0.75%		0.75%	
Retirement Income @ Age 65	$1,600		$2,200	
Age 65 Range of Portfolio Values	$33,240 to $65,045		$46,219 to $83,867	
EXCESS EXPENSE:	**0.50%**	**1.00%**	**0.50%**	**1.00%**
	(1.25% total)	(1.75% total)	(1.25% total)	(1.75% total)
COST OF EXCESS EXPENSE				
Additional Annual Savings Needed	$500	$1,200	$800	$1,700
Delay Retirement by:	1 Year	2 Years	1 Year	2 Years
Reduce Annual Retirement Income by	$100	$300	$200	$400
Increased Risk of Outliving Resources	34%	89%	40%	92%
Reduction to Age 65 Portfolio Values:				
Likely More than:	$798	$780	$949	$944
Likely Less than:	$1,474	$1,474	$1,695	$3,357

Total annual savings is COMBINED annual employee AND employer contribution

AGE 60 WITH CURRENT 401(K) BALANCE OF $25,000

Total Annual Savings	$10,000		$15,000	
Allocation: **80% Stock/20% Bonds**				
Base Comfortable "In Balance" Case:				
Maximum Fair Total Expense	0.75%		0.75%	
Retirement Income @ Age 65	$3,700		$4,900	
Age 65 Range of Portfolio Values	$69,085 to $146,476		$93,267 to $191,168	
EXCESS EXPENSE:	**0.50%**	**1.00%**	**0.50%**	**1.00%**
	(1.25% total)	(1.75% total)	(1.25% total)	(1.75% total)
COST OF EXCESS EXPENSE				
Additional Annual Savings Needed	$1,100	$2,400	$1,100	$2,700
Delay Retirement by:	1 Year	1 Year	1 Year	1 Year
Reduce Annual Retirement Income by	$300	$600	$300	$700
Increased Risk of Outliving Resources	32%	63%	31%	65%
Reduction to Age 65 Portfolio Values:				
Likely More than:	$1,276	$1,252	$1,586	$1,557
Likely Less than:	$2,576	$2,576	$3,221	$6,390

Allocation: **60% Stock/40% Bonds**				
Base Comfortable "In Balance" Case:				
Maximum Fair Total Expense	0.75%		0.75%	
Retirement Income @ Age 65	$3,500		$4,700	
Age 65 Range of Portfolio Values	$71,300 to $131,649		$96,584 to $173,573	
EXCESS EXPENSE:	**0.50%**	**1.00%**	**0.50%**	**1.00%**
	(1.25% total)	(1.75% total)	(1.25% total)	(1.75% total)
COST OF EXCESS EXPENSE				
Additional Annual Savings Needed	$900	$2,200	$1,300	$3,000
Delay Retirement by:	1 Year	1 Year	1 Year	1 Year
Reduce Annual Retirement Income by	$300	$500	$300	$700
Increased Risk of Outliving Resources	38%	80%	38%	79%
Reduction to Age 65 Portfolio Values:				
Likely More than:	$1,335	$1,309	$1,598	$1,537
Likely Less than:	$2,312	$2,312	$2,892	$5,678

Allocation: **45% Stock/55% Bonds**				
Base Comfortable "In Balance" Case:				
Maximum Fair Total Expense	0.75%		0.75%	
Retirement Income @ Age 65	$3,300		$4,500	
Age 65 Range of Portfolio Values	$72,207 to $122,642		$97,718 to $161,239	
EXCESS EXPENSE:	**0.50%**	**1.00%**	**0.50%**	**1.00%**
	(1.25% total)	(1.75% total)	(1.25% total)	(1.75% total)
COST OF EXCESS EXPENSE				
Additional Annual Savings Needed	$800	$2,100	$1,500	$3,100
Delay Retirement by:	1 Year	1 Year	1 Year	1 Year
Reduce Annual Retirement Income by	$200	$500	$300	$700
Increased Risk of Outliving Resources	51%	105%	43%	99%
Reduction to Age 65 Portfolio Values:				
Likely More than:	$1,305	$1,316	$1,618	$1,589
Likely Less than:	$2,181	$2,181	$2,700	$5,355

Total annual savings is COMBINED annual employee AND employer contribution

AGE 60 WITH CURRENT 401(K) BALANCE OF $75,000

Total Annual Savings	$2,500		$5,000	
Allocation: **80% Stock/20% Bonds**				
Base Comfortable "In Balance" Case:				
Maximum Fair Total Expense	0.75%		0.75%	
Retirement Income @ Age 65	$4,100		$4,800	
Age 65 Range of Portfolio Values	$68,367 to $201,376		$80,518 to $222,122	
EXCESS EXPENSE:	**0.50%**	**1.00%**	**0.50%**	**1.00%**
	(1.25% total)	(1.75% total)	(1.25% total)	(1.75% total)
COST OF EXCESS EXPENSE				
Additional Annual Savings Needed	$1,000	$2,600	$1,500	$3,400
Delay Retirement by:	1 Year	3 Years	1 Year	2 Years
Reduce Annual Retirement Income by	$300	$600	$400	$800
Increased Risk of Outliving Resources	28%	63%	25%	58%
Reduction to Age 65 Portfolio Values:				
Likely More than:	$1,970	$1,924	$2,081	$2,032
Likely Less than:	$4,858	$4,858	$5,116	$10,129

Allocation: **60% Stock/40% Bonds**				
Base Comfortable "In Balance" Case:				
Maximum Fair Total Expense	0.75%		0.75%	
Retirement Income @ Age 65	$3,900		$4,500	
Age 65 Range of Portfolio Values	$71,134 to $175,914		$84,272 to $195,138	
EXCESS EXPENSE:	**0.50%**	**1.00%**	**0.50%**	**1.00%**
	(1.25% total)	(1.75% total)	(1.25% total)	(1.75% total)
COST OF EXCESS EXPENSE				
Additional Annual Savings Needed	$1,300	$2,800	$1,300	$3,200
Delay Retirement by:	1 Year	3 Years	1 Year	2 Years
Reduce Annual Retirement Income by	$400	$600	$300	$700
Increased Risk of Outliving Resources	35%	69%	38%	73%
Reduction to Age 65 Portfolio Values:				
Likely More than:	$2,013	$1,965	$2,199	$2,200
Likely Less than:	$4,354	$4,354	$4,529	$8,967

Allocation: **45% Stock/55% Bonds**				
Base Comfortable "In Balance" Case:				
Maximum Fair Total Expense	0.75%		0.75%	
Retirement Income @ Age 65	$3,700		$4,300	
Age 65 Range of Portfolio Values	$73,628 to $156,638		$86,446 to $176,581	
EXCESS EXPENSE:	**0.50%**	**1.00%**	**0.50%**	**1.00%**
	(1.25% total)	(1.75% total)	(1.25% total)	(1.75% total)
COST OF EXCESS EXPENSE				
Additional Annual Savings Needed	$1,200	$2,900	$1,600	$3,400
Delay Retirement by:	2 Years	3 Years	1 Year	2 Years
Reduce Annual Retirement Income by	$300	$600	$400	$700
Increased Risk of Outliving Resources	40%	87%	37%	89%
Reduction to Age 65 Portfolio Values:				
Likely More than:	$2,069	$2,020	$2,227	$2,175
Likely Less than:	$3,946	$3,946	$4,176	$8,267

Total annual savings is COMBINED annual employee AND employer contribution

AGE 60 WITH CURRENT 401(K) BALANCE OF $75,000

Total Annual Savings	$10,000		$15,000	
Allocation: **80% Stock/20% Bonds**				
Base Comfortable "In Balance" Case:				
Maximum Fair Total Expense	0.75%		0.75%	
Retirement Income @ Age 65	$6,000		$7,300	
Age 65 Range of Portfolio Values	$105,814 to $263,857		$130,740 to $307,261	
EXCESS EXPENSE:	**0.50%**	**1.00%**	**0.50%**	**1.00%**
	(1.25% total)	(1.75% total)	(1.25% total)	(1.75% total)
COST OF EXCESS EXPENSE				
Additional Annual Savings Needed	$1,500	$3,700	$1,900	$4,500
Delay Retirement by:	1 Year	2 Years	1 Year	2 Years
Reduce Annual Retirement Income by	$400	$900	$500	$1,000
Increased Risk of Outliving Resources	29%	66%	28%	63%
Reduction to Age 65 Portfolio Values:				
Likely More than:	$2,436	$2,382	$2,707	$2,798
Likely Less than:	$5,632	$5,632	$6,521	$12,919

Allocation: **60% Stock/40% Bonds**				
Base Comfortable "In Balance" Case:				
Maximum Fair Total Expense	0.75%		0.75%	
Retirement Income @ Age 65	$5,700		$6,900	
Age 65 Range of Portfolio Values	$110,550 to $233,256		$136,771 to $273,729	
EXCESS EXPENSE:	**0.50%**	**1.00%**	**0.50%**	**1.00%**
	(1.25% total)	(1.75% total)	(1.25% total)	(1.75% total)
COST OF EXCESS EXPENSE				
Additional Annual Savings Needed	$1,700	$3,800	$2,000	$4,600
Delay Retirement by:	1 Year	2 Years	1 Year	2 Years
Reduce Annual Retirement Income by	$400	$900	$500	$1,000
Increased Risk of Outliving Resources	33%	70%	32%	71%
Reduction to Age 65 Portfolio Values:				
Likely More than:	$2,507	$2,452	$2,856	$2,756
Likely Less than:	$5,105	$5,105	$5,612	$11,117

Allocation: **45% Stock/55% Bonds**				
Base Comfortable "In Balance" Case:				
Maximum Fair Total Expense	0.75%		0.75%	
Retirement Income @ Age 65	$5,400		$6,600	
Age 65 Range of Portfolio Values	$112,676 to $213,436		$138,657 to $251,602	
EXCESS EXPENSE:	**0.50%**	**1.00%**	**0.50%**	**1.00%**
	(1.25% total)	(1.75% total)	(1.25% total)	(1.75% total)
COST OF EXCESS EXPENSE				
Additional Annual Savings Needed	$1,700	$3,900	$2,400	$4,900
Delay Retirement by:	1 Year	2 Years	1 Year	2 Years
Reduce Annual Retirement Income by	$400	$800	$500	$1,000
Increased Risk of Outliving Resources	40%	98%	40%	92%
Reduction to Age 65 Portfolio Values:				
Likely More than:	$2,613	$2,513	$2,847	$2,832
Likely Less than:	$4,609	$4,609	$5,085	$10,073

Total annual savings is COMBINED annual employee AND employer contribution

AGE 60 WITH CURRENT 401(K) BALANCE OF $150,000

Total Annual Savings	$2,500		$5,000	
Allocation: **80% Stock/20% Bonds**				
Base Comfortable "In Balance" Case:				
Maximum Fair Total Expense	0.75%		0.75%	
Retirement Income @ Age 65	$7,600		$8,300	
Age 65 Range of Portfolio Values	$123,259 to $383,380		$136,614 to $402,631	
EXCESS EXPENSE:	**0.50%**	**1.00%**	**0.50%**	**1.00%**
	(1.25% total)	(1.75% total)	(1.25% total)	(1.75% total)
COST OF EXCESS EXPENSE				
Additional Annual Savings Needed	$2,000	$5,000	$2,500	$5,600
Delay Retirement by:	2 Years	3 Years	2 Years	3 Years
Reduce Annual Retirement Income by	$500	$1,100	$700	$1,300
Increased Risk of Outliving Resources	27%	60%	28%	61%
Reduction to Age 65 Portfolio Values:				
Likely More than:	$3,735	$3,634	$3,942	$3,846
Likely Less than:	$9,749	$9,749	$9,716	$19,234

Allocation: **60% Stock/40% Bonds**				
Base Comfortable "In Balance" Case:				
Maximum Fair Total Expense	0.75%		0.75%	
Retirement Income @ Age 65	$7,300		$7,800	
Age 65 Range of Portfolio Values	$129,008 to $330,523		$142,268 to $351,827	
EXCESS EXPENSE:	**0.50%**	**1.00%**	**0.50%**	**1.00%**
	(1.25% total)	(1.75% total)	(1.25% total)	(1.75% total)
COST OF EXCESS EXPENSE				
Additional Annual Savings Needed	$2,800	$5,600	$2,600	$5,600
Delay Retirement by:	2 Years	3 Years	1 Year	3 Years
Reduce Annual Retirement Income by	$600	$1,200	$700	$1,200
Increased Risk of Outliving Resources	33%	69%	35%	69%
Reduction to Age 65 Portfolio Values:				
Likely More than:	$3,861	$3,767	$4,026	$3,929
Likely Less than:	$8,358	$8,358	$8,706	$17,231

Allocation: **45% Stock/55% Bonds**				
Base Comfortable "In Balance" Case:				
Maximum Fair Total Expense	0.75%		0.75%	
Retirement Income @ Age 65	$6,900		$7,400	
Age 65 Range of Portfolio Values	$133,774 to $292,977		$147,256 to $313,275	
EXCESS EXPENSE:	**0.50%**	**1.00%**	**0.50%**	**1.00%**
	(1.25% total)	(1.75% total)	(1.25% total)	(1.75% total)
COST OF EXCESS EXPENSE				
Additional Annual Savings Needed	$2,800	$5,500	$2,400	$5,700
Delay Retirement by:	2 Years	3 Years	2 Years	3 Years
Reduce Annual Retirement Income by	$600	$1,200	$600	$1,200
Increased Risk of Outliving Resources	40%	88%	40%	87%
Reduction to Age 65 Portfolio Values:				
Likely More than:	$3,961	$3,864	$4,138	$4,040
Likely Less than:	$7,559	$7,559	$7,890	$15,613

Total annual savings is COMBINED annual employee AND employer contribution

AGE 60 WITH CURRENT 401(K) BALANCE OF $150,000

Total Annual Savings	$10,000		$15,000	
Allocation: **80% Stock/20% Bonds**				
Base Comfortable "In Balance" Case:				
Maximum Fair Total Expense	0.75%		0.75%	
Retirement Income @ Age 65	$9,600		$10,800	
Age 65 Range of Portfolio Values	$161,036 to $444,244		$185,966 to $486,167	
EXCESS EXPENSE:	**0.50%**	**1.00%**	**0.50%**	**1.00%**
	(1.25% total)	(1.75% total)	(1.25% total)	(1.75% total)
COST OF EXCESS EXPENSE				
Additional Annual Savings Needed	$3,000	$6,800	$3,200	$7,200
Delay Retirement by:	1 Year	2 Years	1 Year	2 Years
Reduce Annual Retirement Income by	$800	$1,500	$800	$1,600
Increased Risk of Outliving Resources	25%	58%	28%	64%
Reduction to Age 65 Portfolio Values:				
Likely More than:	$4,162	$4,065	$4,541	$4,438
Likely Less than:	$10,231	$10,231	$10,777	$21,344

Allocation: **60% Stock/40% Bonds**				
Base Comfortable "In Balance" Case:				
Maximum Fair Total Expense	0.75%		0.75%	
Retirement Income @ Age 65	$9,100		$10,400	
Age 65 Range of Portfolio Values	$168,423 to $390,155		$194,579 to $428,388	
EXCESS EXPENSE:	**0.50%**	**1.00%**	**0.50%**	**1.00%**
	(1.25% total)	(1.75% total)	(1.25% total)	(1.75% total)
COST OF EXCESS EXPENSE				
Additional Annual Savings Needed	$3,000	$6,800	$4,000	$8,000
Delay Retirement by:	1 Year	2 Years	1 Year	2 Years
Reduce Annual Retirement Income by	$700	$1,500	$900	$1,700
Increased Risk of Outliving Resources	35%	72%	36%	75%
Reduction to Age 65 Portfolio Values:				
Likely More than:	$4,399	$4,400	$4,684	$4,579
Likely Less than:	$9,059	$9,059	$9,721	$19,249

Allocation: **45% Stock/55% Bonds**				
Base Comfortable "In Balance" Case:				
Maximum Fair Total Expense	0.75%		0.75%	
Retirement Income @ Age 65	$8,600		$9,700	
Age 65 Range of Portfolio Values	$172,891 to $353,163		$199,316 to $390,147	
EXCESS EXPENSE:	**0.50%**	**1.00%**	**0.50%**	**1.00%**
	(1.25% total)	(1.75% total)	(1.25% total)	(1.75% total)
COST OF EXCESS EXPENSE				
Additional Annual Savings Needed	$3,200	$6,700	$3,300	$7,300
Delay Retirement by:	1 Year	2 Years	1 Year	2 Years
Reduce Annual Retirement Income by	$700	$1,400	$700	$1,500
Increased Risk of Outliving Resources	37%	89%	39%	94%
Reduction to Age 65 Portfolio Values:				
Likely More than:	$4,452	$4,350	$4,787	$4,681
Likely Less than:	$8,354	$8,354	$8,843	$17,656

Total annual savings is COMBINED annual employee AND employer contribution

AGE 60 WITH CURRENT 401(K) BALANCE OF $250,000

	Total Annual Savings		$2,500		$5,000	
Allocation: **80% Stock/20% Bonds**						
Base Comfortable "In Balance" Case:						
Maximum Fair Total Expense			0.75%		0.75%	
Retirement Income @ Age 65			$12,400		$13,000	
Age 65 Range of Portfolio Values			$196,222 to $626,152		$210,036 to $645,131	
EXCESS EXPENSE:		**0.50%**	**1.00%**	**0.50%**	**1.00%**	
		(1.25% total)	(1.75% total)	(1.25% total)	(1.75% total)	
COST OF EXCESS EXPENSE						
Additional Annual Savings Needed		$3,900	$8,600	$4,000	$8,900	
Delay Retirement by:		2 Years	4 Years	2 Years	3 Years	
Reduce Annual Retirement Income by		$1,000	$2,000	$1,000	$2,000	
Increased Risk of Outliving Resources		24%	57%	25%	60%	
Reduction to Age 65 Portfolio Values:						
Likely More than:		$6,091	$5,939	$6,361	$6,204	
Likely Less than:		$16,078	$16,078	$16,333	$32,326	

Allocation: **60% Stock/40% Bonds**					
Base Comfortable "In Balance" Case:					
Maximum Fair Total Expense		0.75%		0.75%	
Retirement Income @ Age 65		$11,700		$12,300	
Age 65 Range of Portfolio Values		$206,335 to $536,567		$219,473 to $558,146	
EXCESS EXPENSE:	**0.50%**	**1.00%**	**0.50%**	**1.00%**	
	(1.25% total)	(1.75% total)	(1.25% total)	(1.75% total)	
COST OF EXCESS EXPENSE					
Additional Annual Savings Needed	$4,200	$9,000	$4,500	$9,000	
Delay Retirement by:	2 Years	4 Years	2 Years	3 Years	
Reduce Annual Retirement Income by	$1,000	$1,900	$1,000	$2,000	
Increased Risk of Outliving Resources	35%	72%	33%	71%	
Reduction to Age 65 Portfolio Values:					
Likely More than:	$6,326	$6,169	$6,490	$6,374	
Likely Less than:	$13,753	$13,753	$14,020	$27,746	

Allocation: **45% Stock/55% Bonds**					
Base Comfortable "In Balance" Case:					
Maximum Fair Total Expense		0.75%		0.75%	
Retirement Income @ Age 65		$11,100		$11,600	
Age 65 Range of Portfolio Values		$214,956 to $475,489		$227,851 to $495,252	
EXCESS EXPENSE:	**0.50%**	**1.00%**	**0.50%**	**1.00%**	
	(1.25% total)	(1.75% total)	(1.25% total)	(1.75% total)	
COST OF EXCESS EXPENSE					
Additional Annual Savings Needed	$4,300	$8,900	$4,100	$8,900	
Delay Retirement by:	2 Years	4 Years	2 Years	3 Years	
Reduce Annual Retirement Income by	$900	$1,900	$900	$1,900	
Increased Risk of Outliving Resources	39%	88%	40%	90%	
Reduction to Age 65 Portfolio Values:					
Likely More than:	$6,574	$6,412	$6,657	$6,496	
Likely Less than:	$12,424	$12,424	$12,680	$25,089	

Total annual savings is COMBINED annual employee AND employer contribution

AGE 60 WITH CURRENT 401(K) BALANCE OF $250,000

Total Annual Savings	$10,000		$15,000	
Allocation: **80% Stock/20% Bonds**				
Base Comfortable "In Balance" Case:				
Maximum Fair Total Expense	0.75%		0.75%	
Retirement Income @ Age 65	$14,300		$15,600	
Age 65 Range of Portfolio Values	$236,367 to $684,882		$259,393 to $726,495	
EXCESS EXPENSE:	**0.50%**	**1.00%**	**0.50%**	**1.00%**
	(1.25% total)	(1.75% total)	(1.25% total)	(1.75% total)
COST OF EXCESS EXPENSE				
Additional Annual Savings Needed	$4,500	$9,600	$5,200	$11,000
Delay Retirement by:	2 Years	3 Years	1 Year	2 Years
Reduce Annual Retirement Income by	$1,100	$2,200	$1,200	$2,400
Increased Risk of Outliving Resources	29%	62%	27%	60%
Reduction to Age 65 Portfolio Values:				
Likely More than:	$6,682	$6,522	$6,824	$6,664
Likely Less than:	$16,365	$16,365	$16,880	$33,423

Allocation: **60% Stock/40% Bonds**				
Base Comfortable "In Balance" Case:				
Maximum Fair Total Expense	0.75%		0.75%	
Retirement Income @ Age 65	$13,500		$14,800	
Age 65 Range of Portfolio Values	$246,016 to $597,863		$271,954 to $637,107	
EXCESS EXPENSE:	**0.50%**	**1.00%**	**0.50%**	**1.00%**
	(1.25% total)	(1.75% total)	(1.25% total)	(1.75% total)
COST OF EXCESS EXPENSE				
Additional Annual Savings Needed	$4,500	$9,900	$5,200	$11,200
Delay Retirement by:	1 Year	3 Years	1 Year	2 Years
Reduce Annual Retirement Income by	$1,100	$2,200	$1,200	$2,400
Increased Risk of Outliving Resources	34%	70%	33%	69%
Reduction to Age 65 Portfolio Values:				
Likely More than:	$6,756	$6,596	$7,196	$6,982
Likely Less than:	$14,512	$14,512	$15,179	$30,048

Allocation: **45% Stock/55% Bonds**				
Base Comfortable "In Balance" Case:				
Maximum Fair Total Expense	0.75%		0.75%	
Retirement Income @ Age 65	$12,800		$14,000	
Age 65 Range of Portfolio Values	$253,791 to $534,053		$279,290 to $576,236	
EXCESS EXPENSE:	**0.50%**	**1.00%**	**0.50%**	**1.00%**
	(1.25% total)	(1.75% total)	(1.25% total)	(1.75% total)
COST OF EXCESS EXPENSE				
Additional Annual Savings Needed	$4,500	$10,000	$5,200	$11,200
Delay Retirement by:	2 Years	3 Years	1 Year	3 Years
Reduce Annual Retirement Income by	$1,100	$2,000	$1,100	$2,200
Increased Risk of Outliving Resources	39%	90%	36%	88%
Reduction to Age 65 Portfolio Values:				
Likely More than:	$7,002	$6,838	$7,309	$7,139
Likely Less than:	$13,305	$13,305	$13,769	$27,252

Total annual savings is COMBINED annual employee AND employer contribution

Appendix B

ABC Plan-401(k) Plan Fee Disclosure Form

ABC PLAN
401(k) PLAN FEE DISCLOSURE FORM
For Services Provided by XYZ Company[1]

Overview

The Employee Retirement Income Security Act of 1974, as amended (ERISA) requires employee benefit plan fiduciaries to act solely in the interests of, and for the exclusive benefit of, plan participants and beneficiaries. As part of that obligation, plan fiduciaries should consider cost, among other things, when choosing investment options for the plan and selecting plan service providers.

This 401(k) plan fee disclosure form may assist you in making informed cost-benefit decisions with respect to your plan. The purpose of this form is to help you determine the total cost of the plan. It is also intended to provide you with a means to compare investment product fees and plan administration expenses charged by competing service providers, regardless of how a particular service provider structures its fees.

The 401(k) plan fees included in this disclosure form represent the following: _____ actual 401(k) plan expenses for the period X/XX/XX through X/XX/XX or _____ estimated 401(k) plan expenses[2] for the period X/XX/XX through X/XX/XX. Additional investment product information regarding fees may be obtained from the product prospectus, annuity contract or other similar documents. Additional information relating to plan administration services and expenses is contained in documentation provided by the service provider, including the contract for plan services. Other plan expenses may include legal fees for initial plan design and ongoing amendments resulting from changes in pension law or plan design and the cost of a mandatory annual audit. You need to contact your legal advisor or accountant to determine these charges.

Selecting a service provider requires that you evaluate and differentiate services offered by competing companies. Cost is one of the criteria, but not the only criterion, for making this evaluation. Other factors of equal or greater importance to consider include the quality and type of services provided, the anticipated performance of competing providers and their investment products and other factors specific to your plan's needs. *The service provider offering the lowest cost services is not necessarily the best choice for your plan.*

Calculation of Fees

In general, fees are calculated in four ways:

- Asset-based: expenses are based on the amount of assets in the plan and generally are expressed as percentages or basis points.
- Per-person: expenses are based upon the number of eligible employees or actual participants in the plan.
- Transaction-based: expenses are based on the execution of a particular plan service or transaction.
- Flat rate: fixed charge that does not vary, regardless of plan size.

Fees may be calculated using one or any combination of these methods. Plan administration-related expenses can also be charged as one-time fees or ongoing expenses. One-time fees are typically related to start-ups, conversions (moving from one provider to another) and terminations of service. Ongoing fees are recurring expenses relating to continuing plan operation.

---

[1] There may be plan expenses incurred by other providers, other than the company completing this form. For a complete list of expenses charged to your plan, please contact all plan service providers with whom you contract or may contract and request fee information with respect to their services.

[2] If you are considering a conversion from an existing plan service provider to a new service provider, you will need to provide the service provider(s) with certain information about the plan, including the number of plan participants, the number of eligible participants and the amount of plan assets in order for the service provider(s) to be able to complete this form. Similarly, if you are considering starting a plan, you will need to provide the service provider(s) with estimates of plan participants and plan assets. When providing potential service providers with information regarding your plan, it is critical that you provide identical information to all of the competing companies in order to ensure equivalent comparisons.

<table>
<tr><td colspan="2">

ABC PLAN
401(k) PLAN FEE DISCLOSURE FORM
For Services Provided by XYZ Company
Total Plan Expenses

</td><td>

Contact Name: _____
Institution: _____
Phone: _____

</td></tr>
</table>

		Amount/ Estimate[3]
I.	**Investment Product Fees (See Schedule A)**	
	A. Collective Investment Fund(s)	$_____
	B. Insurance/Annuity Product(s)	$_____
	C. Mutual Fund(s)	$_____
	D. Individually Managed Account(s)	$_____
	E. Brokerage Window	$_____
	F. Other Product(s) (Specify)	$_____
	Total Investment Product Fees	$_____
II.	**Plan Administration Expenses (See Schedule B)**	
	Total Plan Administration Expenses	$_____
III.	**Plan Start-Up or Conversion Related Charges (See Schedule C)**	
	One Time Start-Up/Conversion expenses	$_____
IV.	**Service Provider Termination Related Charges (See Schedule D)**	
	Service Provider Termination expenses	$_____
	Total Plan Expenses	$_____

For definitions of terms used throughout this disclosure form, see Schedule E.

---

[3] Amounts are calculated based on rates charged, which are identified in attached schedules as applied to relevant information (for example amount of assets or number of participants). Certain calculations may be estimates based on information provided by you, the plan sponsor, and may vary as circumstances change.

ABC PLAN
401(k) PLAN FEE DISCLOSURE FORM
For Services Provided by XYZ Company
Schedule A

Investment Product Fees/Estimates

Collective Investment Fund	Assets (X/X/XX)	Management Fee	Other[+] (Specify)	Total Cost
Fund 1				
Fund 2				
Fund 3				
Fund 4				
TOTAL				

Insurance /Annuity Product	Assets (X/X/XX)	Management Fee	Mortality Risk and Administrative Expense (M&E Fee)	Other[+] (Specify)	Total Cost
Fund 1					
Fund 2					
Separate Account 1					
Separate Account 2					
TOTAL					

Mutual Fund	Assets (X/X/XX)	Expense Ratio[4]	Front-end Load	Other[+] (Specify)	Total Cost
Fund 1					
Fund 2					
Fund 3					
Fund 4					
TOTAL					

Individually-Managed Account	Assets (X/X/XX)	Management Fee	Other[+] (Specify)	Total Cost
Product 1				
Product 2				
Product 3				
Product 4				
TOTAL				

[+] Fees represent product-related charges paid by the plan. Fees associated with participants' transfer of account balances between investment options, including investment transfer expenses and any contingent back-end loads, redemption fees and surrender charges should be included in "other" expenses. In addition, any wrap fees or pricing charges for non-publicly traded assets should be included in the "other" expenses column. For investment product termination fees associated with plan termination or conversion, see Schedule D. Insurance companies incur marketing and distribution costs, which are recouped through charges assessed against the plan.

[4] Includes 12b-1 fee and management fee. (See the fee table in the fund prospectus).

ABC PLAN
401(k) PLAN FEE DISCLOSURE FORM
For Services Provided by XYZ Company
Schedule A, continued

<u>**Investment Product Fees/Estimates**</u>

Brokerage Window[5]	Assets (X/X/XX)	Commission (Range)	Transaction Fee (Range)	Other[+] (Specify)	Total Cost
Total Transactions					

Other Product[6]	Assets (X/X/XX)	Management Fee	Other[+] (Specify)	Total Cost
Product 1				
Product 2				
Product 3				
Product 4				

Total Investment Product Fees $_____

---

[5] When providing potential service providers with information/assumptions regarding the brokerage window plan feature, it is critical that you provide identical information to all of the competing companies in order to ensure equivalent comparisons.

[+] Fees associated with participants' transfer of account balances between investment options, including investment transfer expenses and any contingent back-end loads, redemption fees and surrender charges should be included in "other" expenses. In addition, any wrap fees or pricing charges for non-publicly traded assets should be included in the "other" expenses column. For investment product termination fees associated with plan termination or conversion, see Schedule D. Insurance companies incur marketing and distribution costs, which are recouped through charges assessed against the plan.

[6] Other products could include investment vehicles such as REITs and limited partnerships.

ABC PLAN DISCLOSURE FORM
For Services Provided by XYZ Company
Schedule B

PLAN ADMINISTRATION EXPENSES

Expense Type	Rate/ Estimate[*]	Bundled Service Arrangement (✔)[7]	Total Cost[**]
Administration/Recordkeeping Fees:			
• Daily valuation	$_____	☐	$_____
• Payroll processing	$_____	☐	$_____
• Balance inquiry	$_____	☐	$_____
• Investment transfer	$_____	☐	$_____
• Contract administration charge	$_____	☐	$_____
• Distribution processing	$_____	☐	$_____
• QDRO processing	$_____	☐	$_____
• Participant statements	$_____	☐	$_____
• Plan sponsor reports	$_____	☐	$_____
• VRU/Internet services	$_____	☐	$_____
• Other (specify)	$_____	☐	$_____
Subtotal			$_____
Participant Education/Advice:			
• Participant education materials/distribution	$_____	☐	$_____
• Education meetings (frequency__)	$_____	☐	$_____
• Investment advice programs	$_____	☐	$_____
• Other (specify)	$_____	☐	$_____
Subtotal			$_____
Trustee/Custodial Services:			
• Certified annual trust statement	$_____	☐	$_____
• Safekeeping of plan assets	$_____	☐	$_____
• Other (specify)	$_____	☐	$_____
Subtotal			$_____

---

[*] Amounts represent the method by which the fee is calculated, for example as a percentage of plan assets under management, based upon number of participants or based upon number of transactions. For start-up or take-over situations, fees are based upon estimates and/or certain assumptions, i.e., regarding assets under management and number of participants. When providing potential service providers with information/assumptions regarding your plan, it is critical that you provide identical information to all of the competing companies in order to ensure equivalent comparisons. Without a standardized set of assumptions, service providers will certainly use differing assumptions, defeating the intended purpose of clarifying fee comparisons among service providers.

[7] Services provided under a bundled services arrangement are indicated by a check mark next to the specific service.

[**] Amounts represent flat dollar amount charges or total charges based upon the particular method of calculation. In some instances, these amounts represent estimates based on assumptions provided by you, the plan sponsor.

ABC PLAN DISCLOSURE FORM
For Services Provided by XYZ Company
Schedule B, continued

Expense Type	Rate/ Estimate[*]	Bundled Service Arrangement (✔)	Total Cost[**]	
<u>Compliance Services</u>:				
• Nondiscrimination testing	$_____	☐	$_____	
• Signature ready form 5500	$_____	☐	$_____	
• Annual audit	$_____	☐	$_____	
• Other (specify)	$_____	☐	$_____	
Subtotal				$_____
<u>Plan Amendment Fee</u>:				
• Plan amendment fee	$_____	☐	$_____	
• Plan document/determination letter fee	$_____	☐	$_____	
• Other (specify)	$_____	☐	$_____	
Subtotal				$_____
<u>Loan Administration</u>:				
• Loan origination fee	$_____	☐	$_____	
• Loan processing fee	$_____	☐	$_____	
• Loan maintenance and repayment tracking fee	$_____	☐	$_____	
• Other (specify)	$_____	☐	$_____	
Subtotal				$_____
Total separate charges			$_____	
Total bundled services			$_____	
(Less offsets/credits paid to plan)			$(_____)	
Total Plan Administration Expenses			$_____	

---

* Amounts represent the method by which the fee is calculated, for example as a percentage of plan assets under management, based upon number of participants or based upon number of transactions. For start-up or take-over situations, fees are based upon estimates and/or certain assumptions, i.e., regarding assets under management and number of participants. When providing potential service providers with information/assumptions regarding your plan, it is critical that you provide identical information to all of the competing companies in order to ensure equivalent comparisons. Without a standardized set of assumptions, service providers will certainly use differing assumptions, defeating the intended purpose of clarifying fee comparisons among service providers.

** Amounts represent flat dollar amount charges or total charges based upon the particular method of calculation. In some instances, these amounts represent estimates based on assumptions provided by you, the plan sponsor.

ABC PLAN
401(k) PLAN DISCLOSURE FORM
For Services Provided by XYZ Company
Schedule C

ONE TIME START-UP/CONVERSION EXPENSES

Expense Type	Rate/ Estimate[*]	Total Cost[**]
• Start-up/conversion education program	$ _____	$_____
• Start-up/conversion enrollment expense	$ _____	$_____
• Installation fee	$ _____	$_____
• Start-up/conversion plan document fee/filing fee	$ _____	$_____
• Other (specify)	$ _____	$_____
Total Start-up/Conversion expenses		$_____

---

* Amounts represent the method by which the fee is calculated, for example as a percentage of plan assets under management, based upon number of participants or based upon number of transactions. For start-up or take-over situations, fees are based upon estimates and/or certain assumptions, i.e., regarding assets under management and number of participants. When providing potential service providers with information/assumptions regarding your plan, it is critical that you provide identical information to all of the competing companies in order to ensure equivalent comparisons. Without a standardized set of assumptions, service providers will certainly use differing assumptions, defeating the intended purpose of clarifying fee comparisons among service providers.

** Amounts represent flat dollar amount charges or total charges based upon the particular method of calculation. In some instances, these amounts represent estimates based on assumptions provided by you, the plan sponsor.

ABC PLAN
401(k) PLAN DISCLOSURE FORM
For Services Provided by XYZ Company
Schedule D

SERVICE PROVIDER TERMINATION EXPENSES

Expense Type	Rate/ Estimate[*]	Total Cost[**]
Investment Product Expenses		
• Contract termination charges	$ _____	$ _____
• Back-end load	$ _____	$ _____
• Product termination fee	$ _____	$ _____
• Other (specify)	$ _____	$ _____
Total		$ _____
Plan Administration Expenses		
• Service provider termination charge	$ _____	$ _____
• Service contract termination charge	$ _____	$ _____
• Other (specify)	$ _____	$ _____
Total Termination Expenses		$ _____

---

[*] Amounts represent the method by which the fee is calculated, for example as a percentage of plan assets under management, based upon number of participants or based upon number of transactions. For start-up or take-over situations, fees are based upon estimates and/or certain assumptions, i.e., regarding assets under management and number of participants. When providing potential service providers with information/assumptions regarding your plan, it is critical that you provide identical information to all of the competing companies in order to ensure equivalent comparisons. Without a standardized set of assumptions, service providers will certainly use differing assumptions, defeating the intended purpose of clarifying fee comparisons among service providers.

[**] Amounts represent flat dollar amount charges or total charges based upon the particular method of calculation. In some instances, these amounts represent estimates based on assumptions provided by you, the plan sponsor.

ABC PLAN
401(k) PLAN FEE DISCLOSURE FORM
For Services Provided by XYZ Company
Schedule E

DEFINITION OF TERMS

Administration/Recordkeeping Fee: Fee for providing recordkeeping and other plan participant administrative type services. For start-up or takeover plans, these fees typically include charges for contacting and processing information from the prior service provider and "matching up" or mapping participant information. Use of this term is not meant to identify any ERISA Section 3(16)(A) obligations.

Annual Audit: Federal law requires that all ERISA-covered plans with more than 100 participants be audited by an independent auditor. It is also common to refer to a DOL or IRS examination of a plan as a plan audit. Any charge imposed by a service provider in connection with this audit is reflected on Schedule B.

Back-End Load: Sales charges due upon the sale or transfer of mutual funds, insurance/annuity products or other investments, which may be reduced and/or eliminated over time.

Balance Inquiry: Fee that may be charged each time a participant inquires about his or her balance.

Brokerage Commission: A fee paid to a broker or other intermediary for executing a trade.

Brokerage Window: A plan investment option allowing a participant to establish a self-directed brokerage account.

Bundled Services: Arrangements whereby plan service providers offer 401(k) plan establishment, investment services and administration for an all-inclusive fee. Bundled services by their nature are priced as a package and cannot be priced on a per service basis.

Collective Investment Fund: A tax-exempt pooled fund operated by a bank or trust company that commingles the assets of trust accounts for which the bank provides fiduciary services.

Contract Administration Charge: An omnibus charge for costs of administering the insurance/annuity contract, including costs associated with the maintenance of participant accounts and all investment-related transactions initiated by participants.

Contract Termination Charge: A charge to the plan for "surrendering" or "terminating" its insurance/annuity contract prior to the end of a stated time period. The charge typically decreases over time.

Conversion: The process of changing from one service provider to another.

Distribution Expense: The costs typically associated with processing paperwork and issuing a check for a distribution of plan assets to a participant. May include the generation of IRS Form 1099R. This fee may apply to hardship and other in-service withdrawals as well as to separation-from-service or retirement distributions.

Eligible Employee: Any employee who is eligible to participate in and receive benefits from a plan.

Expense Ratio: The cost of investing and administering assets, including management fees, in a mutual fund or other collective fund expressed as a percentage of total assets.

ABC PLAN
401(k) PLAN FEE DISCLOSURE FORM
For Services Provided by XYZ Company
Schedule E (continued)

Front-End Load: Sales charges incurred when an investment in a mutual fund is made.

Individually Managed Account: An investment account managed for a single plan.

Installation Fee: One-time fee for initiating a new plan or initiating new services.

Investment Transfer Expense: Fee associated with a participant changing his or her investment allocation, or making transfers among funding accounts under the plan.

Loan Maintenance and Repayment Tracking Fee: Fee charged to monitor outstanding loans and repayment schedule.

Loan Origination Fee: Fee charged when a plan loan is originally taken.

Loan Processing Fee: Fee charged to process a plan loan application.

Management Fee: Fee charged for the management of pooled investments such as collective investment funds, insurance/annuity products, mutual funds and individually managed accounts.

Mortality Risk and Administrative Expense (M&E Fee): Fee charged by an insurance company to cover the cost of the insurance features of an annuity contract, including the guarantee of a lifetime income payment, interest and expense guarantees, and any death benefit provided during the accumulation period.

Nondiscrimination Testing Expense: Tax qualified retirement plans must be administered in compliance with several regulations requiring numerical measurements. The fee charged for the process of determining whether the plan is in compliance is collectively called nondiscrimination testing expense.

Participant: Person who has an account in the plan.

Participant Education Materials/Distribution Expenses: All costs (including travel expenses) associated with providing print, video, software and/or live instruction to educate employees about how the plan works, the plan investment funds, and asset allocation strategies. There may be a one-time cost associated with implementing a new plan, as well as ongoing costs for an existing program.

Plan Document/Determination Letter Fee (Filing Fee): Fee charged for a written plan document. Fee can also include the costs associated with preparing and filing IRS required documentation, including the request for a determination letter (document issued by the IRS stating whether the plan meets the qualifications for tax-advantaged treatment).

Plan Loan: The law allows participants to borrow from their accounts up to prescribed limits. This is an optional plan feature.

ABC PLAN
401(k) PLAN FEE DISCLOSURE FORM
For Services Provided by XYZ Company
Schedule E (continued)

Product Termination Fee: Investment-product charges associated with terminating one or all of a service provider's investment products.

QDRO (Qualified Domestic Relations Order): A judgment, decree or order that creates or recognizes an alternate payee's (such as former spouse, child, etc.) right to receive all or a portion of a participant's retirement plan benefits.

Separate Account: An asset account established by a life insurance company, separate from other funds of the life insurance company, offering investment funding options for pension plans.

Service Provider Termination Charge: Plan administrative costs associated with terminating a relationship with a service provider, with the permanent termination of a plan, or with the termination of specific plan services. These may be termed "surrender" or "transfer" charges.

Signature Ready Form 5500: Fee to prepare Form 5500, a form which all qualified retirement plans (excluding SEPs and SIMPLE IRAs) must file annually with the IRS.

Start-up/Enrollment Expense: Costs associated with providing materials to educate employees about the plan, and enrolling employees in the plan. This may be part of, or included in, the education programs. There may be a one-time cost associated with implementing a new plan, as well as ongoing enrollment costs.

Trustee Services: Fees charged by the individual, bank or trust company with fiduciary responsibility for holding plan assets.

VRU: Voice Response Unit.

Wrap Fee: An inclusive fee generally based on the percentage of assets in an investment program, which typically provides asset allocation, execution of transactions and other administrative services.

12b-1 Fee: A charge to shareholders to cover a mutual fund's shareholder servicing, distribution and marketing costs.

About the Author

David B. Loeper is a Certified Investment Management Analyst®, a Certified Investment Management Consultant®, and the CEO of Financeware, Inc. An SEC-Registered Investment Adviser with more than 25 years' experience, Loeper has appeared on CNBC, CNN, and Fox Business and has been a featured contributor on Yahoo! Financevision and Bloomberg TV.

Born in Milwaukee, Wisconsin, Loeper began his career in finance as an investment representative with Century Companies of America in 1984. In 1986 he joined Richard Schilffarth & Associates as an investment consultant and also served as an officer of their broker/dealer, Investment Account Services Corporation.

Loeper joined Wheat First Securities as vice president of investment consulting in 1988, where he served for 10 years. He was promoted to managing director of investment consulting, and then eventually to managing director of strategic planning for the retail brokerage division. He left his position at Wheat First Securities in 1999 and founded his current company, Financeware, Inc., which operates as Wealthcare Capital Management®.

Active in industry associations throughout his career, Loeper has been a member of the Investment Management Consultants Association (IMCA) for more than 20 years, serving on the advisory council for more than 5 years, most recently as chairman. He also served as a founding member of the Asset Consulting Roundtable, an independent group composed of the heads of investment consulting groups from numerous brokerage firms. Loeper has also served on the Investment Advisory Committee of the nearly $30 billion Virginia Retirement System. He received his CIMA® designation in 1990 by completing a program offered through Wharton Business School, in conjunction with IMCA.

Drawing on years of experience in the finance industry, Loeper's book, *Stop the Investing Rip-off: How to Avoid Being a Victim and Make More Money, Second Edition* (John Wiley & Sons, 2012), reveals how so much of the financial services industry may cause you to become a victim and how to protect yourself by asking the secret questions that will expose potential problems beforehand.

Index

Administration and record-keeping fees, of retirement plans, 28, 57
Advertising promises, 79–80
Advice and monitoring (custom), as optional expense, 59–60
Age-based investing. *See* Lifecycle (target date) funds
Alternative investments, funds-of-funds fees and, 32
American Association of Retired Persons (AARP), earnings from product promotions, 135, 136
Annuities, 121–122
  avoiding needless risk and, 128–129
  compared to balanced portfolio returns, 122–127
  emotions, reason and, 127–188
Asset allocation, 96–99. *See also* Investment selection
  scoring model questionnaire, 99–104
  scoring model questionnaire, using information from, 104–107

Brinson, Hood, and Beebower studies, 98
Broker/dealers, 91–92
Bundled fees, 27–28

Center for Retirement Research study, xv–xvi

Certified Wealthcare Analyst™, 80
Comfort and confidence zone, for retirement plans, 50–53, 118–120
Commodity funds, funds-of-funds fees and, 32
Contingent deferred sales charge (CDSC), of mutual funds, 31
Correlation coefficient, performance prediction and, 94
Co-workers, employer plan reform and, 63–68
Custodial costs, of retirement plans, 23, 26–28, 58, 111, 115

Defined-benefit pension plans, xiii, xvii
Department of Labor, 69, 75–76
  contacting, as last resort, 76–77
  Form 5500 of, 75
Diversification, 57–58, 97, 134
  access to diversified funds, 22, 60
  correlation coefficient and, 97
  fiduciaries and, 70, 72–73
Dodd/Frank Financial Reform Bill, 91

Employee Retirement Income Security Act of 1974 (ERISA)
  float and, 36
  prohibited transactions, 15
  standards for reasonable fees, 69–75

Employer, working with to reduce
costs, 55–56
contacting Department of Labor
about, 75–76
determining facts about plan
expenses, 56–60
ERISA standards and, 69–75
good intentions of plan selectors,
55–56, 62, 63
presenting facts about plan
expenses to, 60–62
recruiting co-workers to help
reform plan, 63–68
Exchange-traded funds (ETFs), 97

Fees and expenses, of retirement
plans, 11–37, 115, 118. *See also*
Employer, working with to
reduce fees; *Lifestyle entries*
administration and record-
keeping, 28, 57
compound interest and benefits
of reducing, 6–7
custodial costs, 27–28
expense ratios, 25–26
financial consequences of, xvi
funds-of-funds fees, 31–32
for government and teachers'
unions, 131–136
legal standards for reasonable
fees, 69–75
lifecycle (target date) funds, 32–34
market performance and advisors,
versus index funds, 18–23
mortality and expenses charges,
30–31
mutual fund hidden expenses,
34–36
new disclosure rules, xvii–xviii,
1–2, 11–12
as predictor of performance,
94–95
revenue sharing, 26–27

surrender charges, 31
taking control of, 137–138
thinking about like mortgage
interest, 17–18
value, but lack, of personal
advice, 23–24
wrap fees, consulting, and
advisory fees, 28–30
Fidelity Spartan S&P 500 Index
Fund, 70
Financial advisors, 92
serving their interests, not yours,
79–83
Financial Industry Regulatory
Authority (FINRA),
41, 91–92
Financial services industry, 44–45,
71, 80. *See also* Financial
advisors
Float, as hidden mutual fund fee,
35–36
Form 5500, of Department of
Labor, 75
401(k) plans, xiii–xv, 1–2
lifestyle costs of excessive fee
by age and savings balance,
139–204
plan disclosure form, 205–216
403(b) plans, xiii, xiv, 1–2, 14
fees and expenses of, 131–136
457 plans, xiii, xiv, 1–2, 14
fees and expenses of, 131–136
Four Pillars of Retirement Plans, The
(Loeper), 5
Fundgrades.com, 73, 93, 96
Funds-of-funds fees, 31–32

Google Finance, 96
Government Accountability Office
study, xvii
Government unions. *See* 457 plans
Guaranteed income.
See Annuities

Hayward, Justin, 127
Health, retirement planning and uncertainty about, 89
Hedge funds, funds-of-funds fees and, 32

"In balance" plans. *See* Comfort and confidence zone, for retirement plans
Index funds, 138
  diversification with, 97
  market performance and advisors contrasted, 18–23
Insurance companies. *See also* Annuities
  mortality and expense charges, 30–31
  surrender charges, 31
International index funds, 71
Investment advisory fees, 29
Investment selection. *See also* Asset allocation
  helpful data elements, 94–96
  past performance and, 91–94

Lifecycle (target date) funds, 32–34, 107–109
Lifestyle, current, 39–53
  choices impacting, 79–89
  comfort zone to avoid too much uncertainty and needless sacrifice, 50–53, 118–120
  examples by age and savings balance, 139–204
  market uncertainty and, 40–45
  market uncertainty as manageable but not controllable, 47–50
  scare tactics to increase savings rate, 45–47
Lifestyle, in retirement:
  choices impacting current as well as, 79–89

cost of excess fees to, 12–17, 39–53, 118–120
Lipper, 21, 96

Market uncertainty, 7–8
  as manageable but not controllable, 47–50
  past performance and future results, 40–45
  performance reports versus advisor's advice, 85, 87–88
Material underperformance risk, 95–96
Miller, George, xvii
Morningstar ratings, 20–21, 96
Mortality and expense (M&E) fees, of retirement plans, 30–31
Multidiscipline accounts (MDAs), fees and, 29
Multimanager accounts (MMAs), fees and, 29
Mutual funds:
  hidden expenses of, 34–36
  material underperformance of, 93, 97–98
  past performance and future results, 41
  surrender charges, 31

National Education Association (NEA), earnings from product promotions, 135–136

Ohio, unions and, 131

Participant-directed retirement plans, generally, xiii–xiv. *See also* 401(k) plans; 403(b) plans; 457 plans
Past performance:
  versus advisor's advice, 85, 87–88
  future results and, 5, 21, 40–45, 57, 72
  investment selection and, 91–94

Priorities, changes in and retirement planning, 88–89

Private equity funds, funds-of-funds fees and, 32

Rating services, 72–73, 95

Record-keeping costs, of retirement plans, 28, 57

Retirement. *See* Lifestyle, in retirement; Time horizon

Revenue sharing, retirement plan fees and, 26–29, 55–56, 59–60, 61, 73

Risk tolerance:
in asset allocation scoring model, 100–104, 105
avoiding fees to determine, 138
questions from advisor about, 82

Savings:
comfort analysis for rate of, 83–85, 86
questions from advisor about, 82

Securities and Exchange Commission (SEC), 30, 57

Self-directed brokerage accounts, 34, 58, 59

Statement of additional information (SAI), mutual fund hidden expenses and, 34–35

Stop the Investing Rip-off (Loeper), 8

Surrender charges, of retirement plans, 31

Target date funds. *See* Lifecycle (target date) funds

Taylor, Don, 30

Teachers Insurance and Annuity Association–College Retirement Equities Fund (TIAA-CREF), 70

Teachers unions. *See* 457 plans

Time horizon:
in asset allocation scoring model, 99–100, 104, 105
questions from advisor about, 82

Track records. *See* Past performance

Unions. *See* 403(b) plans; 457 plans

Variance, asset allocation and, 98

Wall Street Journal, 121–122

Wealthcare Capital Management®, 71–72, 128
asset allocation and, 109–114, 116–117
Certified Wealthcare Analyst™, 80
contact information, 52, 85, 111

Wisconsin, unions and, 131

Wrap fees, of retirement plans, 27, 28–30

Yahoo!, 96

Zero Alpha Group study, 35